CENTRAL BANKS AND GOLD

A volume in the series
CORNELL STUDIES IN MONEY

Edited by Eric Helleiner and Jonathan Kirshner

A list of titles in this series is available at www.cornellpress.cornell.edu.

Central Banks and Gold

*How Tokyo, London, and New York
Shaped the Modern World*

Simon James Bytheway
and Mark Metzler

Cornell University Press
Ithaca and London

First published 2016 by Cornell University Press
Printed in the United States of America

Library of Congress Cataloging-in-Publication Data

Names: Bytheway, Simon James, 1969– author. | Metzler,
    Mark, 1957– author.
Title: Central banks and gold : how Tokyo, London, and New York
    shaped the modern world / Simon James Bytheway and Mark Metzler.
Description: Ithaca ; London : Cornell University Press, 2016. | Includes
    bibliographical references and index.
Identifiers: LCCN 2016026968 | ISBN 9781501704949 (cloth : alk. paper)
Subjects: LCSH: Banks and banking, Central—History. | Banks and
    banking, International—History. | Money supply—History. | Gold
    standard—History.
Classification: LCC HG1811 .B98 2016 | DDC 332.4/22209041—dc23
LC record available at https://lccn.loc.gov/2016026968

Cornell University Press strives to use environmentally responsible
suppliers and materials to the fullest extent possible in the publishing of
its books. Such materials include vegetable-based, low-VOC inks and
acid-free papers that are recycled, totally chlorine-free, or partly
composed of nonwood fibers. For further information, visit our website
at www.cornellpress.cornell.edu.

Cloth printing   10 9 8 7 6 5 4 3 2 1

Contents

TABLES AND FIGURES

Tables

Figures

PREFACE

This book presents a series of close-up historical views of national money-creation systems and their international connections. We concentrate on the triangular connections between Tokyo, London, and New York. Early in the twentieth century, the London–New York connection emerged as the main axis of global financial governance. We add Tokyo to this picture and work to develop a view of the little-known Tokyo–London and Tokyo–New York sides of the trilateral. These connections illuminate aspects of the entire international structure that cannot be detected by looking only at the connections between London and New York.

Our focus is on the pivotal age from the late 1890s to the depression of the 1930s. It was then, only a century ago, that the United States established a central bank, and it was then that central banks established regular international connections with one another. This happened quietly and often invisibly, and much of the story has been unknown to historians. Some of our conclusions may surprise even specialists in the subject. Central banks created credit capital for national private banking systems and formed the administrative peaks of national systems of credit creation. At times they also created credit capital for each other. Gold, in theory, defined the unit of monetary account and provided the foundation upon which the system of credit and debt was built. An immense superstructure of social claims and obligations was thus, notionally, built upon the gold bullion stored in central bank vaults. Movements of that physical gold could also have major consequences for much larger structures of credit and debt.

In the 1890s, London was the only one of these three capital cities to function as a truly international center of money and credit creation, and Great Britain was the world's largest creditor country. New York suddenly took a leading international role after 1914, and the United States simultaneously became the world's largest net creditor country. Tokyo emerged as an international financial center only seventy years later, in the 1980s, when Japan replaced the United States as the world's largest net creditor country (as it remains today). As early as 1896, however, Japanese money played a surprising and significant role in London itself. In the 1910s, Japanese financial authorities were already working to establish Tokyo as an international credit center. This book thus reveals the beginnings of processes that have since reshaped flows of resources and the distribution of wealth at a global level.

The creation of money is itself an elaborate social process that is normally presented to the public as a kind of physical fact. Those outside the process see mainly a blank and institutional face, exemplified by the elaborately engraved images on paper banknotes and the colonnaded façades of imposing bank headquarters. To insiders, the process was more personal, founded in exclusive institutional networks and close-knit social circles. Decisions made within these circles, in an age of immense fluctuations in monetary purchasing power, could have enormously outsized effects. This is the picture revealed in the primary documentary sources we utilize here, drawn from research in the historical archives of all three financial centers. The questions we address are also matters of living history and of processes that continue to unfold.

ACKNOWLEDGMENTS

Both authors are responsible for the entire work; our angles of approach sometimes differ, but they also offer a triangulating view of the subject. Our common goal is to open new perspectives not developed by other authors or in our own earlier work and to open new terrain for research and understanding. At some points, we refer interested readers to our earlier books, which offer a comprehensive international financial history of the period especially as seen from the vantage point of Japan.

This book is based on research in the historical archives of the Bank of England (BoE), the Federal Reserve Bank of New York (FRBNY), and the Bank of Japan (BoJ), as well as the National Archives, the London Metropolitan Archives, and the archives of N. M. Rothschild & Sons, HSBC, and Deutsche Bank in London; the Kensei Shiryōshitsu (History of Constitutional Government Archives) in Tokyo (which contain the papers of several Japanese ministers of finance); and the personal papers of Thomas W. Lamont of Morgan and Company, held at the Baker Library of Harvard

Business School. Thank you to the helpful archivists at all these places, with special thanks to Sarah Millard, formerly of the Bank of England archives, Rosemary Lazenby and Joseph Komljenovich at the Federal Reserve Bank of New York archives, and Ōmiya Hitoshi at the Bank of Japan archives. We have combined these archival investigations with a synthesis of some results of the large, highly developed historiographies of all three countries; these intellectual debts are, partially, expressed in the endnotes.

Two parts of this book are developed from papers originally presented at the Institute for Monetary and Economic Studies (IMES) of the Bank of Japan, where special thanks are due to Shizume Masato, Okina Kunio, and Hatase Mariko. We also owe thanks to the talented staff at Cornell University Press, particularly to Roger Haydon, to series editors Eric Helleiner and Jonathan Kirshner, and to the anonymous reviewers for their valuable advice.

We finally thank our families for their constant love and support.

Abbreviations

BIS	Bank for International Settlements
BoE	Bank of England
BoJ	Bank of Japan (Nihon Ginkō)
FRBNY	Federal Reserve Bank of New York
IBJ	Industrial Bank of Japan (Nihon Kōgyō Ginkō)
IMF	International Monetary Fund
MoF	Ministry of Finance (Ōkurashō/Zaimushō)
NCB	National City Bank
YSB	Yokohama Specie Bank

Note on Conventions

Currency

The "$" symbol refers to US dollars, "£" to British pounds, and "¥" to Japanese yen. Under their gold-standard parities,

£1 = $4.8669 = ¥9.763
$1 = £0.2054 = ¥2.006
¥1 = £0.1024 = $0.4985

Easier to remember: this was the era of the 50-cent yen, when 2 yen equaled 1 US dollar, while 10 yen roughly equaled 1 British pound.

Under the "£-s-d" system, 1 British pound (£ or "*l*") equaled 20 shillings (*s*), and 1 shilling = 12 pence (*d*).

Billion here means 1,000 million.

Japanese Names and Words

Names of Japanese people are given in the Japanese order (family name first), except in bibliographic citations for English-language works in which they were originally listed in the Western order.

When rendered into the Latin alphabet, Japanese words are pronounced more or less as they would be in Spanish or Italian.

Central Banks and Gold

INTRODUCTION

Bases of Credit

Modern commercial economies run on credit, created and sustained by a complicated hierarchy of institutions and backed ultimately by the credit-creation activities of central banks. A century ago, when the Federal Reserve System was first established in the United States, central banks based their own creation of money and credit on their holdings of gold. These two institutional practices—central banking, and the use of gold as monetary reserves—were the bases of the world's first truly globalized credit system. This global system was originally centered in London, with the Bank of England at the center of the center. Today, the actions of central banks continue to move economies, perhaps even more than they did a century ago. Gold-backed currencies are a thing of the past, but central banks nonetheless remain the biggest owners of gold, while gold markets seem to have an ongoing monetary significance. These institutions also remain mysterious in many ways. In an effort to understand more, this book explores some interconnections among the central-place financial institutions of Tokyo, London, and New York. Most histories of this subject have had a North Atlantic focus. Bringing Japan into the picture illuminates new aspects of the entire system and suggests that some popular historical judgments need to be reconsidered.

We begin with the question of central bank cooperation. Most scholars date the beginnings of regularized central bank cooperation to the First World War, or to the 1920s. In fact, the Bank of England (BoE) and the Bank of Japan (BoJ) secretly developed a close form of cooperation in the early years of the century. After 1896, as described in chapter 1, the Bank of Japan kept very large balances at the Bank of England, and for much of the period from 1896 to 1914, the BoJ was the Bank of England's largest single depositor. The Bank of England's ability to maintain its global financial position during the decade and a half before 1914 was supported by its ability to manage these Japanese funds and quietly to draw on them in moments of need. On its side, the Bank of Japan accounted these London funds as part of the "specie" reserve for Japan's own national monetary system. The discovery of the details of this connection, based on research into formerly closed archival materials, widens a hitherto Europe-centered view. This financial alliance was the counterpart of the political and military alliance that the British and Japanese empires finalized in 1902. That political alliance was itself financially instantiated in the giant war loans raised in London for Japan's war with Russia in 1904–5. The war was followed by a great boom in 1906 and a great crash in 1907; this was an international movement, but it was most conspicuous in Japan, while its impulses radiated out internationally mainly via London.

Central bank cooperation became a multilateral enterprise during the opening weeks of the First World War, as explored in chapter 2. It was the Bank of England that took the initiative to establish a network of Allied central banks. The US Federal Reserve System was framed in 1913 and went into operation shortly after the war began in Europe. The Federal Reserve Bank of New York (FRBNY) also joined the Allied central bank network as soon as it could, well before the US government entered the war. In early 1915, backed by the FRBNY, US private banks began to finance the enormous military purchasing programs run by the British and French governments in the United States. The close personal friendship between Benjamin Strong of the FRBNY and Montagu Norman of the Bank of England began in the spring of 1916, when Strong visited England as part of a campaign of financial alliance building. A private financial alliance thus preceded the public military alliance. The central banks of the United States and Japan also established their own direct tie during the war, even though their governments were then involved in open rivalry in China, and even though their military establishments each perceived the other as a probable future enemy.

Attention to these wartime developments prompts us to revise some current understandings of the development of financial globalization over time. Many economic historians have recently depicted 1914 as the end of the first era of modern globalization and as the beginning of a phase of "de-globalization" or "globalization reaction." We fully agree that the classical gold standard era (ca. 1873 to 1914) was an age of unprecedented financial globalization. However, contrary to this view of de-globalization, we find that the First World War induced a great *intensification* of global financial governance. The year 1914 itself, with the beginning of the World War and the coincidental opening of the Federal Reserve System, appears as "year one" of American-centered financial globalization. This globalizing movement was not only financial. Culturally and technologically also, the decade after the First World War was the world's first American age. This flourishing of American technological and popular cultural forms, from Henry Ford's production system, to Hollywood movies, to jazz phonograph records, was highly conspicuous to both Europeans and Japanese. A surge of international credit creation by US banks accompanied these movements.

Less well known is the international surge of Japanese credit creation during the war, when Japan emerged, briefly and "prematurely," as one of the world's top three creditor countries. As chapter 3 outlines, Tokyo financial groups lent to Britain and France, as well as to Russia and China. Simultaneously, Japanese central bankers began to build the institutional infrastructure of an international credit center. This initiative was relatively unsuccessful. It did, however, herald the beginning of a structural shift.

After the First World War, Japanese, American, and British central bank policies became aligned as never before, as explored in chapter 4. The gold convertibility of national currencies had been suspended during the war. Prices in each of the three countries doubled, while the purchasing power of gold also declined substantially. The restoration of gold-based monetary systems now seemed to demand deflation and austerity. The "restoration" period that began in 1919 also signified the beginning of a historic increase in the purchasing power of gold. Ultimately, during the 1930s, the purchasing power of gold would reach the highest levels since the sixteenth century. Deflation and austerity were thus integral to the program of central bank cooperation, which we understand as the world's first internationally coordinated monetary policy. The biennium 1919–20 was thus Year One for a new type of multinational financial governance, which has since become hegemonic.

Central bank cooperation involving New York, London, and Tokyo was also, at its inception, highly personal in nature. The governors of the three central banks—Benjamin Strong, Montagu Norman, and Inoue Junnosuke—have each been the subject of considerable study. Theories of economic history have hinged on the interpretation of their actions. Each of them, in turn, took a lead in directing his own country's restoration of the gold standard: Strong in 1919, Norman in 1925, and Inoue in 1930. Each was blamed for the deflation and depression that followed. Benjamin Strong, as governor of the Federal Reserve Bank of New York, directed the first move, the return of the US dollar to gold convertibility on June 26, 1919. One result of this action was a great surge of gold shipments out of the United States. This gold was shipped above all to Japan, where it helped to inflate a great credit bubble. At the same time, the central banks of all three countries began to press forward with deflation policies.

As Strong anticipated, world price deflation began in 1920. This movement appeared first in Japan. Strong, weakened by the illness that would ultimately take his life, took an extended leave from his post before the deflationary wave hit. He was on his way to Japan, where he would vacation as a semi-official guest of the Bank of Japan, when the crisis broke. Other leading American bankers—Thomas W. Lamont of J. P. Morgan & Company, and Frank Vanderlip of National City Bank—made their own separate visits to Japan, which had suddenly emerged as a new financial power, in the spring of 1920. Strong stayed the longest and established the closest connections, becoming especially friendly with Inoue Junnosuke and Fukai Eigo of the Bank of Japan, as recounted in chapter 5.

Chapter 6 describes how Montagu Norman, in partnership with Strong, turned ad hoc wartime cooperation into a formal agenda. The paired ideas that national central banks should be autonomous, and that they should cooperate with each other, were first spelled out in a private "manifesto" that Norman circulated among fellow central bankers in 1921. In fact, what Norman outlined was a kind of central bank sovereignty, encompassing central banks' independence from their national governments, their separation from and avoidance of competition with commercial banks, their supervision of commercial banks within their own countries, and their continuous cooperation with each other. Whether he intended it or not, Norman's quiet declaration of the principles of "central bank independence" and "central bank cooperation" was the announcement of a new international order. Central bank cooperation was internationally recognized as a principle at the 1922 Genoa Conference, and it was also put into practice. Cooperation between central banks began primarily as *informational* cooperation, which includes not only the sharing of information but also the sharing and propagation of worldviews. *Operational* cooperation between central banks, which includes the provision of mutual credit facilities and the coordination of policy actions, was unusual before the World War but became conspicuous in the 1920s. An international network of central banks thus developed out of the war, as did the world's first truly coordinated system of international monetary policy. In these and other ways, financial globalization surged to a new level in the 1920s. As to the actual content of central bank cooperation in the 1920s, much of it focused on the reconstitution of an international system of national gold-based currencies. Assured of American support, but also pressed by American initiatives in South Africa, the source of most of the world's gold, Montagu Norman in 1925 directed Great Britain's restoration of the pound sterling to its prewar gold value. The purchasing power of gold climbed still further.

The Bank of Japan took part in the movement to foster central bank cooperation in the 1920s, and helped support Britain's own restoration of the gold standard. The BoJ likewise contributed to international central bank credits to support the restoration of the gold standard in Belgium and Italy. Japan itself, however, was delayed in returning to the gold standard, first by the great earthquake disaster of 1923 and then by the great banking crisis of 1927. Finally, in the second half of 1929, following an American lead, Inoue Junnosuke took charge of the project of restoring the yen to gold convertibility, also at its prewar par value. This goal was realized in January 1930. Simultaneously, the purchasing power of gold surged still further—meaning that the price of almost everything else declined.

This was the third great round of postwar deflation, a deflation on top of deflation, with disastrous effects on the nonfinancial economy. Inoue has accordingly been viewed as the policy maker most responsible for the "Shōwa panic" of 1929–32, which was the Japanese aspect of the Great Depression.

The deployment of physical gold via the London gold market was quietly at the center of much of this. Chapter 7 opens a window onto the questions of gold production, commoditization, and trade via the hitherto obscure story of how British authorities created a market for this master commodity. During the First World War, central banks came to control most of the world's gold, which could not be freely traded and was no longer a commodity in any normal sense. When the pound sterling formally went off gold and began to float against the US dollar in 1919, the Bank of England invited N. M. Rothschild & Sons to open a "free" market for gold in London. In this marketplace at the center of the international payments system, only five brokers were present, representing anonymous clients. It was a closed, ritualized, and hierarchical affair, and its documentary traces are few; this chapter offers a first examination of just what the London gold market was. London was in fact the channel for some two-thirds of the world's gold production, and international movements of this gold could induce enormous economic shifts.

In 1930 and 1931, there was a great rush to cash in national currencies for gold, as described in chapter 8. This movement began with Japan. Under the press of this run on gold, gold-based credit systems collapsed. Thus, credit-led globalization, in its post–First World War version, gave way to the globally synchronized debt-destruction crisis known as the Great Depression. There was now indeed a many-faceted reaction against financial globalization. In Japan itself, the depression undermined pro-Western liberalism and opened the way for the fascistic turn of national life in the 1930s. The period holds many lessons for our own times. We note in chapter 8 another remarkable fact. Every truly major international financial crisis of the era—1907, 1920, 1929—appeared first in Tokyo, having an onset some three to six months earlier than in New York and London. It seems that the contradictory faces of these world movements were manifested especially sharply in Japan, making Tokyo markets a sensitive leading indicator.

We conclude by considering the hierarchical nature of the markets in capital, which constitute the peak markets of the world capitalist system. We also reconsider the central-bank connections between Tokyo, London, and New York as vital inner links within a larger set of world-city geographies. In a century of violent changes, these "capital city" geographies have been remarkably persistent. The great Tokyo bubble of 1989–90 was the greatest yet of its kind, but it now seems relatively modest next to the New York and London bubbles of 2007–8. Each of these "capital city" bubbles showed a mix of classic and novel features. Each revealed, again, the centrality of the central banks themselves. In the aftermath of the bubbles, the questions unaddressed at the origins of the central bank project, of international financial governance, openness, and democratic accountability, are more pressing than ever. These questions concern the provision of money as an essential public utility. The ability to create credit-money yields enormous profits and creates powerful financial interests. Its governance involves highly specialized knowledge, which is often expressed in language that serves better to hide the real distribution of gains and losses than to make it visible and understood. Our study of historical origins seeks to clarify these issues.

1

THE BEGINNINGS OF CENTRAL BANK COOPERATION

Tokyo and London, 1895–1914

Anxiety about the national gold reserve was in no way abated. . . . Almost the whole civilized world was on the gold basis, so that, through the international banks, claims might be made on London from any, or all, of half a dozen or more financial centres. A centre so new, remote and incalculable as Tokio now kept very large balances in London.

JOHN CLAPHAM, *The Bank of England*, 1944

Cooperation between the Bank of Japan and the Bank of England, as revealed in hitherto obscure archival records, constitutes the first historical example we know of close, regularized cooperation between national central banks. The story starts with the Japanese receipt, in London, of an immense monetary indemnity from China, as an outcome of Japan's victory in the Sino-Japanese War of 1894–95. The indemnity funds were received by the Bank of Japan, at the Bank of England. Using these funds as a reserve, the Japanese government established a British-style gold standard in 1897. Interwoven with this story are the conclusion of the Anglo-Japanese military alliance of 1902 and the issuance, in London, of massive loans to the Japanese government for the war with Russia in 1904 and 1905. The Bank of England made use of Japanese funds to an extraordinary degree during this pivotal period. These operations helped it to maintain its own position at the foundation of Britain's globalized credit structure.

A detailed view of this connection is made possible by examining the governor's daily accounts at the Bank of England, which were not made available to outside researchers until almost a century after the events in question.[1] Even these records are cryptic, as explained below, with the enormous newly opened Bank of Japan accounts being labeled simply "A" and "B," without being otherwise named in the account books. These procedures testify to the great political and financial sensitivity of these accounts. A newly constructed data series based on these accounts is presented here and in appendix A at the end of the book.

The first decade of this central-bank connection was punctuated by wars, including Britain's war in the Transvaal and Japan's war with Russia in northeastern China. This period was punctuated also by financial disturbances, the greatest of which were the financial bubbles of 1906 and the panic of 1907. During these years, the Bank of Japan assisted the Bank of England with enforcing its official discount rate and thereby reinforced the preeminent standing of the pound sterling in international finance. What were the motives and nature of the mutual assistance between the Bank of England and the Bank of Japan? What was the significance of the Bank of Japan's "overseas specie reserve," which supported Japan's gold-standard currency system? And what was the role played by the Bank of Japan in lending short-term funds to the Bank of England?

The Bank of Japan's Foreign Specie Reserve Held in the Bank of England

On cessation of the Sino-Japanese War, the imperial Chinese government agreed to pay the Japanese government an indemnity of 200 million kuping (Treasury) taels, equivalent to 7.5 million kilograms of silver. A further treaty yielded an additional payment of 30 million kuping taels to the Japanese government.[2] Matsukata Masayoshi, Japan's veteran minister of finance, recognized the magnitude of the opportunity provided by the Chinese indemnity as early as May 1895 and petitioned the prime minister concerning the "method and process of payment." Matsukata's bold proposal was that all Chinese indemnity payments be paid in London in pounds sterling, directly convertible to gold, thereby creating the gold reserve necessary for Japan's adoption of the gold standard.[3] On October 6, 1895, the

Chinese government agreed with the Japanese request: regardless of how the Chinese government financed the indemnity, it agreed to make all payments in London, using English currency. Accordingly, the Chinese government was to pay £32.9 million; to this, £4.9 million was added for the retrocession of the Liaodong Peninsula, and a further £82,000 to subsidize the Japanese occupation of the port of Weihaiwei. The total Chinese payment to Japan was thus calculated to be £37.9 million.[4] It can hardly be overstated: the Bank of Japan's overseas specie reserves originated in the payment of these indemnities. Forced to resort to foreign loans to pay for these huge indemnities, the Chinese government turned first to a Franco-Russian bank syndicate.

On July 25, 1895, even before these arrangements were finalized, an account was opened at the Bank of England with the name "Russian Finance Minister," through the agency of the bankers Hottinguer and Company of Paris. On October 31, 1895, the bulk of the funds in this account, some £11 million, were transferred to another Bank of England account named "Chinese Minister," and then transferred into a "Japanese Minister" account as the initial indemnity payment. When the first check was drawn, for the first quarter-payment of the indemnity and ancillaries, it totaled £11,008,857 (often misquoted as being for £32 million or £38 million). It was reputedly, up until that time, the largest bank check to be processed in world history.[5] "On taking charge of this large amount of money belonging to Japan in the Autumn of 1895," as the governor of the Bank of England explained to the chancellor of the exchequer a year later, "we made no special stipulations, presuming that the nature of the operation was a temporary one."[6]

On March 12, 1896, the balance of the "Russian Finance Minister" account was again transferred to the "Japanese Minister" account, via the account of the "Chinese Minister." From this point on, however, a newly formed Anglo-German syndicate, on behalf of the Chinese government, refinanced the Franco-Russian loans and made all further indemnity payments.[7] The Anglo-German syndicate's aggressive takeover and refinancing of the Franco-Russian advance illustrates the way that finance and diplomacy so often converge.[8] The syndicate was led by the Hongkong and Shanghai Bank (the future HSBC) and the Deutsch-Asiatische Bank, which was itself owned by a consortium of German banks. Together they floated two £16 million loans for the Chinese government on the London financial market, the first at 5 percent in March 1896, and a second at 4.5 percent in March 1898.[9] The Bank of England was more deeply involved at this point, via its guarantee of the bonds. As a further outcome of this profitable arrangement, the Hongkong and Shanghai Bank also became the British government's chief financial agent in China.[10] The bulk of the indemnity was thus financed or refinanced in London. The Anglo-German syndicate included the Reichsbank, Germany's central bank, and the Disconto-Gesellschaft as a junior partner; they assisted by floating two loans worth £5.1 million each on the Berlin financial market in May 1896 and May 1898. The participation of the Reichsbank is significant, as it marked a starting point for the Bank of Japan to develop relations with the German central bank.[11]

After the fact—in the form of the Chinese indemnity—capital funds raised in European markets thus paid Japan's expenses in the Sino-Japanese War of 1894–95. The Chinese were left with the bill. For China also, this marked a turning point. Before this time, the external debt of the Chinese government was quite small. But now, as Charles Addis of the Hongkong and Shanghai Bank noted, China was having to borrow some £40 million to pay the indemnity. The annual debt service would henceforth cost the Chinese government about £3 million per year—and "that sum would nearly absorb all her maritime [customs] revenues, of which formerly six tenths were used in the provinces, four-tenths for the imperial exchequer."[12] The implication of Addis's statement, concerning the fiscal aggravation this might cause in the provinces especially, was prescient. By 1910, the Qing government was facing a comprehensive fiscal crisis, which created the conditions for its overthrow in the revolution of 1911.[13] Altogether, between October 1895 and May 1898, the Japanese government received in London a total of thirteen indemnity payments through the auspices of the Franco-Russian and then the Anglo-German financiers.

We have seen how the funds were raised. How were they received? First, in whose name would the Japanese account be held? In initial negotiations between the Bank of England and the Yokohama Specie Bank (YSB, Japan's parastatal foreign exchange bank), the Bank of England had refused to countenance the opening of an account for the Japanese bank.[14] By October 31, 1895, however, Bank of England objections to opening a Japanese account had obviously been overruled, presumably at the very highest levels of the British government. Nevertheless, it would take almost another six months for the Yokohama Specie Bank's negotiators (primarily Nakai Yoshigusu, but also Takahashi Korekiyo and others) to find a way around the Bank of England's intransigence.[15] In this context, it is notable that the Bank of Japan in 1897 requested to send two trainees to the Bank of England, and the request was brusquely turned down. These trainees were Inoue Junnosuke and Hijikata Hisaakira, who interned instead at Parr's Bank in London; both would serve in turn as governors of the Bank of Japan in the 1920s.[16]

In the end, Nakai Yoshigusu asked the Bank of England to open an account for Japan's central bank, the Bank of Japan, instead of for the Yokohama Specie Bank. Thus, on April 16, 1896, the account was retitled as "Bank of Japan," though it continued to be administered by the Yokohama Specie Bank as the London agents of the Bank of Japan. This account was the central reservoir of the Bank of Japan's overseas specie reserve; it was without doubt the most important account the Bank of Japan held at another bank.

Arguably, the Bank of Japan account was also the most important central bank account held by the Bank of England in the two decades prior to the First World War. In fact, for a time in late 1896, the Japanese account alone was equivalent to more than half of the Bank of England's entire gold reserve (see table 1.1). On May 18, 1896, the Bank of Japan account was split into two accounts: a normal "A" account held by the Bank of Japan head office, and a special "B" account, held by the Bank of Japan as its own convertible banknote reserve.[17]

Thus, the division of the Bank of Japan account into "A" and "B" accounts seems initially to have reflected the dual use of the indemnity payments as both a source of funds for foreign exchange and as an overseas specie reserve supporting the convertibility of the Bank of Japan's own banknotes.[18] This was a preparatory step in the establishment of the yen on a gold-standard basis; that happened on October 1, 1897, meaning that Bank of Japan notes were now convertible into gold rather than into silver as formerly. Later, in the early 1920s, when the Bank of Japan deposited a large $20 million and then $40 million fund at the Federal Reserve Bank of New York, it asked again for the same kind of dual account.[19] All of this suggests that the dual account arrangement had a particular significance or orthodoxy in Japan's international finances. But these "overseas specie reserves" were not something that Bank of Japan or Japanese Ministry of Finance officials discussed in public, and much concerning these arrangements remains obscure.[20]

Turning to the "A" and "B" accounts themselves, the first thing we notice is the enormity of their initial sizes (see table 1.1). The significance of the Bank of Japan's two accounts was not lost on the Bank of England; indeed, Bank of England officials in their daily account books entered the "A" and "B" balances in red ink under the bank's own account totals. For example, on June 1, 1896, following the big Chinese indemnity loan in London in March, the combined balances of the two accounts totaled over £20 million. This sum was equivalent to 53 percent of the Bank of England's entire gold reserve. Japan's balance at the Bank of England was also significantly higher than the value of all the other (British) bank balances held at the BoE at that time. On December 18, 1896, the Bank of England's governor A. E. Sandeman wrote to Chancellor of the Exchequer E. W. Hamilton to explain that after the bank received the large Japanese funds in the autumn of 1895, "numerous transactions have since taken place, and lately the Japanese Government have withdrawn a certain amount in gold for export." The Japanese had done this "in a very discreet manner," he said, "but, should these withdrawals assume large proportions, and become generally known, they might easily create alarm at a time like the present," when the financial markets were "in a very sensitive condition." The governor concluded that "unless some arrangement can be come to with the depositors," the money market would be seriously imperiled.[21] By January 1, 1897, the Bank of Japan's account balances were equivalent to 64 percent of the Bank of England's gold reserves, and were equivalent to 72 percent of total (British) bank balances held at the BoE. Clearly there was a need for the British government to accommodate Japanese finances, for while Sandeman refrained from discussing it in public, London's streets buzzed with rumors of Japan's "enormous (£11, £32, or £38 million!?) account" and how its withdrawal threatened the gold standard and the finances of Great Britain and the empire.[22]

It is therefore striking that the great bulk of the Bank of Japan's account does in fact appear to have been paid out in quick order. According to the Bank of England's daily accounts, there were no withdrawals from the Bank of Japan's accounts during 1895, but during 1896, £8,084,779 was withdrawn. The Japanese then withdrew almost double that amount, £15,459,576, during the twelve months of 1897.[23] Accordingly, the special "B" (convertible bank note reserve) account was closed at the request of the Bank of Japan on November 8, 1897. Japanese withdrawals continued, and after 1900, the Bank of England temporarily ceased to specially note the Bank of Japan's "A" account underneath its own daily account totals.

How did the agents of the Bank of Japan manage to move these enormous funds without disrupting London's financial market? The direct export of gold from the Bank of England to the Bank of Japan could have caused financial panic and had the potential to destabilize the British economy. The Yokohama Specie Bank therefore scoured the world's financial markets to purchase bills of exchange payable in Japan from late 1895 to early 1903. In this way, funds were remitted to Japan, while in London demand for bills of exchange, payable in Japan, did not seem unusually large. In the midst of these operations, during 1897, the Bank of Japan discreetly withdrew £6,018,048 from the "B" account for use as its convertible bank note reserve, in the lead-up to the adoption of the gold standard on October 1, 1897.[24] Simultaneously, the Yokohama Specie Bank went to great lengths to reduce the discounting in London of trade bills for imports to Japan, in order to discourage the Japanese import trade and ameliorate Japan's trade deficit with Great Britain.[25]

Table 1.1 summarizes the course of the Bank of Japan's accounts at the Bank of England over their first four years. In 1900, the Japanese balances were withdrawn from the Bank of England. Then, from the time of the Russo-Japanese War loans in 1904, the Bank of Japan again began to keep an account with the Bank of England, which mainly fluctuated around a level of between £1 million and £4 million from September 1904 through 1909, and thereafter held to lower levels (appendix table A.1). As discussed below, the Bank of Japan's balance at the Bank of England continued to be important to both parties.

Ultimately, from January 11, 1896, to March 31, 1899, Chinese indemnity funds worth £30.5 million, 80 percent of the total, were quietly withdrawn through the efforts of the Yokohama Specie Bank and, to a lesser extent, the Bank of Japan. The form in which these payments were transferred is telling. Some 52 percent (or £15.8 million) of these funds were withdrawn as Bank of England gold-convertible banknotes; this was the method most advantageous to the Bank of England. Another 10 percent (£3 million) was taken in the form of silver bullion (at a time when silver remained the ultimate form of settlement for the bulk of intra-Asian trade). Only 38 percent (£11.6 million) was taken as gold bullion "London Good Delivery" bars. To support Japan's new gold standard, two-thirds

TABLE 1.1. Bank of England reserves and Bank of Japan accounts, 1896–1900 (in thousands of British pounds)

	A	B	C	D	E
Date (year in quarters)	Total BoE reserves	Bank of England gold reserve	Bank of Japan "A" account (red-inked under "other private deposits")	Bank of Japan "B" account	BoJ balances as a proportion of BoE gold reserve ($C+D / B \times 100$)
1896 Apr. 16	45,075	38,186	9,057	0	24%
June 1	45,014	37,999	14,478	5,804	53%
Sep. 1	41,797	33,114	12,525	5,804	55%
Dec. 1	33,129	26,103	9,758	5,804	60%
1897 Mar. 1	36,434	29,653	7,138	4,220	38%
June 1	33,598	25,243	3,912	0	15%
Sep. 1	33,448	24,521	2,038	1,316	14%
Dec. 1	29,913	21,834	2,735	0	13%
1898 Mar. 1	31,427	23,730	889	0	4%
June 1	34,786	26,046	7,331	0	28%
Sep. 1	32,680	23,516	91	0	0%
Dec. 1	29,545	21,100	391	0	2%
1899 Mar. 1	31,552	23,762	1,019	0	4%
June 1	28,109	19,084	143	0	1%
Sep. 1	33,759	23,356	2,297	0	10%
Dec. 1	28,981	18,641	269	0	1%
1900 Mar. 28	34,186	22,156	98	0	0%

Source: Bank of England Daily Accounts, C1/44 to C1/48, Bank of England Archives, London.

of this gold bullion, equivalent to £7.7 million, was immediately minted as new gold yen coins, and stored by the Bank of Japan to be used as its convertible bank note reserve.[26] (In fact, Japanese monetary authorities largely reserved this gold for making international payments.)

Some large gold transactions certainly took place, as seen above, but records of these transactions seem to have disappeared. Wakatsuki Reijirō, the future prime minister, started his career as a financial bureaucrat and was posted to London as Japan's overseas financial commissioner from April 1907 to July 1908. He later wrote in his memoirs that Japan agreed to import gold from Australia in order to avoid direct shipments from

Britain, and that "not one ounce of gold left London bound for Japan."[27] The veracity of Wakatsuki's recollections requires further study. The first sale of Australian gold to the Japanese government for which records remain occurred in 1902, when the Japanese bought freshly minted gold specie worth £250,000 from the Royal Perth Mint.[28]

Alliance and War: London Lends to Japan

Anglo-Japanese financial cooperation was a product of interrelated financial and diplomatic objectives. Japanese efforts to raise a long-term loan in London began almost immediately after the adoption of the gold standard in October 1897. In the spring of 1898, Finance Minister Inoue Kaoru sent the vice president of the Yokohama Specie Bank, Takahashi Korekiyo, to London in a mission that resulted in the Japanese government's first large overseas bond issue in June 1899. The Japanese bonds sold poorly, owing to Britain's own impending war in the South African gold country. Nonetheless, the operation did open up an important channel for future borrowing in London. The Anglo-Japanese alliance was concluded on January 30, 1902, and in October 1902 a small Japanese bond issue was financed in London, this time with the "inscribed" guarantee of the Bank of England. With the outbreak of the Russo-Japanese War, on February 10, 1904, the Japanese government became desperate to find sources of funding. The Japanese government turned to the London financial market, where it ultimately took out a series of massive war loans.[29]

Britain's military alliance with Japan specified that Britain would come to Japan's aid if Japan faced a war with more than one country. Britain therefore remained neutral in Japan's war with Russia but in fact provided major assistance. Most decisive was the assistance of the London financial market: A consortium of London banks, jointly with a New York group organized by Kuhn, Loeb & Company, arranged four giant bond issues during the war, totaling £82 million. The first loan was issued in March 1904 and the last in July 1905. The Japanese government issued a fifth great loan of £25 million soon after the war, in November 1905, to refinance its earlier war bonds. £6.5 million of the November 1905 loan was taken out in London. Because of France's alliance with Russia, Paris markets were closed to Japanese borrowing during the war. With the conclusion of the war and with the participation of the Paris Rothschilds, the Paris markets were now opened to Japan, and £12 million was borrowed there. The remaining £6.5 million was divided equally between New York and Berlin.

Less is known, however, about how Japan's financial agents struggled to finance purchases for war matériel prior to these trophy loans, when victory was not assured. In fact, one of the first financial effects of the Russo-Japanese War was the transfer of balances to London by both belligerent governments, in order to pay for armaments, coal, and stores. It appears also that the Yokohama Specie Bank received two bridging loans of £500,000 from the Bank of England in October 1904, in order to facilitate its armament purchasing operations.[30] In this context, it became obvious to the Japanese government that a sizable working account should remain deposited at the Bank of England in London. This type of balance was later referred to as a "special" or "security" reserve. It is what after the Second World War would be referred to as a "compensating balance": as a condition for further borrowing, this balance would remain at the lending bank and would not be spent by the borrower. Such an arrangement is familiar in both Japanese and US practice.[31] The Bank of Japan's account balance was therefore increased by the Bank of Japan to the point that from July 2, 1904, the Bank of England again began to note the balance of the Bank of Japan's "A" account directly under its own daily accounts. The Bank of England's daily monitoring of the Bank of Japan's "A" account balance thereafter continued for almost twelve years, until May 2, 1916, when the account appears to have become dormant.[32]

The Bank of Japan "A" account balance, although diminished in comparison to its earlier enormous size, was still significant to the Bank of England, especially in the turbulent period from late 1904 to the end of 1910. Throughout this period, the Bank of Japan account averaged over £2 million. This amount represented around 10 percent of the Bank of England's gold reserve, and around 10 percent of total (British) bank deposits held at the Bank of England. At its second peak, on April 1, 1906, following the Japanese government's immense war bond issues in London, the Bank of Japan account equaled 33 percent of the Bank of England's gold reserve and 30 percent of its total bank deposits.[33] Thus, the Bank of Japan balance was often the largest of all bank balances—domestic or foreign—held at Bank of England in the first decade of the twentieth century. The Bank of England did not pay interest on deposits, but they were able to compensate depositors by providing other services beyond the reach of ordinary banks. These included the ability to support the issuance of large Japanese loans by easing market conditions at the appropriate moment.[34] Moreover, as we shall see, a balance the size of the Bank of Japan's "A" account could facilitate further central bank cooperation, in ways that the Japanese government could not have foreseen.

Tokyo and New York: Weaker Connections

The link between the Bank of England and the Bank of Japan, as described further below, appears to be the first case of regularized and continuous central bank cooperation between sovereign states. In contrast, high-level financial connections between Tokyo and New York developed more slowly and were never comparably close during the period before the First World War. Later, in the 1920s, the connection between New York and Tokyo did become closer; ultimately, this connection strengthened the hand of pro-austerity policy makers in Japan, in a way that greatly magnified the effects of the Great Depression. We discuss that moment in later chapters. Here we note that these Tokyo–New York connections originated as a Japanese initiative, and the first Japanese efforts were rebuffed.

The United States, for reasons tied to its federalist formation, did not establish an enduring central bank until 1914, decades after many less industrialized countries set up their own central banks. The Bank of England was founded in 1694, as the world's second central bank (after the Swedish Riksbank in 1668). The Bank of Japan was founded in 1882, designed to operate a national monetary system much as the Bank of England did. The Bank of Japan's legislative framework was modeled closely on the Belgian central bank.[35] The Bank of Japan was also the only central bank outside of Europe. In the United States before 1914, the US Department of the Treasury was responsible for the currency as well as for managing the debt of the federal government. The private firm of J. P. Morgan & Company took on some of the roles of a central bank, most conspicuously during the run on US gold reserves in 1895, when Morgan & Company made an emergency gold loan of $65 million to the US Treasury, thereby protecting the American gold standard.[36] Morgan & Company was able to act as a lender of last resort owing to its close London connections and ability to draw on the London capital markets. Morgan's role was also politically notorious, and it aroused widespread public criticism. When Japanese representatives first attempted to establish high-level Wall Street connections, it was to Morgan & Company that they turned.

These efforts began as early as 1897, simultaneously with Japan's new initiatives in the London financial world. It is notable that at the same moment, Japanese financial officials were also setting up the first of the Japanese colonial central banks, in Taiwan (meaning that the Bank of Taiwan also is one of the world's older central banks).[37] Effective October 1, 1897, as described already, the Japanese yen was placed on the same gold-convertible basis as the British pound and the US dollar, thus fixing the yen's exchange rate vis-à-vis the gold-standard currencies. A main goal in doing this was to establish Japan's national credit and enable it to borrow in Western financial markets.[38] The Japanese government immediately sought to raise large overseas loans in both London and New York. Japanese officials now attempted to establish a relationship with J.P. Morgan senior—"the king of the financial world," as Mitsui Bank president Ikeda Shigeaki called him. In 1897, Kaneko Kentarō, the Harvard-educated minister of agriculture and commerce, employed Edwin Dun, who had just retired as the American minister to Japan, to establish a connection. Dun sought a meeting with Morgan, but Morgan put him off, saying that Japan's business ought to go through London.[39] In March 1898, Kaneko secretly sent a second emissary, Sugiyama Shigemaru, to New York. Sugiyama's mission was to sound out Morgan & Company about helping to fund a "special" (*tokushu*) parastatal bank. This was the projected Industrial Bank of Japan (IBJ; Nippon Kōgyō Ginkō), whose mission would be to provide long-term finance for Japanese industry by issuing bonds at home and abroad. That bank was actually founded in 1902, but without foreign help. In 1898, Sugiyama succeeded only in meeting with Morgan's general counsel, telling him that he wanted $100 million to $130 million for the project. At the time, this was an immense sum, approximately equal to the Japanese government's entire general account budget. Morgan again sent word that the time was not right, given the impending US war in Cuba and the stringency in European capital markets.[40]

London was much more accommodating to Japanese borrowers. As mentioned, it was also in the spring of 1898 that Yokohama Specie Bank vice president Takahashi Korekiyo went to London and succeeded in arranging the Japanese government's first large overseas bond issue. No capital would be forthcoming for Japan from Morgan & Company for another twenty-six years. Thus Japan entered Britain's financial orbit.

Japan's 1904 war with Russia was a turning point in US-Japan relations also. During the war, American news media and public opinion broadly supported the Japanese side.[41] The Russo-Japanese War was also the occasion for the Japanese government's first borrowing from Wall Street, also arranged by Takahashi Korekiyo, now vice-governor of the Bank of Japan. Again, however, Takahashi was rebuffed on his first effort at raising a war loan in New York. He then went to London, where he met Jacob Schiff of the New York investment bank Kuhn, Loeb & Company, a rival of Morgan & Company. Takahashi contracted with Schiff to arrange a series of giant war loans in 1904 and 1905. The personal friendship between Takahashi and Schiff extended to a friendship between their families.[42] Their connection also constituted a main axis of Tokyo–New York financial relations for the next decade, illustrating the highly personal nature of these critical international ties during their early phase. These war loans were the first big long-term American loans to Japan. It is significant, however, that the operation was a fifty–fifty Anglo-American undertaking. The loan funds were denominated in sterling, not in dollars, and they were arranged by intermediaries in London. These facts confirm London's continuing financial centrality, and the de facto American support for it. These war loans were among the largest international loans of their times. They were critical for Japan's winning the war and establishing a colonial empire on the Asian mainland.

In the United States itself, this decisive financial support was followed by an anti-Japanese turn after the Russo-Japanese War, when both the US government and public opinion began to view an ascendant Japan as a strategic and racial threat.[43] These tensions also surfaced in finance. During the August 1905 peace treaty negotiations, the "railroad king" E. H. Harriman, a close associate of Jacob Schiff, visited Tokyo. His goal was to leverage Schiff's initiative by forming a joint US-Japan venture that would own and operate the formerly Russian-owned Chinese Eastern Railway line that formed part of Japan's war booty. The Japanese government at first agreed to but then rejected Harriman's plan. Instead it reorganized the railway in 1906 under the control of a new parastatal company, the South Manchurian Railway Company, thereby fixing the focus of Japan's empire-building program in China. US relations with Japan took on an aspect of rivalry and suspicion.[44] South Manchurian Railway Company debentures were thereafter effectively shut out of the New York financial markets. Jacob Schiff himself took a personal vacation to Japan in 1906, when he was lavishly hosted and honored by the Japanese government. During this visit, he tried and failed to revive Harriman's railway venture. After this, Kuhn Loeb took the American lead in only a single further bond issue for Japan, again jointly with London, in 1912.

In a contrary movement, Anglo-Japanese relations became closer after the Russo-Japanese War. The Anglo-Japanese military alliance was rewritten in much stronger terms after Japan's 1905 victory. British investment in Japan also became much more active. Japanese borrowers in London now included not only the central government but also several municipal governments, the Industrial Bank of Japan, the Oriental Development Company, and the South Manchurian Railway Company. Much of this borrowing went to help build Japanese infrastructure. Much of it also went to build the new Japanese empire in Korea and South Manchuria. Indirectly British lending also supported the maintenance of Japan's gold standard, by helping the Japanese government and its parastatal banks maintain larger sterling balances in London. Japan's sterling deposits in London also formed part of the "foreign specie reserve" (*zaigai seika*) against which new yen could be issued in Japan.

Japan Lends to the World's Bank of Banks

Before 1914, the Bank of England dealt almost entirely with British clients; the historical record does not seem to support some of the more enthusiastic statements made in recent histories of globalization claiming that the Bank of England acted as a kind of world central bank. As Bank of England historian John Clapham described it in 1944, only "a few centrally placed banks in the Empire and a few in foreign countries of secondary importance" had accounts at the Bank of England before 1914. Clapham listed only six: Greece, Japan, Spain, Turkey, New Zealand, and Australia.[45] Of these, only Japan and Spain could be considered to have had practical economic independence. Greece came under foreign, primarily British and French, debt administration in 1898. The Ottoman Empire functioned under a similar form of international debt administration, while the Imperial Ottoman Bank, which functioned as a central bank, was owned by French and British interests. Australia and New Zealand were parts of the British Empire. When the Bank of England dealt with "Indian" funds, to take another instance, the dealings were with the British officials who administered those funds. In this context, the relations that developed between the Bank of England and the Bank of Japan after late 1905 appear all the more extraordinary.

As a matter of law, the Bank of England was required to maintain the convertibility of its banknotes to gold. "Bank rate"—the interest rate the Bank of England charged when lending to other banks—was commonly described as the Bank of England's chief means of protecting its gold reserves. As the Bank of England explained in 1909: "The Bank rate is raised with the object either of preventing gold from leaving the country, or of attracting gold to the country."[46] Rate increases were the decisive action, with rate decreases being something like a system reset. Higher interest rates also increased the cost of doing business and could depress domestic business activity. In practice, the central bank regularly combined its bank rate increases with operations to quietly withdraw funds from the markets, in order to "make bank rate effective."[47] Thus, in managing the purportedly automatic gold standard, the Bank of England intervened routinely in the London credit markets.

The Bank of England also employed the so-called "gold devices," which were BoE interventions in the London gold market in order to increase gold reserves and discourage gold exports. These devices were highly effective because the Bank of England was actually much more than the London gold market's buyer and seller of last resort—the bank itself constituted the center of the market, as discussed further in chapter 8. Among the devices at the bank's disposal were the buying of gold at a price above its fixed statutory level; offering interest-free loans to gold importers; raising its selling price for foreign gold coins; or refusing to sell gold bars. All these tools together gave the Bank of England significant power to manage movements of gold into and out of the London markets. The bank resorted to these devices frequently; they were effective because of London's central place in the world's gold trade. Even during the British war in South Africa, when the BoE gold reserve fell to a low level, the Bank of England "had the first of the gold" from the Klondike, Kalgoorlie, and elsewhere.[48] With the end of the South African war, these methods were still more effective, with the bank in a position to manage the world's largest gold flows.[49]

In the Bank of England's credit-market interventions, India Office funds were enormously useful as a pool of short-term capital that the bank could pull out of the markets on quick order, thereby contracting the supply of funds and forcing borrowers to resort to the Bank of England. This ability to force borrowers "into the Bank" was a great source of flexibility to the Bank of England.[50] The BoE made regular use of Indian funds for this purpose, typically borrowing £1 million or £2 million. Secrecy and timing were critical here, but using India Office funds involved British agencies other than the Bank of England itself, meaning that news of the bank's actions could leak out. The Bank of England was also competing with a variety of City interests for these funds.[51] Connections with the Bank of Japan thus recommended themselves to the Bank of England for their confidentiality, and this is where the Bank of Japan's London funds entered the picture. Nevertheless, rumors of these operations—that the Bank of England made its rate effective by gaining "control of a considerable amount of Japanese money"—did make it into the press.[52]

This cooperative relationship began in late 1905, following the giant Japanese war loans of March 1904–November 1905. Thereafter, the Bank of England regularly made use of Japanese funds for its market interventions. These were formal loans, in which sums as high as £10 million were borrowed at negotiated rates for fixed periods, which were often extended. The first of these loans was in December 1905 (see table 1.2).[53]

The Bank of England made especially active use of the Bank of Japan's London funds during 1906 and 1907. Although the Bank of England changed its bank rate frequently, in the years after 1874 it enforced an extended period of high (over 5%) rates only twice. Both times are significant for the present discussion. The first episode of high rates was from October 1906 to February 1907. The second was later in the same year, from October 1907 to January 1908. These episodes of high bank rate thus framed the international financial panic of 1907.[54] The Bank of England's orientation may have been primarily British, but the effects of its policies were much more widely felt, and these rate increases put pressure directly on the United States and other countries.

This period of pressure began in September 1906, when heavy demand in New York was pulling large amounts of gold from London. The Bank of England again began to borrow Japanese funds—that is, it pulled these funds from the London markets—and raised its bank rate in October from 4 to 6 percent. Bank of England borrowing of Japanese funds became heavier in early 1907 (table 1.2). At this point, there were already signs of financial trouble in Japan. A postwar "victory boom" got under way in Japan in the second half of 1906, and the speculative frenzy reached a peak in January 1907. There was a banking crisis in Japan from March to May, and the country entered an extended period of postwar recession in April. The international crisis of 1907 thus appears to have broken out first in Japan. As Clapham described the view from London, "Japan had lost her economic head after victory over Russia, and was paying the sort of penalty that Germany paid in 1873, collapse following an orgy of promotion."[55] The London–to–New York gold flow also reversed in early 1907, as London now pulled funds from New York. In New York, there was also an initial wave of panic selling on the stock market in March 1907, followed by an apparent recovery from May to September. In late August, the Bank of England resumed heavy borrowing from the Bank of Japan. This continued to mid-September. Sayers makes the remarkable statement that, at this point, the Bank of England was fighting speculation—in New York!—to which British funds had been flowing in high volume. This interest in curbing speculation was itself something new in Bank of England doctrine.[56] In New York, the great financial panic broke out on October 22, 1906, and there was again an enormous demand for gold from London. In combination with its steps to pull funds from the markets, the Bank of England between October 31 and November 7 raised the bank rate from 4½ to 7 percent. "There had not been a single day of 7 since 1873."[57] The bank maintained its lending rate at 7 percent in November and December. There was now an enormous flow of gold into London, and renewed panic in Japan and other countries.

Japan's war with Russia thus had global financial effects, but these effects actually radiated out not from Tokyo but from the world's financial center in London. The war, and more particularly Russia's defeat, also had political effects, as seen in the revolutions of 1905–6 in Russia, Iran, and other countries. As a global moment of war, revolution, inflationary boom, and deflationary bust, these years foreshadowed the still greater and more globalized cascade of events of 1914–20.

The crisis of 1907 also highlights the connection between international financial centers. Japan has scarcely been noticed in this context, nor has it been noticed that the Bank of Japan functioned during these years as the Bank of England's leading lender. The detailed, often daily shifts in the Bank of England's borrowings of Japanese funds (for which it did pay interest), beginning in December 1904, suggest the Bank of England's management in detail when it came to advising the Japanese where and when to place their funds. It also suggests the central bank's careful governance of and detailed interventions in the London capital markets.

Cooperation between the Bank of England and the Bank of Japan was significant for Japan in another way, because the establishment of the Bank of Japan's "overseas specie reserve" after 1905 became the basis for Japan's own national monetary system. On paper, Japan had an orthodox gold standard, but in a de facto way, it was actually a sterling exchange standard. In other words, the Bank of Japan was counting its pound sterling balances as being equivalent to gold.[58]

We can add some additional relevant facts here. Japan was the largest foreign government borrower in the London capital markets during the years from 1900 to 1913, accounting by itself for more than 20 percent of London's foreign government loan issues during these years.[59] By 1913, Japan's total long-term foreign borrowing added up to roughly £200 million, a large sum to have run up in just fifteen years. Japan held the largest official sterling balances of any country in 1913. Although well down from their peak levels of a few years earlier, Japan's sterling holdings in London then still amounted to £39 million (or US$189 million; including Yokohama Specie Bank and Japanese government holdings). This sum exceeded even the London funds of the British government of India (£28 million [$136 million]), and these Indian funds have been described as a critical element in Britain's maintenance of its international financial position in the early twentieth century.[60] We can compare these numbers to the total officially reported foreign reserves that *all countries* held in London in 1913—£89 million (equal to US$432 million). Between them, Japan and India thus held 75 percent of the total. *By this measure, the international predominance of the pound sterling as a reserve currency was an Asian phenomenon.* This fact by itself demands a rethinking of the international financial history of the period.

TABLE 1.2. Summary of Bank of England borrowings from the Bank of Japan (amounts of about £1 million or more, red-inked at bottom of Daily Account pages)

Date (mm/dd/yy)	Amount (in millions of British pounds)
December 1904–January 1905	
12/28/04 to 1/11/05	1.0
September 1905–April 1906	
9/20/05 to 10/5/05	1.0–1.6
10/6/05 to 10/19/05	3.8–5.5
10/20/05 to 12/14/05	1.5–4.0
12/15/05 to 12/31/05	6.6–10.1
1/1/06 to 1/12/06	4.6–4.9
1/13/06 to 2/20/06	6.8–10.8
2/21/06 to 2/25/06	4.6
2/26/06 to 3/15/06	1.6–2.6
September 1906–February 1907	
9/13/06 to 11/18/06	2.0–5.5
11/19/06 to 11/24/06	0.9–1.6
11/25/06 to 1/3/07	1.6–2.2
1/16/07 to 1/17/07	0.9–2.9
1/18/07 to 1/30/07	4.3–5.2
1/31/07 to 2/13/07	3.1–3.4
2/14/07 to 2/15/07	0.9–1.4
October 1907	
10/16/07 to 10/21/07	1.6–2.2
October 1909–December 1909	
10/17/09 to 11/3/09	4.5–5.8
11/4/09 to 11/30/09	6.1–7.8
12/1/09 to 12/19/09	5.5–5.9
12/20/09 to 12/28/09	2.3–4.3
October 1910–December 1910	
10/21/10 to 11/1/10	1.2–4.6
11/2/10 to 11/23/10	5.4–6.4
11/24/10 to 11/30/10	3.6–4.6
12/1/10 to 12/9/10	1.0–2.9

Note: A day-to-day series is given in table A.2.
Source: Bank of England Daily Accounts, C1/44 to C1/64, Bank of England Archives, London.

It also compels a rethinking of the history of central bank cooperation. Central bank cooperation, as we discuss in the next chapter, is often seen to have originated during the First World War and then developed in the 1920s. It is also seen as a movement that primarily involved Great Britain, the United States, and sometimes France. Some writers describe central bank cooperation as having become substantive only in 1961, with the establishment of mutual credit lines and a large "swap" network between major central banks.[61] The example of the Bank of Japan and the Bank of England illustrates that it occurred much earlier than that. Indeed, from the Bank of England's perspective, cooperation with the Bank of Japan had a still earlier precedent, in the Bank of England's close connections with Britain's colonial and territorial monetary authorities, and particularly in the Bank of England's handling of the massive reserves of the colonial government of India. The centralization of other countries' gold holdings in London thus began before the First World War. In an ad hoc and untheorized way, the Bank of England, as a central reservoir for gold, took on some of the functions of an international central bank. Out of this experience, in the matrix of war, a more conscious and explicit "forward" policy began to emerge.

2

World War and Globalization

The modern banking system has been likened to a huge sky-scraper based on
a comparatively small foundation of gold, and the many superimposed stories
are represented by the immense number of all obligations payable in gold
which, ordinarily, are settled by clearings of credits. . . .

. . . Under a modern system, there are two entirely different duties to be
performed by the general banking institutions and the central organ. The
former must see to it that they can command cash credits to meet their
demand obligations, but it is the duty of the central reservoir to see to it that
these cash credits be always transformed into actual cash when required. . . .

. . . The duty to transform credit into cash resting on the central organ, *it
alone is concerned in the holding of adequate gold reserves . . .*

PAUL WARBURG, on "Circulating Credits," July 1914

Around the world, the First World War brought about an enormous am-
plification of credit creation. In the United States, a new central banking
structure, the Federal Reserve System, began to operate only a few weeks
after war broke out in Europe. As the warring countries of Europe embargoed gold exports, and as the financial markets of London closed their
doors to the needs of foreign businesses, the new Federal Reserve Bank
of New York immediately faced ample challenges and opportunities. International gold shipments became tightly regulated during the war. At
the same time, new credits for international purchases changed hands in
a flood of exchanges. This flood of credit created a heavy burden of debt,
which would dominate the economic character of the years that followed
the war. These metaphors are incongruous—the liquid metaphors so often
associated with credit, and the metaphors of heavy material burden so

often associated with debt—and this incongruity suggests some of the social contradictions of the process itself.

The greatest volume of international credits was created to fund the purchase inside the United States of an enormous volume of agricultural and industrial production. These credits were created by the Wall Street money-center banks, led by J. P. Morgan & Company, now backed by their new, jointly owned central bank. By 1915, US banks were thus engaged not only in the biggest international financial operations in their own history but in some of the biggest international financial operations yet seen. Simultaneously, National City Bank of New York established, in a matter of months, the first great international branch network of any American bank. It did this by moving into overseas financial markets that had formerly been oriented toward London. The year 1914 thus signified the sudden beginning of the era of US-centered financial globalization. As chapter 3 will describe, Japanese banks also moved for the first time into large-scale international lending.

Central banks also gained new powers. Domestically, in almost every country, wartime financial demands greatly enhanced the administrative authority and reach of central banks. And, within days of the beginning of war in August 1914, the Bank of England began to put into action a program of international central bank cooperation.

De-globalization after 1914?

How can we understand the long-run timing of financial globalization? Was it characterized by cyclic intensifications, and cyclic reversals? Recently, many historians of economic globalization have described the First World War as the *end* of the first great age of modern globalization and the beginning of a phase of "de-globalization" or "globalization backlash."[1] This view of history does not describe what happened in international finance. It is also a Europe-centered view of history, and a foreshortened one, which lumps together the 1920s with the 1930s—two decades that differed radically in their international financial character. In the view we offer here, financial globalization actually intensified in the 1920s, partly as a *result* of the First World War. London-based globalization was indeed set back by the war in several ways. Crucially for our account, however, even in the view from London there was a great leap forward in respect to central bank cooperation. In fact, this was the period when the Bank of England led the first campaign for multilateral central bank cooperation. Berlin, Frankfurt, and Hamburg indeed lost their standing as international credit centers, while the place of Paris was much diminished. But seen from the standpoint of New York, and from the standpoint of Tokyo as well, the First World War accelerated financial globalization in practically every respect. "Whole world" globalization outside Europe developed to an entirely new level, notwithstanding the disruptions of trade in Eastern and Central Europe and the higher trade tariffs imposed after the war by many countries.

The World War also marked the beginning of a much more explicitly *managed* form of globalization. In this movement, international monetary and financial management played a leading but often unpublicized role. During the 1920s, this management was predominantly British and American. Ultimately, it was a movement whose own internal dynamics led to the international financial collapses of the early 1930s.

A US Central Bank

At this point, it is good to step back and survey some of the circumstances of the formation of the Federal Reserve System itself. Our focus here is on the international dimension.[2] Margaret Myers, writing in 1931, put it categorically: New York was "not equipped" to be an international money market until the passage of the Federal Reserve Act in December 1913. Then, "the establishment of the Federal Reserve system made it possible for New York at last to take its place among the money markets of the world and indeed, by virtue of war conditions, to become their leader."[3]

This new international leadership was personal as well as institutional. Here, Benjamin Strong (1872–1928), as founding governor of the Federal Reserve Bank of New York, was the leading figure.[4] Strong himself advanced into the top circles of American banking not only because of his capability and drive, but also owing to his close relationship with J. P. Morgan & Company. This relationship itself goes far in explaining Strong's influence. From the latter part of the nineteenth century, Morgan & Company connected the peak levels of the New York and London financial worlds. In 1900, Morgan handled the first large US loan to Great

Britain, to help finance the conquest of the Transvaal. Morgan's London partner, Edward Grenfell, became a Bank of England director in 1905 and remained a member of the Bank of England court until 1940. The central bank connections that developed after 1915 thus arose out of the matrix of Morgan & Company networks. Benjamin Strong entered this network on the basis of personal connections, made early in his banking career when he moved into the exclusive neighborhood of Englewood, New Jersey. There, he became friends with Henry P. Davison (1867–1922) and Thomas W. Lamont (1870–1948), joining the same clubs and community organizations. Davison helped found the Morgan-linked Bankers Trust, helped frame plans for the Federal Reserve System, and then became the leading partner at Morgan & Company. Lamont was Davison's protégé and later succeeded him as the leading partner and chief diplomat for Morgan & Company. Davison adopted Strong too as a protégé, and Strong's career thereafter progressed one step junior to Lamont's.

Bankers Trust itself was created in 1903 as a "bankers' bank." It was owned by other banks, held some of their reserves, and served them as a lender of last resort. It thus served as a kind of private central bank for the New York City banking world, in advance of the establishment of the Federal Reserve Bank of New York. It was also at Bankers Trust that both Lamont and Strong rose to senior positions in the banking world. In 1904, Lamont was made vice president of Bankers Trust. Strong succeeded Lamont as secretary and treasurer of Bankers Trust. Strong's professional success was joined with personal tragedy. In 1905, perhaps suffering from postpartum depression, Strong's wife, Margaret, committed suicide. They had two young sons and two young daughters. Their elder daughter then died in 1906. The three other children were brought up in Davison's family.[5]

During the October 1907 financial panic, J. P. Morgan, James Stillman, and other top New York bankers put Davison in charge of the bailout effort. Davison tasked Strong with heading the committee that decided which banks to save.[6] Also in 1907, Strong married Katherine Converse, the twenty-year-old daughter of the president of Bankers Trust. In 1909, Davison became a Morgan partner. Lamont then also left his position as vice president of Bankers Trust, to fill Davison's former position as vice president of the Morgan-linked First National Bank of New York. Strong in turn filled Lamont's former post as vice president of Bankers Trust. In 1911, Lamont himself joined Morgan & Company as a partner.

Strong was also one of the framers of America's new central bank system, together with Henry Davison, Paul Warburg of Kuhn, Loeb & Company, and Frank Vanderlip of National City Bank. Strong's involvement in the project went back to a ten-day meeting at the Jekyll Island resort in Georgia in November 1910, hosted by the powerful and corrupt Senator Nelson Aldrich, chair of the Senate Finance Committee (and father-in-law of John D. Rockefeller Jr.). The bankers traveled together in a private railway carriage dressed as duck hunters, not wanting stories to get into the newspapers that the bank plan was cooked up by a group of Wall Street bankers. Like the others, Strong, in his own words, "[had] always been in favor of a central bank, as distinguished from this regional bank plan." He was further convinced that "if we are to have a central bank, it must be run from New York."[7] Strong was appointed president of Bankers Trust in 1914. In October of the same year, when Europe's Great War was already under way, he was elected governor of the newly established Federal Reserve Bank of New York, which opened for business in November. It was chiefly Davison and Warburg who persuaded Strong to take the job as FRBNY governor.

The title of "governor" was borrowed from British central bank practice, and its use is significant. On paper, the FRBNY was one of twelve new reserve banks. In many ways, however, Strong functioned as America's first, de facto central bank governor. Strong's personal qualities, his personal history as part of Wall Street, and his bank's location and role made the FRBNY the first among the formal equals in the Federal Reserve System. Strong led the system especially when it came to the Federal Reserve's relations with the central banks of other countries. This balance of forces shifted under Strong's less forceful successor, George L. Harrison, when the great transformation of the 1930s brought power to the Federal Reserve Board, and more than that, back to the US Treasury, both headquartered in Washington, DC.

Like the members of the Morgan firm, and like Inoue Junnosuke in Japan, Strong was Anglophile in orientation. For this he was later criticized for having divided loyalties. Herbert Hoover later blasted him as "a mental annex to Europe," in the blame game that followed the Great Depression.[8] Strong's pro-English orientation mirrors the strongly American orientation of Strong's counterpart in London, Montagu Norman.

Wartime Origins of Multilateral Central Bank Cooperation

The widening of central bank cooperation began immediately after the outbreak of war in August 1914, at a time when the Bank of England was engaged in an unprecedentedly large bailout of the London financial markets. It was then that central banks first established standing bilateral agreements.[9] By the end of the year, an Allied central bank network was in place. Coincidentally, the Federal Reserve Bank of New York went into operation in November 1914. Within months of the bank's founding, its new governor, Benjamin Strong, worked to assist this Allied central bank network, and he took steps to join it formally a year in advance of the US government's entry into the war.

The view that multilateral central bank cooperation was a wartime innovation is supported by the work of Kenneth Mouré (1992) and Marc Flandreau (1997). Under the classical gold standard, central banks provided reserves to each other in an ad hoc way, and this provision of reserves was at times critical, as Barry Eichengreen has emphasized. But in regard to ongoing cooperation, Mouré has concluded that "the pre-war gold standard offered neither justification nor opportunity for continuous central bank co-operation." Flandreau goes further, arguing that central banks scarcely cooperated before the First World War. Therefore, he concludes, "the alleged collapse of central bank cooperation" in the 1930s "looks very much like business as usual."[10] The type of multilateral cooperation that began during and after the First World War was something new.

The movement to organize an international network of central banks began with the Bank of England. When Britain entered the war on August 4, 1914, the London gold market was effectively closed and gold exports informally embargoed. (As explained further in chapter 7, the Bank of England in many ways *was* London's gold market.) On August 8, the Defence of the Realm Act prohibited the private export of gold. Financial authorities maintained the pretense that Great Britain remained on the gold standard.[11] In fact, other countries could not repatriate their gold from London; the British pound was no longer as good as gold.

To aid in settling international payments in these new circumstances, the Bank of England turned to central-banking techniques that it had long used in order to settle accounts between British banks at the national level.

A prime example was its use of that "most valuable adjunct of the clearing house," the Private Drawing Office, which extended short-term credit and facilitated remittances between banks, seeking to minimize actual transfers of currency. (The Public Drawing Office handled British government accounts.) In August 1914, the Bank of England lost no time in putting the Private Drawing Office to work. In John Clapham's description,

> War also brought some novelties in the "Private" Drawing Office. On the day that the first Ways and Means Advances were sanctioned [August 13, 1914], the opening of a drawing account for the Bank of France was approved. Then on 20 August, an account was opened for the Banca d'Italia. . . . In September the name of the National Bank of Switzerland appears. The ally, a potential ally, and the most honourable and resolute of neutrals are linked with the world's second greatest reserve of wealth and credit, in London. Before the end of the year, the governments of France, Belgium and Serbia, allies, and of Chile, a friendly neutral, all have drawing accounts; and so have the National Banks of Belgium and Serbia, with those of Norway and the Netherlands—both neutrals well disposed but, for geographical reasons, not always able to be openly helpful.[12]

By December 1914, the Bank of England thus set up a mechanism for direct transactions with seven foreign central banks and with four foreign governments, using the facility of a drawing office similar to what British banks maintained to conduct their own clearings with each other. Already, the Bank of England's network included most of Western Europe. (Chile's inclusion is also notable, for Chile was the world's chief exporter of sodium nitrate, used to produce high explosives.)

Having an account at the BoE's Private Drawing Office enabled a private financial institution (or agent for a government) to carry out and settle all manner of transactions without having to use banknotes or coins. Avoiding the physical use and movement of currency, and restricting the unit of settlement to British pounds, greatly supported the Bank of England's own credit-creation power. It also increased the speed of transactions and reduced the risks of loss. Now, emergency wartime clearing arrangements allowed the Private Drawing Office to extend credits, or advances, free of charge. The Private Drawing Office also received and supplied various forms of foreign exchange and offered custody of valuables, also without charge.[13] In theory, any private individual or institution could open an account at the Private Drawing Office, but the usual catch was the Bank of England's insistence that the client deposit a sufficient "remunerative balance" in proportion to its liabilities. There were no fixed rules concerning how large these compensating balances should be, but they should reflect the type, size, and frequency of business proposed. In practice, approximately 20 percent seems to have been sufficient.[14] These dormant balances would later be termed "special security" or "security reserves," and were usually discussed behind closed doors. The Bank of England's Private Drawing Office maintained close liaison with the bank's Chief Cashier's Office and with the Treasury and other departments of the central government.[15]

In 1916, the Bank of England and the Bank of France regularized and deepened their connections, also establishing a direct telegraph link between the offices of the two governors. It was also in 1916 that the Federal Reserve Bank of New York joined this financial alliance. Even before this, Benjamin Strong deployed the new capacity of the FRBNY to discount trade bills as a means of Allied war finance.

Thus, central banks opened their own diplomatic channels during the war, in a new kind of quasi-public, quasi-private diplomacy. This central bank diplomacy was highly personalized, and it developed out of the shared social circles and conventions of the world of private high finance. Benjamin Strong was the leading American practitioner of this new diplomacy. In turn, the new salience of international financial relations greatly enhanced Strong's position as America's first de facto central bank governor.[16] Strong had already made a trip to Europe shortly before the war, in May and June of 1914, after the Federal Reserve legislation was passed but before he himself had agreed to serve as governor of the New York bank. In July 1915, Charles Addis of the Hongkong and Shanghai Bank visited Strong in New York. Addis, an experienced financial diplomat, would join the Bank of England's Court of Directors in May 1918.[17] In September 1915 the first gigantic American war loan was floated by J. P. Morgan & Company, a $500 million issue for the British and French governments. Strong made his first trip to Europe as FRBNY governor in February–April 1916, going to Britain and France to strengthen ties. In the midst of these undertakings, 1916 was another year of personal crisis for Strong. His second wife, with their two young daughters, left him, and they later divorced. It was also in June 1916, after returning from his trip to Europe, that Strong learned that he had tuberculosis, which was to remain chronic for his remaining twelve years.[18]

Of the greatest significance for these institutional ties was Strong's friendship with Norman. Norman himself was an insider's insider, descended on both sides of his family from former governors of the Bank of England. He was an army officer during the South African war and worked as a merchant banker in New York and London.[19] These New York and South African connections are notable in the context of the present study. Norman joined the Bank of England's Court of Directors in 1907, became BoE deputy governor in 1917 and then governor in 1920. Before the First World War, governors of the Bank of England, as a rule, had served two-year terms. The five-year wartime term of Walter Cunliffe from 1913 to 1918 was itself unprecedentedly long. But the historical record goes to Norman, who began his term as governor in March 1920 and ultimately remained in office until 1944. The friendship between Norman and Strong began during Strong's three-month sojourn in 1916. Their friendship deepened in 1920–21, after which Strong and Norman regularly spent extended vacations together. Both men were bachelors, married to their institutions. Both suffered from ill health. When Strong died in office in 1928, it seemed he had already lived longer than he expected. Norman, who remained a bachelor until age sixty-two, was a remote and mysterious figure interested in occult forms of spiritualism. The two men developed an intimacy that at least verged on the romantic.[20] Their personal friendship involved a great informal exchange of information; hence Sayers's comment that Norman often shared more with New York—meaning Benjamin Strong—than with his own people.[21] Their friendship also meant operational cooperation that may have gone to the extent of systematic public deception, as discussed in chapter 6.

Thus, acting for the Federal Reserve System, Benjamin Strong initiated a formally private and extraconstitutional track of financial diplomacy. Following Strong's meetings in Europe, the FRBNY appointed the Bank of England as its foreign agent in December 1916. As Strong confidentially expressed it to Norman, the goal was to establish "the closest possible relationship between your great institution and our new one . . . even tho extensive transactions are not undertaken at this time, we should nevertheless perfect our arrangements and put the plan in operation so that the relationship will be fait accompli." This happened at a moment of

US-British tensions, including a public warning over massive British borrowing by the Federal Reserve Board in Washington (with President Wilson behind them). Strong apologized for this to Norman.[22] In February 1917, the FRBNY also designated the Bank of France as its agent.[23] The establishment of correspondent relations between the FRBNY, the Bank of England, and the Bank of France ultimately involved the central banks opening accounts for one another and arranging the purchase of bills of exchange for one another, enabling interbank transfers to substitute for gold shipments. The role of central banks in acting as each other's "agents" would become an explicit part of Norman's theory of central bank cooperation, discussed further in chapter 4.

Thus, a de facto alliance of central banks was inaugurated in advance of any constitutionally sanctioned foreign alliance on the part of the US government. Inside the Federal Reserve System, Paul Warburg vigorously but unsuccessfully opposed Strong's initiative as being a violation of the US government's neutrality policy. Strong argued that it did not violate neutrality because both the FRBNY and the Bank of England were private banks.[24] On April 6, 1917, the United States Congress declared war on Germany.

Benjamin Strong also sought to bring the Bank of Japan into the FRBNY's new international network. There was no military alliance between the United States and Japan, but after April 1917 both countries were wartime allies of Great Britain. Japan had entered the war on August 23, 1914. In November of that year, Japanese forces completed their occupation of the German territorial concessions in Shandong, and in January 1915 the Tokyo government presented the Beijing government with its Twenty-One Demands, calling for political, military, and economic concessions that would have radically subordinated the Chinese government to the Japanese. The Japanese state behaved "like a thief at a fire," as historian Shimazaki Kyūya put it.[25] As we will see, the Japanese government also organized a consortium of Japanese banks and undertook an extraordinary campaign of overseas lending. American suspicions of Japanese intentions in China intensified greatly.

American financiers were more interested in cooperation. In June 1917, Benjamin Strong sent a message to the Bank of Japan representative in New York indicating that the FRBNY had established connections with the British and French central banks and proposing a similar connection with the Japanese. The Bank of Japan was interested, and instructed its New York representative office to negotiate a formal connection. The Japanese were represented in Washington by Baron Megata Tanetarō, the former minister of finance, and by the New York representative of the BoJ. (A decade earlier, Megata had taken the lead in organizing a Japanese-controlled central banking system in Korea.) The Japanese and US central banks accordingly opened business relations on January 9, 1918.[26]

New York as an International Financial Center

International credit creation by US banks suddenly surged after 1914. The context of this expansion was the boom in wartime exports, which began in 1915, when the United States accumulated an annual export surplus of $1 billion. This historical record was followed by export surpluses of more than $3 billion a year in 1916, 1917, and 1918, and more than $4 billion in 1919.[27] Practically the whole world outside of Europe took part in the export boom, as did European neutral countries such as Spain. Japan, relative to the size of its existing industrial base, boomed more greatly than any other large country. The industrial base of the United States was many times larger than Japan's, and in absolute terms the United States gained the most of all. There was a great increase in agricultural and industrial production, and a great increase in prices and wages.

Unlike European currencies, the US dollar remained convertible into gold after August 1914, and gold remained freely exportable. Enormous though it was, the creation of bank credits and long-term loans covered only part of Allied purchasing in the United States, and Great Britain now shipped enormous volumes of gold to the United States. For New York City especially, it was a kind of gold rush, comparable in its scale, suddenness, and inflationary effects with the California gold rush of 1849–50. During the first phase of the war, before the United States entered the war in April 1917, $1 billion in gold came into the United States. Americans simultaneously paid off their current foreign debt, owed mainly to British investors. They also aggressively repurchased foreign-held US securities. American banks also arranged the lending of more than $2 billion abroad.[28]

Most of the gold delivered to the United States to settle British accounts actually came by way of the British dominion of Canada. In the year

1915, net gold imports to the United States came to $420 million. Of this, $207 million came from Canada and $109 million directly from Britain. In 1916, the net gold inflow was $530 million; $571 million in gold came from Canada and only $51 million came direct from Britain.[29] These gold shipments to the United States were partially offset by large gold exports; by 1917, the largest destination for US gold exports was Japan. Hence some of the interest of US bankers in Japan.

Making a Market: The Trade in Trade Credits

When they planned the Federal Reserve System, Paul Warburg, Benjamin Strong, Henry Davison, and Frank Vanderlip shared the aim of creating a market for discounting trade bills in New York. Their goal was to take over the financing of American import and export trade from London and to extend the international usage of the US dollar, thereby opening immense new fields for lending and credit creation by US banks. They were thinking specifically of a market for dollar acceptances, to finance international trade in competition with sterling bills, which were the main vehicle for financing global trade up to 1914.

The shutting of London markets to the trade-financing needs of other countries after August 1914 turned this plan into a pressing necessity of trade and greatly accelerated its realization. US banks thus filled in, partially, by financing trade bills where European credit facilities were withdrawn. For the banking world, this taking up of business formerly dominated by London was the equivalent of the surge of import-substitution industrialization seen in so many countries during the war years. It was Benjamin Strong at the Federal Reserve Bank of New York who took the lead in sponsoring and regulating this new market.[30] Almost immediately, Strong also used the FRBNY's new facility for discounting trade acceptances to provide de facto long-term credits to the British and French governments. This happened in advance of the first large war loan organized by Morgan & Company in September 1915. These financial commitments worked as factors promoting the US entry into the war.

Emulation, gentlemanly business rivalry, and quiet informal understandings were thus all elements in Strong's relationship with British finance.[31] In fact, the first subject of correspondence between Norman and Strong concerned this very point—informal understandings. Shortly before his visit to London in the spring of 1916, Strong in December 1915 queried the Bank of England about the rules governing commercial bills connected to actual shipments of goods versus bills for general financing. This issue was at the heart of the struggle between Strong and Warburg over war finance. Norman avoided saying anything definite in response, but he did offer a general statement that exemplified his entire approach, which was based on unwritten "tradition," "elasticity," and the cultivation of uncertainty over the central bank's intentions.[32]

In London, sterling bills had owed their convenience and liquidity (meaning their ease of cashing at banks) to the large secondary market for discounting them. This market was ultimately backed by the Bank of England, which stood ready, in a cash crunch, to temporarily buy up top-quality bills. The writers of the Federal Reserve Act wanted to re-create such a market for dollar acceptances in New York.[33] An acceptance is a kind of promissory note, an order for a bank to pay a specified amount after a certain time, based in turn upon a commercial debt owed to the bank by a merchant. Acceptances could also be traded in a secondary discount market. Thus, banks created credit in the form of acceptances, which were based on commercial bills, which were based upon actual shipments of goods. Other banks and financial institutions would buy these acceptances at a discount, and the Federal Reserve banks (mainly the New York bank) stood ready to buy them in an emergency. With this system in place, New York banks could finance trade between third countries that did not involve American companies. This had been London's business before the war. By the end of the war, New York was catching up fast, and in the 1920s, New York's acceptance business would surge. As J. Peter Ferderer concluded, the dollar acceptance, "a financial instrument created almost from scratch," rose to "challenge the mighty sterling bill," a major step in making New York City the world financial center.[34]

The market in bankers' acceptances also originated as a market made by and for the Morgan group and National City Bank. The very first issues of the *Federal Reserve Bulletin* named the banks discounting acceptances. At the top of the list were Bankers Trust, Strong's former employer, and Guaranty Trust, also of the Morgan group, joined by National City Bank. Later numbers of the bulletin often omitted this information.[35]

The question of trade acceptances was thus from the beginning a political one. From early in the war, Strong enabled the provision of open-ended credits to the Allies by quietly turning trade acceptances into revolving credits, as Priscilla Roberts indicates in an important study of the subject. These were de facto unsecured loans no longer tied to any particular consignment of goods. In doing this, Strong also asserted, through the FRBNY's chief legal counsel, that America's new central bank was a private institution, owned by its member banks, and therefore free to deal with foreign banks without violating the US government's neutrality policy.[36] In pushing this policy, Strong represented, de facto, the financial group centered on Morgan & Company. He was resisted by Paul Warburg, who had intimate family and business ties in Germany and who viscerally opposed US involvement in the European war. More than genuine trade acceptances, these revolving credits had become "finance bills drawn by foreign governments masquerading as acceptances." Warburg thus opposed the creation of credits that were not based on a particular trade transaction and hence were not self-liquidating.[37] This latter point deserves special notice: these acceptances had become a pure creation of new purchasing power unconnected to any specified material economic activity. Warburg was joined in his opposition to this use of acceptances by Frank Vanderlip of National City Bank. The Federal Reserve Bank of New York itself bought up large volumes of these acceptances, although many of them ended up on the books of other Federal Reserve banks and did not appear in the published statistics as FRBNY purchases. Accordingly, there was a huge creation of new credits via the new mechanism of bankers' acceptances in the latter part of 1915. This creation of new purchasing power was, of course, inflationary.

Strong and the Morgan firm, represented by Henry Davison, thus enthusiastically funded and supported the war, which Warburg hated.[38] Although Warburg won some tactical victories in the struggle over acceptance credits, he lost the war, as it were. In 1918, now stigmatized as a German, Warburg had to resign from his position as vice-governor of the Federal Reserve Board.

Creating a Global Commercial Bank: Frank Vanderlip and National City Bank

American banks took quick advantage of the forced retreat of British finance during the First World War by opening up their own operations overseas. The new Federal Reserve Act permitted national banks to open overseas branches. The first to take advantage of this provision was National City Bank of New York (NCB), the future Citibank and later Citigroup, led by Frank Vanderlip (1864–1937). During the wartime surge of US business overseas, Vanderlip made National City Bank into the most international of American banks.[39]

The business of international branch banking by US banks was actually pioneered just after the turn of the century by the International Banking Corporation (IBC), which was chartered by the state of Connecticut. The International Banking Corporation established its first branch, in the Philippines, shortly after the US conquest. It served as the depository of colonial government funds. In the context of a political structure that was then highly federal, the new US overseas colonialism stands out also as a frontier of federal government expansion, with the Philippine colonial government itself being under the US Department of War's Bureau of Insular Affairs. The International Banking Corporation began to do business in Shanghai in 1902. Here, too, the IBC did business as the agent of the US government, collecting the Boxer indemnity funds paid by the Chinese government. As with the overseas advance of Japan's Yokohama Specie Bank, politically led processes were intertwined with commercially led processes. By the early 1910s, the IBC had a network of branches scattered through the foreign treaty-port settlements of East Asia. This network would later be taken over by National City Bank.

National City Bank became the largest US bank by assets in the 1890s. As Standard Oil's main bank, National City Bank was within the circle of the Rockefeller interests. There were family ties here as well, as both daughters of NCB chairman James J. Stillman married into the Rockefeller family. Stillman and National City Bank were close to E. H. Harriman and to Jacob Schiff of Kuhn, Loeb & Company, but the bank also became close to Morgan & Company. It thus maintained good relations with rival financial empires.[40] The expansion of National City Bank went into overdrive during the war years, under the leadership of Frank Vanderlip, the bank's president from 1909 to 1919. Vanderlip began his career as a journalist and publicist. Thomas W. Lamont of Morgan & Company had likewise started out as a journalist. So too did Ikeda Shigeaki of Mitsui Bank (hence in a popular Japanese account of world finance, Vanderlip was called "America's Ikeda Shigeaki"). Vanderlip entered the US Treasury

Department in 1897, and as assistant secretary of the treasury gained a rep-
utation in financial circles by his success in selling war bonds for the 1898
war against Spain, working closely with his mentor, Treasury Secretary
Lyman J. Gage.[41] Gage later joined Vanderlip and his party on a 1920 jun-
ket to Japan, as described in chapter 5. Vanderlip also wrote several popular books, including such titles as *The American "Commercial Invasion" of
Europe* (1902), which was translated immediately into both German and
Japanese. The year 1902 was also when Vanderlip joined National City
Bank. He became the bank's president in 1909. National City Bank took
part in the Morgan-led syndicates for lending to Latin America and China,
also formed in 1909. In the 1920s, the same four-bank group, known as the
"New York Group," would become active in organizing lending to Japan.
As mentioned, Vanderlip participated with Henry Davison, Benjamin
Strong, and Paul Warburg in the famous secret meeting at Jekyll Island in
1910 and helped frame the first plan for the US Federal Reserve System.
National City Bank was the first shareholder in the new Federal Reserve
Bank of New York in 1913.[42]

Enabled by the Federal Reserve Act, National City Bank set up its first
overseas branch in November 1914, in the historically British financial
domain of Buenos Aires. This was the same month that the Federal Reserve
Bank of New York opened its doors. In the South American countries that
had historically been in the financial orbit of London, this North American banking advance was purely a matter of business. Closer to US shores,
this banking advance was also intertwined with gunboat diplomacy. Haiti
presents a striking example. The government of Haiti had fallen under a
multinational financial administration run by France, Britain, the United
States, and Germany, the same creditor countries that made up the four-
country consortium in China. With Europe at war and renewed stirrings
of revolution in Haiti, the United States in December 1914 asserted unilateral control over Haitian finances, as Secretary of State William Jennings
Bryan agreed to the requests of Haiti's American bankers—National City
Bank—and of the foreign-controlled National Bank of Haiti, to remove
the Haitian government's gold reserve. The gold was taken aboard a US
warship to the safety of NCB's New York City vaults. US armed forces
subsequently occupied Haiti in July 1915. National City Bank later took
control of the National Bank of Haiti itself.[43] Here, again, state and private
initiatives were intertwined.

US international branch banking was belated in comparison not only to that of Britain but also compared to France, Germany, and Japan. National City Bank swiftly made up for lost time. In 1915, National City Bank bought the International Banking Corporation, and the two subsequently operated as a single entity. By 1918, National City Bank had forty-one overseas branches. Of these, twenty-four were IBC branches, including fifteen in Asia. Seventeen were direct NCB branches, of which fourteen were in Latin America. Within just four years, National City Bank thus established one of the largest international bank branch networks in the world. It was also the leading American bank in East Asia. In November 1915, Vanderlip directed another international initiative, also directed toward Asia, in the form of the American International Corporation (AIC), whose vice president was Willard Straight. Straight himself had close connections with both Morgan & Company and Benjamin Strong.[44]

NCB was especially active in trade finance and foreign exchange, and the wartime export boom meant a tremendous increase in the bank's trade financing business. By 1919, National City Bank was the first US bank to claim $1 billion in assets. In the 1920s, as a member of the "New York Group," NCB took part in bond issues for the Japanese central government, municipal governments, and corporations.[45] As we will see, National City Bank also helped launch the run on Japanese gold reserves in January 1930—opening the first act in the "gold rush" that ended in the collapse of the international gold-standard system.

Still more internationally significant was the transformation of J. P. Morgan & Company into a global investment bank. In 1915 and 1916, Morgan & Company financing was critical to British and French war supply. Morgan & Company was the official purchasing agent for the British and French governments, and the gains of both Morgan & Company and of Morgan's Guaranty Trust were very large.[46] Morgan & Company added Tokyo to its network after 1920, at the same moment that Benjamin Strong was forming a personal connection with the Bank of Japan. (We treat the activities of Morgan & Company less in the present book because they are covered extensively in the book *Lever of Empire*.) After the war, again in partnership with the FRBNY, Morgan & Company engaged in a series of "stabilization" loans, in a style much like that later followed by the IMF, swaying the course of the national histories of Japan, Germany, Italy, and other countries.[47]

Wartime: The State-Bank Nexus

In the late nineteenth century, in the absence of a central bank or of regular, authoritative state involvement, Wall Street developed as America's
peak banking center. The organization of the Federal Reserve System in
1913–14 created an entirely new level of financial system governance, and,
via the special role of the FRBNY, helped to institutionalize the position
of Wall Street within what was in effect an extended state-bank structure.
There remained major obstacles to the extension of Federal Reserve authority. Although national (federally chartered) banks were required to
join the new system by the Federal Reserve Act, banks and trust companies chartered by the states initially held back. American entry into the war
in April 1917 brought a sudden and extraordinary change. The Federal
Reserve banks now indeed appeared as agencies of a central state with authoritative powers of surveillance and control. This was part of a panoply
of controls, as described in a 1920 statement by historian Frederic Paxson:

> By September 1918, the organization of the American war government was
> complete. By the side of the normal civil agencies with restricted powers, it
> comprised a series of boards and administrations exercising dictatorial au-
> thority over economic and social matters. It marked, in the term of eighteen
> months, a genuine attempt at a complete transition from the doctrine of in-
> dividualism and free competition to one of *centralized national co-operation*.[48]

Paxson was celebrating rather than criticizing this emergency response.
"Nearly three thousand separate agencies" were involved in this network
of state control.

The Federal Reserve Bank of New York was indispensable in this program of "centralized national cooperation." The United States government restricted gold shipments by presidential order on September 7, 1917,
in effect suspending the US gold standard. (The biggest gold shipments
had been to Japan, as detailed further in chapter 3.) The Federal Reserve
Board was put in charge of administering gold shipments. The FRBNY's
own powers of regulation and guidance extended to an extraordinary daily
monitoring and control over the banks' lending decisions.

In Tokyo, in May 1920, Benjamin Strong explained these changes to
an audience of Japanese bankers, saying that America's entry into the
war brought the imposition of governmental controls over production,

transportation, consumption, and credit. The Federal Reserve System had a key role, raising war loans and controlling credit in cooperation with the Treasury. "But we could not rely upon [interest] rates alone to control credit," Strong explained. Therefore, "understandings were entered into with the New York Stock Exchange, and the principal New York banks, by which the amounts of borrowings and lendings were reported daily." These reports were made to a committee chaired by Strong. "With this information in hand, the Committee . . . was able to regulate the amount of credit employed on the Stock Exchange. Every day the amount to be loaned was determined, and the loans apportioned among about 65 banks." In this way, the FRBNY practiced an intensive form of what the Bank of Japan would later call *window guidance*.[49]

Strong reported that these lending controls began on September 10, 1917. This was three days after the US gold embargo was put in place, although Strong did not mention this connection. It was also from this same point, in the first week of September 1917, that Strong was in regular close contact with the Bank of England concerning interest rates and other matters.[50] As Strong did report in Tokyo, his committee regulated hundreds of millions of dollars in lending, while keeping interest rates steady at about 6 percent. In fact, this wartime experience of "window guidance" gave Strong and his bank an unprecedented authority over the New York banks. It also provided an unprecedented access to financial information, which greatly enhanced the power of the new FRBNY vis-à-vis the banking community. As Strong noted in his speech in Tokyo, "we have in our possession the most complete files of credit reports in the country; an invaluable asset when banking becomes less easy to conduct."[51] To put it mildly, Strong, who already knew a lot about such things, learned all the more about the business of the private banks. The dense web of personal obligations between Strong and the rest of the New York banking community grew still tighter. Remarkably, this episode of direct central-bank credit control, and its considerable implications, go unmentioned in most financial histories.[52]

In the late summer of 1918, a time of inflation and labor protests around the world, Strong's committee acted to restrain stock market speculation. They continued to do so until the spring of 1919. "It was successful in a large measure," Strong reported in May 1920, "but finally the pressure to remove restrictions became so great that our control of the borrower was discontinued about a year ago."[53] As we will see, the spring of 1919 was also when an international inflationary boom got underway. In respect to the New York financial markets, the FRBNY may temporarily have deployed more power over its client banks than did the Bank of Japan. Strong's own evaluation, however, was that the "Bank of Japan has always kept such a very close relationship with ordinary banks as finds no equivalent in other countries." And in fact, the Bank of Japan was during the war engaged in operations that show significant parallels to those Benjamin Strong was undertaking in New York.

3

Japan Emerges as an International Creditor, 1915–1918

> Of all materials required for war, credit is the easiest to manufacture. One
> stroke of the pen on the books of a bank, one revolution of the printing
> press, and bank deposit or note currency is produced. The banking machine
> responds to the demands of higher prices and sometimes of Finance
> Ministers, almost it seems with a note of joy.
>
> Benjamin Strong, speaking to the Tokyo Bank Club, May 1920

During the First World War, the United States abruptly replaced Great
Britain as the world's largest creditor nation. Some seventy years later,
around the year 1985, Japan abruptly replaced the United States as the
world's largest creditor nation. These facts are well known and have been
extensively researched, although Japan's present-day place in the international credit system remains an open historical situation, whose nature and
significance are not yet truly understood. In contrast, Japan's first venture
into the role of international creditor is almost unknown.[1]

With its incorporation into the London-centered world economy of
the nineteenth century, Japan became a peripheral, debtor nation. Japan's
external debts remained relatively small until the Russo-Japanese War,
after which they became very large. With the great European war of
1914–18, this position was suddenly reversed. Japan was temporarily transformed into the country with the second-largest surpluses, after the United
States, and Japanese financial institutions held large balances overseas.
The yen was one of the world's strongest currencies. Like their American

counterparts, Japanese financial authorities also managed to finance their own wartime trade, owing especially to the efforts of the Yokohama Specie Bank and the Industrial Bank of Japan.[2] These two parastatal banks, which functioned as a designated foreign exchange bank and a long-term industrial-investment bank, had key roles in the administration of Japan's capital imports and exports. They were established to realize national policy goals, to mobilize domestic funds, and to build Japan's standing in international finance.

What's in a Center?

During the European war, the question of the shifting of international financial centers attracted much attention. Speaking in June 1918, in the context of the surge of Japanese overseas lending described in this chapter, Inoue Junnosuke, then president of the Yokohama Specie Bank, discussed the question of what makes an international financial center. As "absolute requirements," he said, a fully developed "financial central market" must have

1. a clearing center for international settlements;
2. a credit center with abundant capital for overseas investment;
3. an accumulation of large overseas investments and surplus investment capital;
4. an abundant foreign trade; and
5. a free market for gold—this was "the first absolute condition."[3]

This "first absolute condition" turns out to be anything but natural or simple, as we will see in chapter 7, which looks at the actual workings of the "free market" in gold in London itself.

As Inoue saw it, the development of a financial central market was a question both of institutional infrastructure and of quantitative accumulation. As seen in Tokyo's rise as a financial center, this was a domestic process as well as an international one. In fact, it was only in the late 1910s that Tokyo truly became Japan's premier *national* commercial and financial center. That position had been held by Osaka since the seventeenth century, and Osaka continued to lead in many fields of business enterprise into the early twentieth century. Indeed, Tokyo was not completely dominant as a national financial center until after the great banking panic of 1927, which, in combination with the revised banking law, led to a great concentration of the banking sector, strongly centered on Tokyo.[4]

An early step toward making Tokyo an *international* financial center was the creation of an international branch network by the Yokohama Specie Bank. The YSB was founded in 1880. By 1902, the YSB had ten branches in Asia and another sixteen branches in Japan, in addition to its headquarters. (The British Hongkong and Shanghai Bank had twenty-four branches in Asia at the same date, and, as we have seen, US overseas banking was only beginning.) Japanese conquest of an overseas empire in northeast Asia brought another kind of financial expansion, with the founding of colonial central banks. In 1897, at the same moment that Japanese financial authorities set the yen on a gold standard basis, they also established a central bank in their new colony of Taiwan. In 1904, when Japanese military forces occupied Korea during the Russo-Japanese War, a senior Ministry of Finance official, Megata Tanetarō, took control of Korean government finances and established the local branch of Shibusawa Eiichi's Dai-ichi (First) Bank as Korea's de facto central bank.[5] In 1909, the Japanese set up the Bank of Korea (Kankoku Ginkō) as a central bank. It was renamed the Bank of Chosen (Chōsen Ginkō) in 1911, when Japan annexed Korea as an outright colonial possession. Gold shipments from Korea also provided a significant support for the Japanese gold standard (see chapter 8). But the truly great shipments of gold that flowed into Japan in the late 1910s were the result of the export boom.

According to Inoue Junnosuke, Japan's foreign debts in 1913 stood at ¥1.94 billion, or approximately £200 million. The bulk of this debt had been accrued in the 1904–5 war with Russia. To service a debt of this size required annual interest payments of ¥130 million, or roughly £13.3 million.[6] This was equivalent to about 20 percent of the Japanese general account budget at the time. The "substitute production" boom of the First World War, when Japan filled in for the shortfall of European production, supplied Japan with enough financial resources to potentially liquidate these foreign debts.[7] The United States used wartime surpluses to liquidate its own debts, which were owed above all to British investors. Japanese officials did not do this, though there was substantial Japanese repurchasing of Japanese government foreign-currency bonds originally floated in

London and New York. Japan did follow another American example, by extending credits to its new wartime allies, Britain, France, and Russia. It also concluded a series of highly ambitious and politicized loans in China. Initially, this lending conformed to economic and financial imperatives, but later loans to Russia, and loans to China especially, strongly reflected the diplomatic and political intrigues of Japan's wartime government.

Under the terms of the Anglo-Japanese alliance, Japan entered the war against Germany but confined its military operations to China and the Pacific. In November 1914, Japanese forces seized the German concession in Shandong and took over the Qingdao–Jinan railroad. Filling in for the Royal Navy, Japanese naval patrols extended much further—as far as the coast of British Columbia, northern Australia, and the Mediterranean. The presence of Japanese warships caused alarm in Australia particularly.[8]

In the wartime context of very limited specie exchange, Japanese trading companies struggled to remit their growing trade profits and to fund their transactions on the world's disrupted markets. With the effective closing of London to the needs of third-party trade financing, gold was all the more critical as a means of settlement, particularly for Japanese cotton mills' purchases of raw cotton from India. Japan's ability to pay for Indian cotton hinged upon payment for its trade surpluses with the United States in the form of gold, and then export of the gold onward to the wholesalers in India.[9] Large gold shipments from the United States to Japan began in 1917; in the first eight months of the year, $155 million in gold was shipped to Japan—$140 million from May to September alone—out of a net US gold outflow of $181 million. On September 7, 1917, the US government embargoed gold exports. The Japanese government responded with its own gold embargo five days later.[10] In these circumstances, the Bank of Japan, the Yokohama Specie Bank, and other financial institutions undertook various schemes to facilitate trade. As it was with the United States, Japan's international extension of credit to Britain, France, and Russia was also a means to fund its own export trade.[11] Citing the American example, Inoue Junnosuke in 1917 also promoted loans to European allies as a prudent form of financial insurance against anticipated postwar deflation, readjustment, and recession. Foreign lending potentially served also to "sterilize" monetary inflows and restrain domestic note issue. For Inoue, this was also part of a wider vision of turning Tokyo into a true international financial center, a "London of the East." Leading members of the

Terauchi cabinet, in office from October 1916 to September 1918, were more concerned to use Japanese loans to seize the moment and grasp the levers of influence in China.

Lending to Wartime Allies

Table 3.1 gives an account of Japanese wartime lending to European allies. The lending began in November 1915 with an issue of long-term military bonds for the French government, supported by a coalition of Japan's leading entrepreneurs and bankers. These loans were followed by a large ¥50 million loan to the Russian government in February 1916 and a second Russian loan, for ¥70 million, in September 1916. These bond issues were a new departure for the Tokyo financial world, which had previously lacked an institutional infrastructure for issuing international loans. For the February 1916 loan, the Japanese government enlisted the services of the Yokohama Specie Bank, to organize an eighteen-member syndicate of commercial and parastatal banks. This syndicate subsequently took part in seven further international loans, with a face value of ¥542 million. In total, the syndicate raised over 60 percent of all capital loaned to the British, French, and Russian governments.[12]

Upon receiving an official request from the British government, the Japanese government, through its Ministry of Finance, also undertook to organize capital loans to its hitherto major creditor, a historic about-face. The first British loan was on July 25, 1916, in the form of the British (Six Per Cent) Sterling Treasury Bills, totaling £10.0 million (¥94.6 million), with a short, one-year maturity.

These amounts were very great in Japan's experience but were small compared to Allied borrowing in the United States. By late 1916, British and French purchases in the United States alone were running at the astounding pace of $10 million per day. In November and December, there was a crisis in Allied war funding, so severe that members of the British political establishment began to consider a negotiated end to the war.[13] At this critical time, in October 1916, the British government was encouraged by the Sale & Frazer Company and the Industrial Bank of Japan to issue British Treasury bills on Japan's financial markets. These were the one-year British (Five Per Cent) Treasury Bills, followed in December by the

TABLE 3.1. Japanese lending to wartime allies, 1915–1918

Issue date (year.month)	Country	Name of loan	Interest (per year; %)	Maturity (years/months)	Issue amount (in millions of yen)	Issue amount (in millions of francs, rubles, pounds)	Issuers
1915.11	France	French Military Bonds (1st series)	5.0	15/0	¥0.9	fr 2.3 [£0.1]	Franco-Japanese Bank
1916.2	Russia	Russian Gov't Treasury Bills (1st series)	5.0	1/0	¥50.0	rub 51.6 [£5.3]	Japanese "eighteen bank" syndicate
1916.7	Britain	British Sterling Treasury Bills	6.0	1/0	¥94.6	£10.0	Ministry of Finance Deposit Bureau
1916.9	France	French Military Bonds (2nd series)	5.0	15/0	¥0.2	fr 0.6	Franco-Japanese Bank
1916.9	Russia	Russian Gov't Treasury Bills (2nd series)	6.0	1/0	¥70.0	rub 72.3 [£7.4]	"Eighteen bank" syndicate
1916.10	Britain	British Treasury Bills	5.0	3/8	¥5.2	£0.5	Sale & Frazer Co.
1916.10	Russia	Russian Gov't Short-term Military Bonds (1st–3rd series)	5.0	1/0	¥11.9	rub 12.3 [£1.3]	Sale & Frazer, and Russo-Chinese Bank
1916.10	Russia	Russian Gov't Liberty Bonds	5.0	1/0	¥2.7	rub 2.8 [£2.9]	Sale & Frazer, and Russo-Chinese Bank
1916.12	Britain	British Military Bonds	5.0	3/0	¥3.8	£0.4	Sale & Frazer, and Industrial Bank of Japan
1916.12	Britain	1916 British Gov't Yen Treasury Notes	6.0	3/0	¥100.0	£10.6	"Eighteen bank" syndicate
1917.2	Russia	Russian Gov't Treasury Bills (3rd series)	6.0	1/0	¥50.0	rub 51.6 [£5.3]	"Eighteen bank" syndicate
1917.3	France	French Yen Treasury Bills (4 issues)	6.0	1/0–1/9	¥26.2	fr 67.7 [£2.8]	MoF Deposit Bureau
1917.4	Russia	Russian Gov't Treasury Bills	5.0	0/6	¥15.5	rub 16.0 [£1.6]	MoF Deposit Bureau
1917.7	France	1917 French Gov't Yen Treasury Notes	6.0	3/0	¥50.0	fr 129.0 [£5.3]	"Eighteen bank" syndicate & Franco-Japanese Bank
1917.9	Russia	Russian Gov't Treasury Bills (4th series)	6.0	1/0	¥105.0	rub 108.4 [£11.1]	"Eighteen bank" syndicate
1917.10	Russia	Russian Gov't Treasury Bills	6.0	0/8	¥15.5	rub 16.0 [£1.6]	MoF Deposit Bureau
1917.10	Russia	Russian Gov't Treasury Bills (5th series)	6.0	1/0	¥66.7	rub 68.8 [£7.0]	"Eighteen bank" syndicate
1917.11	France	French Military Bonds (3rd series)	4.0	25/0	¥0.4	fr 0.9	Yokohama Specie Bank & Franco-Japanese Bank
1918.1	Britain	British Yen Treasury Bills	5.0	1/0	¥80.0	£8.5	MoF Deposit Bureau
1918.11	France	1918 French Gov't Yen Treasury Notes	6.0	3/0	¥50.0	fr 129.0 [£5.3]	"Eighteen bank" syndicate & Franco-Japanese Bank

Source: Okurasho [Ministry of Finance, Japan], *Meiji Taishō zaisei shi*, vol. 17 (1940), pp. 593–638.
Note: The "eighteen bank" syndicate consisted of: Dai-ichi Bank, Mitsui Bank, Daihyaku Bank, Industrial Bank of Japan, Bank of Chosen, Dai-san Bank, Yokohama Specie Bank, San-juyon Bank, Naniwa Bank, Mitsubishi Goshi Banking Division, Ju-go Bank, Sumitomo Bank, Konoike Bank, Kajima Bank, Bank of Taiwan, Yasuda Bank, Omi Bank, and Yamaguchi Bank.

Five Per Cent British Military Bonds. Together these totaled ¥9 million, or £0.95 million. Significantly, the Ministry of Finance's Deposit Bureau (Yokinbu) underwrote Britain's yen and sterling bill issues in Japan. In December 1916, the Japanese government tasked the Yokohama Specie Bank and the eighteen-bank syndicate with a much larger British loan of ¥100 million, equivalent to roughly £10 million. The Japanese government was now lending funds, in its own currency, to the world's banker—something that would have been unthinkable just two years earlier. Simultaneously there was an enormous increase in Bank of Japan credit creation, also in the month of December 1916, when BoJ advances on foreign bills jumped suddenly from ¥50 million to ¥122 million. The BoJ's other loans and advances simultaneously jumped from ¥88 million to ¥156 million.[14]

Following the success of the December 1916 operation, all subsequent wartime loan issues supported by the Japanese government were denominated in Japanese yen. On January 21, 1918, a further issue of British (Five Per Cent) Yen Treasury Bills, totaling ¥80 million, was organized by Japan's Ministry of Finance. In total, short-term bills, bonds, and notes worth ¥284 million, or £30 million, were raised in Japan for the British government.[15]

In lending to France, three series of military bonds were issued, for a total of ¥1.5 million, or 3.9 million francs. These bonds had interest rates of 4 to 6 percent, with long fifteen- to twenty-five-year maturities. The Banque Franco-Japonaise, founded in 1912, was a key institutional player in these transactions. The Japanese Ministry of Finance also offered to issue yen Treasury bills on behalf of the French government beginning in March 1917. Consequently, four series of French Yen Treasury Bills were issued, yielding ¥26 million, or 67.7 million francs. The eighteen-member bank syndicate also floated two large issues of French Government Yen Treasury Notes in 1917 and 1918, for a total of ¥100 million. Thus, in the three years from November 1915 to November 1918, Japanese financial markets provided ¥128 million in bills, bonds, and notes to support the French war effort.[16] Again, it is remarkable that Japan was lending capital, denominated in yen, to the prewar world's number-two creditor nation.

By the end of 1917, lending to cash-strapped Russia threatened to eclipse total Japanese lending to Britain and France combined. Miraculously, Japan and Russia had made the transition from enemies to something approaching military allies in the years after 1907. But why was the

Japanese government so eager to extend credit to a country that was clearly the biggest credit risk of all the great powers, particularly after the February Revolution of 1917? As with Britain and France, economic and financial imperatives were important. Japanese suppliers sold the Imperial Russian Army large amounts of ammunition and weapons, worth ¥80 million in 1915 alone. Here, too, lending to Russia in yen was a form of export finance. In the summer of 1916, after the first large Japanese loan of ¥50 million but before the second loan of ¥70 million, the Russo-Japanese alliance of July 7, 1916, was signed, and the Russian government agreed to cede the Changchun-Sungari branch line of its Chinese Eastern Railway to the Japanese government in exchange for military supplies. Clearly, there were important diplomatic and political dimensions to Japan's lending to Russia.[17]

The bulk of Japanese lending to the Russian government was raised by the same eighteen-member syndicate that lent to Britain and France, and it was planned with the guidance of the Ministry of Finance and its Deposit Bureau. From February 15, 1916, to October 8, 1917, the Japanese syndicate raised a series of five Russian Government Treasury Bills, which totaled ¥373 million, or 385 million rubles, an extremely large sum in the Japanese financial context. These loans all had one-year maturities. In October 1916, Japan's financial markets also funded three issues of Russian Government Short-term Military Bonds, totaling ¥12 million, and Russian Government Liberty Bonds of ¥2.7 million, both with one-year maturities. The Sale & Frazer Company and the Russo-Chinese Bank, along with a number of private financiers, issued and underwrote these public bond issues. In April 1917, the Ministry of Finance's Deposit Bureau issued its own Russian loans, the Russian Government (Five Per Cent) Treasury Bills totaling ¥15.5 million, with a six-month maturity. Six months later, in October 1917, this loan was rolled over at a 6 percent rate.[18] Altogether, Japanese lenders issued bills, bonds, and notes with a face value of ¥387 million for the Russian war effort.

In this way, a significant share of Japan's wartime earnings were expended in foreign loans, a large part of them to former creditors, rather than in accelerated redemption of its own earlier war debts. As for the loans to Russia, hopes of repayment effectively ended with the October Revolution in 1917.[19]

Or did they? In the wake of the October Revolution, the Terauchi cabinet's determination to intervene in Siberia may be seen as an attempt to recoup losses incurred from lending to Russia, as if Siberia and its rail-way lines were acceptable collateral for Russia's outstanding loans.[20] If so, Japan was not alone in such concerns. In Omsk, Admiral Alexander Kol-chak, the British-sponsored leader of the "white" regime in Siberia, had seized £80 million in gold stocks of the former Russian government. He expressed a desire to expatriate this gold, and to deposit it with the Hong-kong and Shanghai Bank. British authorities' interest in getting hold of this gold appears to have been an additional motive for British interven-tion in Siberia.[21] Ultimately, more than seventy thousand Japanese troops were dispatched to Siberia, accompanied by large numbers of Japanese civilians. Despite the initial successes of Japan's military advances in the latter half of 1918, Bolshevik and other partisans provided fierce resistance across the region. Given the delicate military balance in East Asia, Japa-nese forces were almost immediately joined in Siberia by vigilant Ameri-can forces, who soon sought to neutralize any advantages Japan hoped to win. The realization that Japan might remain in Siberia acted as a strong incentive to drive the Allies toward dealing with Japanese demands at the Paris Peace Conference. However, like the extension of credit to Russia itself, the Siberian intervention became a political liability and was to her-ald future Japanese failures on the Asian continent.[22]

The root of the Terauchi cabinet's failures abroad are to be found in the establishment of its own "transcendental" foreign affairs agency on June 5, 1917, which effectively usurped the primacy of the Foreign Ministry to act as the Japanese government's representative in East Asia. The executive-level Special Foreign Policy Research Council (Rinji Gaikō Chōsa Iinkai), as it was called, had among its members Prime Minister Terauchi, For-eign Minister Motono Ichirō, Home Minister Gotō Shinpei, the heads of the three major political parties, imperial army and navy representatives, Privy Council representatives, and influential elder statesmen.[23] The coun-cil's proceedings were strictly secret, and direct accounts of its delibera-tions were censored over its sixty-four-month life. "China Affairs" and the Siberian intervention were the council's preoccupations; indeed the coun-cil's very formation was entwined with Chinese and Siberian issues. Power was eventually wrestled away from it by the resurgent Foreign Ministry in 1922.[24] In this way, Japanese lending to Russia stands in between the more businesslike approach of Japanese lending to Britain and France and the frenzy of secretive political lending in China.

Lending to China

In 1895, Sergei Witte, Russia's long-serving minister of finance, is said to have stated quite openly in conversation "his hope that China might fail to meet her engagements *punctually* in which case Russia would obtain the rights of *interfering directly* in the administration of Chinese finance."[25] Were Japan's leaders thinking something similar, some twenty years later, when they extended credit to Duan Qirui and his Anfu regime? Significantly, the sordid episode of Japanese lending to China happened at the time that the Foreign Policy Research Council was the arbiter of Japan's foreign relations with China.

The context of this lending was a great surge of Japanese commercial and industrial activity in China. The war had halted European investment in China. Japan, by contrast, had nearly twice as much direct investment in China in 1920 as in 1914, as Japanese enterprises enlarged their industrial and commercial operations in China and founded many new ventures. The business of the Yokohama Specie Bank in China was already large, and it now expanded greatly. The Specie Bank's issue of banknotes in China more than doubled from 1915 to 1916. Bank balances held at YSB branches in China increased much more than that. The scale of increase in the YSB's total operations is reflected in the increase of its global balance sheet total from £32 million in 1915 to £115 million in 1918, to a peak of £139 million in 1920.[26]

Japan's wartime lending to the Republic of China came on the coattails of the Twenty-One Demands secretly delivered to the Yuan Shikai regime on January 18, 1915. Engineered by Foreign Minister Katō Takaaki, with broad support by Prime Minister Ōkuma Shigenobu and his cabinet, these demands were presented under five basic headings. The first group concerned itself with the transference of German rights in Shandong Province to Japan. The second group called for the acknowledgment of Japan's "paramount interests" in southern Manchuria (Manshū) and eastern Inner Mongolia (Mōkyō). The third group dealt with the surrender of control of China's largest iron and coal mining conglomerate (the Hanyeping Konsu) to Japanese creditors. In the fourth group, Japan forbade China from ceding or leasing any further coastal or island concessions to other foreign powers. Still more offensive demands were made in the fifth and final group, which, among other things, obligated the Yuan Shikai regime to employ Japanese political, financial, and military advisers. If granted, these demands would have allowed Japan a hegemonic level of influence in China.[27]

The first of Japan's wartime loans to the Chinese government in Beijing was the Armament Loan of December 1915, which was issued shortly following the issue in Tokyo of the first French military bonds. In January 1917, during secret treaty negotiations with Great Britain, Japan offered to use its good offices to encourage China to enter the war against Germany.[28] China's declaration of war against Germany was the signal for a series of Japanese loan projects. Prime Minister Terauchi sent his personal representative Nishihara Kamezō to Beijing on February 13, 1917. Nishihara met Cao Rulin and Liang Qichao, two of the Duan regime's most important members, and immediately began to negotiate war, railway, and resource-development loans.[29] Prime Minister Terauchi Masatake, Minister of Finance Shōda Kazue, and businessman Nishihara Kamezō were the key proponents of "financial expansionism" in China.[30] Between February 13, 1917, and September 28, 1918, Nishihara, acting under Terauchi's instructions as a secret personal emissary, and without the knowledge or approval the Foreign Ministry, arranged what would become known as the "Nishihara loans."[31] He also acted outside of established Japanese financial channels in China, which were coordinated especially by the Yokohama Specie Bank. Competition over China was thus a source of friction within the Japanese political and financial establishment.

Following the outbreak of war in Europe, competition over China was also a great source of friction between Tokyo and Washington. For the government of the United States, the issues were the preservation of China's independence and territorial integrity, along with the continued operation of the so-called "open door" free-trade system and equal-opportunity principles. Anxious to allay American concerns, the Japanese government appointed Ishii Kikujirō as special ambassador to the United States. He arrived in Washington on September 1, 1917, to immediately begin discussions with Secretary of State Robert Lansing. (It was also at this point, on September 7, that the US government embargoed gold exports.) In the Lansing-Ishii Agreement of November 2, 1917, Japan reiterated support for China's territorial independence and for equal access to its open door. In return, Japanese negotiators gained an American recognition "that territorial propinquity creates special relations between countries, and consequently, the Government of the United States recognizes that Japan has *special interests* in China, particularly in the part to which her possessions are contiguous."[32]

US acknowledgment of Japan's "special interests" was watered down from Ishii's initial demands for the words "paramount interest." But combined with the announcement that America planned to join other powers in reestablishing a financial consortium to control the flow of capital to China, this recognition fueled the ambitions of the Terauchi cabinet and the so-called China experts in the Imperial Japanese Army. Prime Minister Terauchi authorized loans to the Chinese premier, Duan Qirui, and his government, as a means to justify Japan's increasing economic penetration into the Chinese mainland and further Japanese aims of political hegemony.[33]

Table 3.2 lists Japanese wartime loans to China. The Nishihara loans consisted of a war loan and seven railway and resource-development loans, which totaled ¥145 million.[34] The Industrial Bank of Japan, the Bank of Chosen, and the Bank of Taiwan extended and underwrote these loans. All three were parastatal "special banks," the latter two being the Japanese-run central banks of Korea and Taiwan. The loans carried annual interest rates between 7 percent and 8 percent, generally with short half-year and one-year maturities, using nothing other than government-guaranteed bonds as security.[35] The Nishihara loans were backed by Minister of Finance Shōda receiving, in March 1918, Diet approval to issue ¥100 million in government-guaranteed bonds from the Industrial Bank of Japan as collateral. The Ministry of Finance's Deposit Bureau provided an additional ¥40 million of capital, allowing the three issuing banks to invest just ¥5 million of their own capital in extending their loans.[36]

It was also in March 1918 that the former Japanese finance minister Sakatani Yoshiro came to China, at Chinese government invitation, as an adviser on monetary reform. Sakatani's mission provoked a strong US protest and forced the resignation of the Japanese minister to Washington. Japan's unilateral financial advance in China also prompted the State Department to ask Morgan & Company to revive the prewar China consortium, in order to bind Japan back into a multilateral financial cartel. This was the context of Thomas Lamont's mission to Japan in the spring of 1920.[37]

In addition to the loans mentioned above, the Nishihara loans are sometimes considered to include an additional series of four short-term

TABLE 3.2. Japanese lending to China, 1915–1918

Issue date (yr.month)	Name of loan	Interest (per year) (%)	Maturity (yrs./mos.)	Issue amount (in millions of yen)	Purpose	Issuers
1915.12	1st Armament Loan	9.0	5 yr.	¥2.4	Armament supply and production	Mitsui Bussan, Mitsubishi Gomei, Kawasaki Zosensho, Taipei Group
1917.1	1st Banking Facilities Loan	7.5	1 yr.	¥5.0	Financial assistance	Industrial Bank of Japan (IBJ), Bank of Taiwan, Bank of Chosen
1917.9	2nd Banking Facilities Loan	7.5	1 yr.	¥20.0	Financial assistance	IBJ, Bank of Taiwan, Bank of Chosen
1917.11	2nd Armament Loan	9.0	2y/10mo.	¥0.9	Armament supply and production	Mitsui Bussan, Mitsubishi Gomei, Kawasaki Zosensho & Taipei Group
1917.12	3rd Armament Loan	9.0	2y/9mo.	¥15.4	Armament supply and production	Taipei Group
1918.2	Naval Wireless and Telegraph Loan	10.0	30 yr.	¥5.2	Wireless and telegraph extension	Mitsui Bussan
1918.4	Telegraph Cable Loan	8.0	5 yr.	¥20.0	Telegraph extension	IBJ, Bank of Taiwan, Bank of Chosen (via Exchange Bank of China)
1918.6	Kirin-Kainei (Hueining) Railway Preliminary Loan	7.5	6 mo.	¥10.0	Railway construction	IBJ, Bank of Taiwan, Bank of Chosen
1918.7	4th Armament Loan	9.0	2y/2mo.	¥12.5	Armament supply and production	Taipei Group
1918.8	Mine and Forestry Loan	7.5	6 mo.	¥30.0	Mine and forestry development	IBJ, Bank of Taiwan, Bank of Chosen (via Exchange Bank of China)
1918.9	Manchuria-Mongolia Four-Way Railway Loan	8.0	10 yr.	¥20.0	Railway construction	IBJ, Bank of Taiwan, Bank of Chosen
1918.9	Santo Two-Way Railway Preliminary Loan	8.0	6 mo.	¥20.0	Railway construction	IBJ, Bank of Taiwan, Bank of Chosen
1918.9	War Participation Loan	7.0	1 yr.	¥20.0	Wartime financial assistance	IBJ, Bank of Taiwan, Bank of Chosen

Source: S. J. Bytheway, Nihon keizai to gaikoku shihon: 1858–1939 [The Japanese economy and foreign capital], Tokyo: Tōsui (2005), 127.

Armament Loans, and the long, thirty-year Naval Wireless and Tele-graph Loan of February 1918. These were extended to the Chinese army and navy by the Japanese government through private intermediaries, for a further ¥36.5 million.[38] (These latter loans have been included in further calculations in this chapter, because they were provided by representatives of the Japanese government and its armed forces.) In addition to these loans, the Duan clique requested Japan's financial support on at least two occasions not listed in table 3.2, on May 27 and June 1, 1917. Although the transactions that followed are shrouded in secrecy, and not always recognized as direct Japanese government intervention, clearly the Duan clique enjoyed generous financial assistance through both formal and informal Japanese channels. Nishihara held no official post, and often his participation was the only common element the loans shared. Thus, the Nishihara loans were conceived and negotiated with a number of policy objectives in mind, and worked to further Japanese interests in China on several different fronts.[39]

Nishihara's colonial adventurism culminated in a ¥100 million flurry of questionable loans in the last six months of the Terauchi cabinet.[40] In Japan, the summer and early autumn of 1918 was a time of high infla-tion, strikes, and rice riots across the country, leading finally to the senior oligarchs' move to change the cabinet. Against this background, the loans were frantically concluded. Nishihara signed off on three loans on Septem-ber 28, 1918, the very final day of the Terauchi cabinet. "Really, the last day of the Terauchi cabinet was such a dangerous time," as Nishihara recalled in his 1965 memoir, *My Seventy-Plus Year Dream*.[41]

Apart from subsidizing the apparently sympathetic Duan regime, the Nishihara loans also seemed to offer a means to attenuate popular Chinese resistance against the advance of Japan's imperial interests in China. A new bilateral framework of Sino-Japanese cooperation held out for Japan the tantalizing prospect of a Chinese recognition of Japan's "paramount inter-ests'" in Manchuria and Shandong, won without recourse to great power negotiation and approval.[42] In addition, the Nishihara loans contributed to the development of a yen bloc that could potentially extend across East Asia. That is, from its base in Korea and China's northeast, the Japanese government was attempting to expand the circulation of yen-denominated currency, especially Bank of Chosen banknotes, throughout China. (Here, there was also a strong element of internal discord between the Yokohama

Specie Bank and the Bank of Chosen.) From the standpoint of the Western powers, linking China monetarily to Japan also threatened the "open door" and conflicted with British interests particularly. While not without economic and financial dimensions, the extension of credit to China was ultimately dominated by Japan's geopolitical, imperial objectives.[43]

Some Failings of Yen Diplomacy

Given the secrecy surrounding Nishihara's financial operations, the lack of political recognition of Premier Duan's regime, and the war in Europe, it took time before the great powers were aware of the extent of Japanese loans to China. Once alerted to Nishihara's efforts, however, the Western governments cooperated to terminate these loans, which had been carried through in disregard of established imperialist protocols in regard to China. With the exception of a token repayment of ¥5 million, the Japanese government was humiliatingly forced to write off the loans, and the Ministry of Finance had no option but to bail out the three special banks that had underwritten them.[44] The great bulk of the Nishihara loans were never accounted for. Moreover, it is alleged that the only people who benefited from them were corrupt officials.[45] What is certain is that Japan's yen diplomacy generated intense Chinese antipathy and drew attention to Japanese hegemonic ambitions in China.[46] The Terauchi cabinet's actions thus tended to damage Sino-Japanese relations, already under great stress after the Twenty-One Demands, and tarnished Japan's diplomatic standing in the wider world.[47]

Japan's attempt to establish itself as a creditor nation also largely failed. Some ¥559 million of ¥980 million, or 57 percent of Japan's total value of loans to European allies and China, was completely unrecoverable by the time of the cessation of hostilities in Europe on November 11, 1918.[48] Against the odds, Japan's emergent financial-military complex managed to lose money at a time of unprecedented national prosperity.

Inoue Junnosuke in June 1918 perceived the limits of Japan's position and judged that it would take another fifty or sixty years for Japan to establish itself as an international financial center.[49] Inoue's vision is remarkable in itself. Despite the scarcely imaginable intervention of an astounding series of national crises—the rise of fascism and militarism (and Inoue's own assassination); a second world war; the firebombing of Japanese cities; defeat and military occupation by the United States—Inoue's rough prognosis was on the mark, as Tokyo did become an international financial center in the 1980s. As for Inoue's idea that a free market in gold was an "absolute" requirement for an international center, Tokyo would not have anything like a gold market until 1982, and by that time gold no longer had an officially recognized place in global monetary arrangements.

Thus, Japan briefly emerged from the First World War as one of three big creditor nations. This sudden access of financial power ran in parallel to Japan's simultaneous emergence as a Pacific empire and one of the world's three naval powers. But this financial position reflected the extraordinary results of the war more than it reflected a permanent structural shift. Moreover, Japan's new overseas lending was dwarfed by an enormous surge of US lending during the First World War. New York City also emerged during the war as a central financial emporium for Japan. It was now that Japanese financial policy began to align with American policy, with many unintended consequences.

4

Postwar Alignment

In these past ten years, . . . the great contributors who have grabbed the
great powers by their ears and led them to cooperate are the Bank of England
and the Federal Reserve Bank of New York, as I suppose many people know.
The Bank of England is not only the "Bank of Banks" of England itself;
in the world of international finance, it exercises the authority of a great
head temple.

Inoue Junnosuke, "Norman: In Disguise, the Great Heads
of International Finance Hold Secret Talks," 1930

The pressures of war led the Bank of England to organize a network of
allied and neutral central banks, beginning immediately in August 1914.
This was the first step in creating a formal, multilateral framework for
central bank cooperation. On the hardware side, this network was connected by direct and presumably secure telegraphic links. (British firms
controlled most international submarine cables, and the British secretly
monitored other nations' telegraph traffic during the war.)[1] On the organizational side, the new cooperative framework included provisions for regular mutual reporting. Among the central banks of the Allied countries,
this informational form of cooperation extended into active operational
cooperation. Out of this wartime matrix, in the context of postwar financial and monetary problems, there developed the world's first full-fledged
multilaterally coordinated monetary policy.

The critical decisions that shaped these outcomes were taken by a
remarkably small number of men—the "governors" of the system.[2] Both
Benjamin Strong and Montagu Norman served long terms and had
extraordinary influence as central bank governors. They were joined by

other exceptionally influential central bankers such as Dr. Gerard Vissering, governor of the Nederlandsche Bank from 1912 to 1931, and Dr. Hjalmar Schacht, who directed the German Reichsbank from 1923 to 1930 and then again, under the Hitler regime, from 1933 to 1939. By public repute, these bankers were masters of strange, unseen powers. Norman was dubbed "the alchemist," and Schacht, "the old wizard." Inoue Junnosuke, as governor of the Bank of Japan from 1919 to 1923 and again in 1927–28, was also brought into this exclusive club, a connection that had profound significance for Japan as well. If we consider it abstractly, the new central bank cooperation of the 1920s might appear as a triumph of enlightened internationalism. In its substance, however, it represented a socially narrow standpoint, as privately owned central banks, reflecting the outlook and interests of private banking circles, worked together to preserve the enormous structure of debts created by the war. The effort to maintain this structure of debts produced some of the greatest economic, social, and political disasters in modern history.

A Typology of Central Bank Cooperation

Central bank cooperation was a significant new concept in the world after the war. Associated concepts of world federation and world money were in the air, while practical programs of international cooperation were arising in numerous areas of activity. As Leonard Woolf saw it in 1916, "in every department of life the beginnings, and more than the beginnings, of *International Government* already exist."[3] These forms of elite-based internationalism happened simultaneously with a tremendous surge of radical and oppositional international movements. These new forms of social globalization, as we can call it, included international movements for women's rights, for national liberation from colonial empires, and for world proletarian revolution.

As originally conceived by Montagu Norman, central bank cooperation was a doctrine and a program, a prescription of how things *should* be. But as this program developed, the concept came to be useful as a description of actual realities. Here, we can begin by adapting Richard Cooper's categorization, and dividing central bank cooperation into *informational* and *operational* types of cooperation. Informational cooperation is often overlooked in narrow definitions of what constitutes cooperation. Such informational cooperation encompasses the critical but unquantifiable factors of central bankers' sharing of worldviews, social networks, loyalties, and senses of self-identity. Gianni Toniolo emphasized this aspect in his history of the Bank for International Settlements (BIS), and we emphasize it here. Following Cooper, *informational cooperation* may include, in order of increasing intensity,

1. exchanging information on such things as outstanding credits, new borrowings, and central bank regulations;
2. standardizing concepts and categories of information collected;
3. exchanging views on "how the world works" and on central bank policy;
4. sharing views on the economic outlook; and
5. standardizing regulations.[4]

This latter point, the standardization of regulations, verges into the operational area.

In fact, most of the actual *operations* of central banks could be called informational operations. That is, money and credit are themselves "information," of a socially potent kind: they are social assignments of purchasing power. Money and credit are thus not so much things as relationships, and ultimately, "purchasing power" is realized in acts of buying and hiring. The information encoded in monetary statements was preserved and transmitted by means of an elaborate variety of paper certificates, bank balance books, telegraphic messages, and so on. The authority to designate and validate these monetary claims is at the heart of what central banks do.

Specific *operational cooperation* between central banks included the following, again listed in order of increasing intensity:

1. giving other banks advance notice of upcoming actions;
2. providing mutual financial support;
3. coordinating actions such as the buying and selling of foreign exchange and the altering of discount rates;
4. requiring prior approval of actions; and
5. establishing rules of behavior including proscriptions, for example concerning how and where foreign-exchange reserves will be held.[5]

The latter two points involve the subordination of one central bank to the external control of other central banks or multilateral institutions. In practice, this kind of subordination usually implies outright colonial or quasi-colonial control.[6] Such subordination happened many times in the 1920s, typically in the context of what was called "controlled" or "conditional" lending by private bank groups, primarily in New York and London, to national governments around the world.

These forms and ideas of central bank cooperation go back to the 1920s. In the "BIS view," an institutional basis for central bank cooperation was established at the end of the 1920s with the creation of the Bank for International Settlements; its potential, however, was largely unrealized until after the Second World War.[7] The BIS itself, headquartered in Basel, embodied this program. It had a Federal Reserve–style structure in that it was a "bank of banks," owned by its own member banks. The original members were an early "Group of Seven": Great Britain, France, Belgium, Germany, Italy, Japan, and the United States. Every country was represented by its central bank except for the United States, which was represented by a private banking group led by J. P. Morgan & Company. In practice, the Federal Reserve Bank of New York was closely involved; the first president of the BIS was the chairman of the board of directors of the FRBNY, Gates W. McGarrah.[8] Many of the points listed above concerning central bank cooperation were laid out in the fifth annual report of the BIS in 1935. There, the BIS listed seven areas of collaboration, in addition to exceptional measures of financial aid. These were: (1) to evolve a common body of monetary doctrine; (2) to understand the difficulties of neighboring central banks; (3) to avoid doing harm to one another; (4) to gather and exchange monetary and economic data; (5) to improve inter–central bank practice (including lending to one another); (6) to assist in the creation of new central banks and to aid smaller central banks in following sound policies; and (7) to work out technical improvements to the international monetary system.[9] By the time the 1935 report was written, this was also an outline of a program that had largely failed.

These points will reappear in the discussion that follows. Here we should also repeat two important criticisms of this kind of cooperation. First, it often happened behind the backs of the public and of elected national legislatures.[10] In this, central bank cooperation was in line with many of the new technocratic tendencies of the age. Second, in terms of its actual policy content, the new central bank cooperation after the First World War was directed toward the maintenance of unsustainably high levels of international indebtedness arising out of the war and early postwar periods. To that end, cooperation was directed toward the enforcement of deflationary, depression-inducing policies that were socially destructive and ultimately self-defeating. Accordingly, a vision of international monetary cooperation that was both more public-spirited and more expansive was conceived after the Second World War.

A Market-Making Initiative in Tokyo

Benjamin Strong's role in creating a New York market for trade acceptances has already been introduced. Strong's personal friendship with Montagu Norman served as an important axis of central bank cooperation in the 1920s. His friendship with Inoue Junnosuke of the Bank of Japan established another channel of connection. The question of the thinking and mutual relationship of these three central bankers thus takes on a wide significance.

Inoue Junnosuke has been written about in numerous accounts in Japanese that range from the scholarly to the popular, but his name is not well known outside his homeland.[11] Inoue entered the Bank of Japan in 1896 and began his central banking career as a trainee in London, from 1897 to 1899. As noted already, he was hosted by Parr's Bank after the Bank of England refused to take on a BoJ trainee. In London, Inoue carefully studied the discount market, and he wrote two reports on it shortly after his return to Tokyo.[12] Inoue retained a strongly pro-British orientation throughout his life. Inoue was again posted overseas in 1908–10, to take charge of the Bank of Japan's New York agency. Within the larger world of New York finance, this was then a relatively modest position, and Inoue did not form executive-level connections with American bankers. With relatively little to do, he spent his time in a focused study of American banking practices. Inoue was subsequently dispatched from the Bank of Japan to serve as vice president of the Yokohama Specie Bank, Japan's parastatal foreign-exchange bank. In that capacity, Inoue in 1912 negotiated Japan's entry into the Euro-American bank cartel that controlled international lending to China. As president of the Yokohama Specie

Bank during the First World War, Inoue became known as Japan's foremost specialist in international financial relations.

During the war, when London could no longer finance international trade and settle international payments, Japanese trade finance faced an immediate crisis, and Japanese business began to turn to New York. "Japan, largely as a result of the war, has drifted into an unexpected economic dependence on the United States," was how Benjamin Strong described it, in a report to his New York headquarters during his 1920 trip to Japan. "We are the bankers who finance their trade, and with whom their surplus bankers' and Government balances are principally carried."[13] For Japanese bankers, reliance on sterling or dollar means of trade settlement also implied the payment of a continual "tribute" to foreign banks and a lack of financial independence. Within Japan, the lack of a market for discounting yen trade bills also meant a lack of integration between exchange banks (preeminently the YSB) and commercial banks. Commercial banks were flush with funds during the war boom. In these circumstances, the Bank of Japan was unable to guide market interest rates and was instead forced to follow the markets by lowering rates in 1916 and 1917. The fact that commercial banks had few funds on deposit at the Bank of Japan also made it harder for the BoJ to control credit. At the same time, the Yokohama Specie Bank was severely pressed for operational funds and had to rely on short-term loans from the Bank of Japan. The YSB was getting three-quarters of the Bank of Japan's lending at the time. Inoue understood all of this in detail, and he was eager to develop new remedies.

In March 1919 Inoue was appointed as the ninth governor of the Bank of Japan. Significantly, he was the first career Bank of Japan man to rise to the post of bank governor. His appointment was itself an indication of the professionalization of the bank's executive cadre and of the central bank's growing independence from the world of private banking. As BoJ governor, Inoue immediately undertook to foster a market for discounting trade bills, to be centered on the Bank of Japan. Inoue's plan to develop a London-style discount market thus appears to have followed Strong's lead, further suggesting Inoue's close watchfulness of Anglo-American trends.[14]

Inoue's first step was to introduce the bankers' acceptance (BA), and beginning on May 22, 1919, the Bank of Japan began to discount bankers' acceptances at its most preferential discount rate. As described in chapter 2, bankers' acceptances had been introduced by the Federal Reserve banks only a few years before. Inoue's plan was that commercial banks would invest their surplus short-term funds in BAs, thereby making funds available to the exchange banks for trade financing and simultaneously giving the Bank of Japan more control over the markets.[15] Inoue followed this initiative by introducing another new credit instrument, stamped trade bills, in August. In line with Bank of England theory, he described these new credit instruments as a means to ease the financing of trade but also as a tool that could enable the central bank to contract credit, when the need arose, and make its interest-rate policy more effective.[16] Simultaneously, the Bank of Japan promoted the usage of the yen as an international currency by asking Japanese trading companies and bank agencies to use yen-denominated trade bills for payments. As described in the previous chapter, the government began in 1915 to organize bank consortia and attempted to develop a market for yen-denominated foreign bonds in Tokyo, in an ambitious effort to establish Tokyo as a center for international lending. None of these initiatives really succeeded, at least not in the short run.

Thus, as Benjamin Strong strove to realize his vision of establishing New York City as the London of the West, Inoue Junnosuke dreamed of making Tokyo the London of the East. Strong's policies and Inoue's were similarly conceived but had very different degrees of success. Strong largely achieved his goal within the first five years of the new US central bank. But in Tokyo, Inoue's "London of the East" reforms had little effect, despite his technical ability. At most, he developed a vision of future financial development. Here we see a parallel to the failures of Japanese international lending described in the previous chapter. This result underlines Inoue's earlier conclusion that, financially speaking, Japan remained many decades behind England, and that Tokyo could not hope to become an international financial center for another fifty or sixty years.

Spring Tide: A Flood of Gold

The spring of 1919 was a watershed in international social and political history. There was then a tremendous, international wave of price inflation. There was also an international labor revolt, as hundreds of thousands of workers in dozens of countries joined unions and workers' councils, held mass rallies and marches, went on strike, and seized factories. This work-ers' rebellion was conspicuous in the United States, Great Britain, and Japan; for Japan, it was the first great industrial strike wave in the country's history. Mass-based political revolutions and anticolonial movements si-multaneously broke out in a dozen or more countries. Within Japan's new empire, peaceful demonstrators calling for Korea's independence initiated a national movement on March 1, 1919. It was put down with great vio-lence by Japanese military and police forces in the weeks that followed. In their own empire, British authorities faced mass demonstrations demand-ing national independence in Egypt and India. In Beijing, students who assembled in front of the Tiananmen Gate on May 4, 1919, were targeting especially the pro-Japanese minister Cao Rulin, who had helped arrange the loans described in chapter 3. The Chinese national movement included a movement to boycott Japanese goods and to boycott Japanese banknotes as well.[17] In Italy, Germany, and Austria, there was something close to so-cial warfare during the same months. Further east in Europe, open wars and civil wars continued. News of the negotiations in Paris helped pro-voke several of the national movements of 1919, and in this turbulent con-text the Versailles Treaty was signed on June 28. Less well remembered by historians is the fact that June 1919 was also a great watershed in monetary history, with the opening of the floodgates for gold shipments out of the United States.[18] The direct and indirect effects were profound.

In the historiography of the United States, this globally pivotal event—the de facto restoration of the US gold standard—is profoundly unrec-ognized. This lack of recognition points to a great difference between historical understandings of the restoration of the gold standard in the United States as opposed to understandings of the restoration of the gold standard in almost every other country, including Britain and Japan. During the 1920s, a dozen or more countries experienced "gold restora-tion depressions." This was one of the most significant world-historical movements of the postwar decade, though this movement itself has not been well recognized as constituting a single coordinated movement.[19] In the case of Great Britain, it took six years to return to the gold standard. When British authorities led by Montagu Norman did restore the gold convertibility of the pound sterling at the old prewar par in April 1925, it left the British pound overvalued relative to other currencies, hurting Brit-ish exports and generating price deflation, industrial depression, and social crisis. This was the subject of Keynes's famous 1925 critique, which was widely disseminated in Japan by the economic journalist Ishibashi Tanzan.[20] Britain's return to the gold standard in 1925 also generated global-level deflationary pressure.

In Japan, the return to the gold standard took even longer, eleven years. When Japanese authorities led by Inoue Junnosuke did restore the yen to gold convertibility at its old prewar par in January 1930, the effects on the domestic economy were even more severe than what Britain went through after 1925, as the Japanese government's action forced additional deflation in the midst of the worldwide deflation now known as the Great Depression. Inoue's restoration of the gold standard was afterward universally understood as a disaster. In Japanese history books, the phrase "lifting the gold export embargo" (*kin kaikin*) is practically interchangeable with "Showa panic" (*Shōwa kyōkō*), which is the term for Japan's own experience of the world depression.

Here, then, is the historiographical question: the United States in June 1919 was the first country to return to the gold standard after the war, but US historians usually give the event a bare mention, or none at all. They certainly have not taken it as a historical landmark. In a global view of history, they ought to, for it was indeed a great watershed, fully as significant as Britain's return to the gold standard six years later.

The first effect of the US lifting of the gold export embargo was one of inflationary stimulus, as sudden large gold flows out of the United States helped initiate a tremendous international boom in 1919–1920. The peak of these shipments of gold out of the United States was concentrated in the months June 1919–March 1920, when about $400 million in gold was shipped out. As had happened in the first part of 1917, the single largest outflow went across the Pacific to Japan.

Officials at the Federal Reserve Bank of New York anticipated this and took steps to forestall it before the lifting of the US gold embargo, when they asked for and received the Bank of Japan's assurance that the BoJ would refrain from taking large gold shipments out of the United States.[21] These interactions appear as a case of explicit policy coordination, with the Japanese central bank providing concrete operational support for the US return to the gold standard. Despite these assurances, however, gold shipments to Japan became enormous, totaling ¥885 million (US$443 million) in the three years 1919–21.[22] Close to half of this gold appears to have come from the United States. It may be that the Bank of Japan simply lacked the administrative authority to control most of these flows. Thus, the US gold embargo was fully lifted by the end of June 1919, and, BoJ assurances notwithstanding, "the dreaded gold exports to Japan began in July," as Ralph Hawtrey of the British Treasury put it.[23]

Although the Bank of England was not yet in a position to restore the pound sterling to gold convertibility, on September 12, 1919, the British government also began to allow the export of gold, under license. Simultaneously, as described in chapter 7, a revived "free" gold market, under N. M. Rothschild & Sons administration with Bank of England direction, was opened in London. In fact, a large part of the gold shipped to Japan came from Britain, at least indirectly, because US gold outflows were balanced by a huge inflow of gold from Great Britain in 1920 (see table 7.2 in chapter 7). In net terms, Japan received $195 million in gold from the United States in the two years 1919–20. The net outflow of gold from the United States to the whole world for those two years was $197 million.[24] Once again, suddenly, Japan had a seemingly outsized international financial role that surprised people at the time.[25] That role, having been forgotten, may also surprise present-day historians.

In Japan in the second half of 1919 there arose, on the basis of this movable foundation, a great volume of new credit creation. The sudden repatriation of export earnings that had been trapped overseas by wartime specie embargoes thus helped set off a speculative boom and bubble in Japan. This movement also helps explain why the international financial panic of 1920 broke out first in Japan.

Much of the speculation was in the commodities markets. Wholesale prices in Japan jumped upward some 60 percent in the ten months from May 1919 to March 1920, according to the Bank of Japan's index. By comparison, British wholesale prices increased during the same period by 35 percent, while US wholesale prices increased by 17 percent.[26]

In the United States, these specie shipments also came at a moment when enormous amounts of new credit had recently been thrown into economic circulation, and they also created significant pressures. Thus, as gold exports commenced, the FRBNY began to press for higher interest rates in order to stem the outflow. Other central banks did the same. Even as the rush of gold helped feed the bubble in Japan, the central banks' movement for higher interest rates worked to bring on the counter-reaction of 1920.

Trilateral Deflation: Crises Cooperatively Induced

At the level of ideas and policy consciousness, the international depression of 1920 was the first of the internationally coordinated "stabilization" recessions of the decade. These consciously induced depressions were themselves a novel feature of the financial globalization of the 1920s. This international policy alignment can be explained as an alignment of circumstances, but it was also an alignment of policy consciousness. For this reason also, the US return to the gold standard in 1919 is a historical watershed.

As we have seen, central bank cooperation between the Federal Reserve Bank of New York and the Bank of Japan began during the First World War with informational cooperation, following the connection established in January 1918. A tacit kind of operational cooperation followed in the second half of 1919, when the Bank of Japan aligned its deflation policy with the postwar deflation policies simultaneously adopted by the Bank of England and the FRBNY. Japan, together with the United States and Britain, was thus a first mover in the international deflation movement. This policy alignment continued in a broad sense through the deflationary decade of the 1920s. It culminated in the final crisis of the revived gold standard system in late 1931.

Inoue Junnosuke began to press for higher interest rates soon after he became governor of the Bank of Japan in March 1919. This idea was resisted by Finance Minister Takahashi Korekiyo. In Britain, the Bank of England governor in August and September 1919 also began to press the chancellor of the exchequer to allow the raising of interest rates, in order to rein in inflation and prepare for an early return to the gold standard.[27] This play between national treasuries and central banks was a pattern seen in many countries. It was the central bankers who pushed for higher interest rates and deflation. National treasuries in Europe and the United States wanted to keep interest rates low to help in refinancing large war debts, and so they first resisted but later came around to the deflation line.[28]

In this connection, Benjamin Strong noted the Bank of Japan's position on his visit to Japan in May 1920: "Their relations with the Treasury [i.e., the Ministry of Finance] are much the same as ours, and unless I am mistaken they have encountered much the same difficulty that we have, with possibly less actual independence of position than we enjoy."[29] This judgment was correct. In fact, the Bank of Japan, having historically been much

more directly under Ministry of Finance authority, had much less independence than Strong's Federal Reserve. In October and November 1919,
Finance Minister Takahashi did allow the BoJ to raise rates. Although the
Bank of Japan does not appear to have explicitly coordinated its rate hikes
with the American and British banks, it acted more or less simultaneously
with the Bank of England.[30] For their parts, Strong and Norman were
in direct personal communication concerning their own rate increases.[31]
The postwar movement for deflation—and the international depression
that followed from it in 1920—was thus a coordinated transnational event
rather than a mere conjunction of national events. The central banks of
Japan, Great Britain, and the United States raised their rates as follows:[32]

> *Bank of Japan*: On October 6, 1919, from 6.57 percent to 7.30 percent;
> then to 8.03 percent on November 19. This high rate was main-
> tained until April 1925.
>
> *Bank of England*: On November 6, 1919, from 5 percent to 6 percent;
> then to 7 percent on April 15, 1920. This high rate was maintained
> until April 1921.
>
> *FRBNY*: November 3–December 30, 1919, from 4 percent to 4¾ per-
> cent; then to 6 percent in January 1920, and to 7 percent in June
> 1920. This high rate was maintained until May 1921.

The Bank of England now had its eyes mainly on interest rates in New
York.[33] Reflecting the new international role of the gold-backed dollar,
gold prices in the new London gold market, as described in chapter 7, were
also governed primarily by fluctuations in the dollar–sterling exchange
rate. But the Bank of England was now watching Tokyo also, as reflected
in an internal BoE memorandum of February 1920, at a point when its
own bank rate had already been raised to 6 percent:

> The Federal Reserve Bank's rate for commercial Bills is already 6%, and in
> the other principal creditor country, Japan, rates are already much higher than
> ours. Indeed even now London is to some extent financing American business
> and any slight reduction in our money rates would intensify this anomaly.[34]

In this Bank of England view, Japan was thus, with the United States
and Britain, "the other principal creditor country." The timing of this

statement—February 1920—is significant, for the crisis was just about to break in Tokyo and Osaka. One of its triggers, as we will see, was a historic shift in British currency policy. This was also the moment when Benjamin Strong, Thomas W. Lamont, and Frank Vanderlip were all preparing to travel to Tokyo. Japan's status as an international creditor turned out to be temporary and somewhat anomalous, given Japan's relatively modest industrial base in comparison to the European industrial powers. But in the longer run, it was a true sign of things to come.

Also notable here is the idea that "London is to some extent financing American business"—that is, higher interest rates in New York were pulling in funds from London. Neither London nor New York had this kind of close connection with Tokyo—there was then no "yen carry trade"—no yen-denominated borrowing by foreign banks in Tokyo in order to lend abroad. Nor were there dollar or sterling "hot money" flows from these centers to Tokyo. But there was, on Inoue's part, a kind of parallel policy making, which later moved closer to overt policy coordination.

Thus, in New York, in order to lower prices and in order to defend America's restored gold standard, Benjamin Strong adopted the credit-restriction policies that were primarily responsible for inducing the great deflation of 1920–21. This was the first expression of the doctrine of induced depression that was to guide international "stabilization" policy for the next decade.[35] As discussed further in chapter 6, Strong and Norman were largely of one mind concerning this policy, though Strong was more concerned with the wider social repercussions. In Tokyo, in sympathy with this movement, Inoue Junnosuke simultaneously enforced his own deflation policy. This de facto alignment of central bank policies at a time of sharp geopolitical rivalry between Japan and the United States indicates also the way that political and financial diplomacy diverged.[36]

The common thinking within the three central banks extended to a stated desire to control "extravagance" and to induce economic "adjustment" and "liquidation." These ideas and this language were parts of a complex of moral-economic imperatives that would dominate international financial orthodoxy for the next decade. Male policy makers frequently expressed their choice in gendered language, describing high prices and inflation as a feminine disorder and deflation as a masculine restoration of order.[37]

Left out of this discussion was the fact that the economic extravagances originated largely in new credit creation, which had been supported by the central banks themselves. In a story that can be told of most great bubbles, financial innovation played an important enabling role. In the Federal Reserve System's first partial year of operation, 1914, the total of all bills discounted by the Federal Reserve banks was $10 million. This volume ballooned in 1917 and 1918. In New York, bankers' acceptances particularly served as a new instrument of credit creation supporting the speculative expansion of 1919. Data compiled by Ferderer shows a great peak in the creation of bankers' acceptances around December 1919, when the volume of acceptances reached $1 billion. The total of all bills discounted reached a peak of $2.7 billion in 1920. By this measure, Benjamin Strong's reforms had produced an amazing success; but it was a bubble. By 1922, the volume of acceptances had collapsed to less than half of its bubble peak.[38] A second, greater peak in the creation of acceptance credits would come at the next bubble peak, in 1929–30, as discussed further in chapter 8.

The international commodity boom continued into early 1920. One factor in the continued boom was the pent-up demand for clothing and other consumption goods, following the austerity of the war years. Another factor, directly connected to the surge of credit creation (as both cause and effect) was the competitive stockpiling of and speculation in raw materials by merchants and industrialists. This international movement reached a peak early in the year 1920.

The silver trade was part of this speculative movement. As the second monetary metal after gold, silver also had its central market in London.[39] In 1919, silver prices rose to the highest level since the early 1870s. The increase in silver prices meant that the value of the silver in the subsidiary coinage of many countries threatened to exceed the coins' face value. Large volumes of silver coins were already being smuggled out of many countries to be melted down and sold as silver bullion.[40] In India, British authorities repeatedly increased the exchange value of the rupee in order to maintain it as a token coin. They also increasingly substituted paper money for the circulation of silver coins. By January 1920, a record gap had appeared between spot and future prices for silver. Large amounts of German and other silver coin were now being melted down and sent to London for sale. In what was thought to be a record for a single shipload, 10 million taels (worth £4 million) arrived at Shanghai, enough to cause Shanghai silver prices to fall back. By the last week of January 1920, news reports from many countries told of impending reductions of silver content or the elimination of silver subsidiary coinage owing to the high price of silver.[41] Early in February, British authorities decided on another historical departure, announcing that the silver content of British subsidiary coinage would be reduced from the old "sterling silver" standard of 92.5 percent silver to a standard of 50 percent silver, effective March 20, 1920. This information set off violent international repercussions. Other countries took similar steps to reduce the silver content of their coinages— in traditional monetary terms, it was a wave of currency debasements. Global demand for silver for monetary use was thus suddenly reduced. World silver prices reached a great peak on February 11, 1920, at 89½ pence per ounce on the London exchange, and then began to slide. If we were to view this movement simply in terms of gold and silver, one could say also that gold was now beginning another historic wave of appreciation, comparable to the great appreciation of gold after 1873. Nor was this a matter of gold:silver ratios alone. Gold now began a phase of rapid appreciation vis-à-vis goods in general, and vis-à-vis national currencies that were not pegged to gold.

Benjamin Strong's contractionary measures would later be blamed for initiating the US depression of 1920–21, which was the first policy-induced depression in Federal Reserve history.[42] Strong anticipated some of this, and in poor health, he did not wait around to witness those consequences personally but rather took a leave of absence in January. In April he left the country, taking ship for Japan as the first stage in a round-the-world tour.

As it happened, it was in Japan that the postwar boom first broke and the postwar deflation began. In March, there was a first wave of panic selling in the commodity and stock markets of Osaka and Tokyo. Renewed panic in April caused financial authorities to shut down the stock exchanges and commodities markets for a month. They remained closed at the time of Strong's arrival. Thus the international postwar depression began in Japan. US commodity prices also reached a peak around the same time and began to fall back, then collapsed in the second half of the year. For the United States, this was the sharpest price deflation since 1865–66, and it remains the sharpest since then, surpassing that of 1929–30. It was thus at the crest of a great economic wave that Wall Street came calling in Japan.

WALL STREET DISCOVERS JAPAN, SPRING 1920

> I shall return well posted on Japan. We have seen every side of it, lived with
> the people, of all stations of life, even picked up a bit of the language, and
> I could write a book on the subject. Of one thing I am sure. This is a great
> nation, they have a population of such industry, patience, and docility, that
> their future may be almost anything their leaders wish, —so long as they
> don't try to go too fast, —as they have been doing recently in their whole
> policy of political and trade expansion.
>
> BENJAMIN STRONG, writing home from Japan, July 1920

The spring of 1920, when commodity and financial markets crashed in
Osaka and Tokyo, was a turning point in multiple fields of activity. Economically speaking, it marked the end of the greatest industrial boom yet
experienced in Japan's history. At the height of the financial bubble that
arose on top of this great boom, in a modest pre-play of the late 1980s, an
interest in Japan suddenly appeared among Wall Street leaders. Ironically,
they came to Japan just at the moment the postwar economic bubble was
beginning to collapse.

The First World War brought a parallel set of economic transformations to Japan and the United States. Both countries registered great
export surpluses and piled up a great volume of claims on foreign financial
centers. The bankers of both countries ventured into overseas lending in
a way unprecedented in the history of either country; in both countries
there were new initiatives to develop an international financial center on
the model of London. At the same time, the effective closure of London

financial markets diverted Japanese business to New York. New York did begin to take over many of London's functions, and Japan appeared a very promising market for American companies and banks. The war also intensified rivalry between Japan and the United States, over China.

In the spring of 1920, three of Wall Street's top bankers—Thomas W. Lamont of J. P. Morgan & Company, Frank A. Vanderlip of National City Bank, and Benjamin Strong of the Federal Reserve Bank of New York— made separate voyages to Japan. These bankers, all ambitious to build a new world more open to American business, had already crossed paths the year before in London and Paris, where they were involved in planning postwar European affairs. Their Tokyo tour of 1920 was thus a follow-on to a European tour in 1919. Wall Street financiers subsequently became key actors in shaping US-Japan relations during the decade of the 1920s. Financially speaking, this was the beginning of Japan's first "American" age. This era ended abruptly and violently in the autumn and winter of 1931–32.

The present chapter focuses on the inception of this new bankers' diplomacy and investigates especially the ideas of America's de facto central bank governor, Benjamin Strong, whose ties to Japan were the most intimate of the three, and whose ideas were the most perceptive and wide ranging. If we look at the international lines of force that bore upon these personal encounters, and the developments that sprang from them, the moment appears as a pivot in US-Japan relations.

Three Wall Street Missions

As described in chapter 1, it was the Japanese government that first sought to gain the interest of a relatively disinterested Wall Street, beginning as early as 1897. The Russo-Japanese War was the first great moment of cooperation; Jacob Schiff of Kuhn, Loeb & Company then took the lead in arranging giant war loans for the Japanese government. Morgan & Company remained aloof and in fact was somewhat hostile. By 1919, Morgan & Company, like Wall Street in general, was much friendlier and more interested in doing business with Japan.[1]

In March 1920, Thomas W. Lamont of J. P. Morgan & Company led a first Wall Street mission to Japan. At the Paris Peace Conference the year before, Lamont had been an adviser to the US delegation. His primary mission in Japan, undertaken at the private urging of the US State Department, was to negotiate Japan's entry into a revived, American-led international banking consortium—an international bank cartel intended to control lending to the Chinese government.[2] His chief Japanese interlocutor was Inoue Junnosuke, governor of the Bank of Japan.

The second mission to Japan was led by Frank A. Vanderlip, now recently retired as chairman and president of America's largest and most international bank, National City Bank of New York. (National City Bank had, like Japan's government-backed bank syndicate, made big purchases of Russian government war bonds, and it too was burned by the Bolshevik government's repudiation of Tsarist government debts. Vanderlip was blamed for the losses and forced to resign.) Vanderlip too had recently returned from Europe and had already published a popular book about his trip. Vanderlip led a party that included half a dozen prominent US business leaders, who came at the invitation of the most highly placed members of Japan's business elite. Like Lamont's visit, Vanderlip's visit was understood in Japan as a matter of high state concern.

Figure 5.1. The governors (*left to right*): Bank of Japan governor Inoue, FRBNY governor Strong, BoJ deputy governor Fukai. Taken in front of the Bank of Japan building, 1920. Courtesy of the Archives of the Federal Reserve Bank of New York.

At the beginning of May, Lamont's longtime associate Benjamin Strong also came to Japan, where he ended up spending three months of his 1920 vacation. From the time of his 1920 visit, Strong worked to bring the Bank of Japan, and Inoue Junnosuke personally, into the international central bankers' club that he and Montagu Norman were organizing. As the records of his visit reveal, it was Strong who formed the closest personal connections in Japan.

Lamont, Vanderlip, and Strong were, together with Paul Warburg, the most influential individual framers of US international financial leadership at the dawn of the age of international dollar hegemony. All three developed an enthusiasm for Japan and established friendly relations with Japanese financial leaders. The political context of this flurry of top-level semiprivate visits was the alarm in US government circles over the Japanese government's aggressive moves to gain financial leverage over the government of China, discussed in chapter 3. US officials hoped to use American financial power to co-opt and contain this Japanese advance. Government and banking concerns thus merged in a dual public-private diplomacy. The result of this diplomacy was a mutually satisfactory settlement between financial interests in New York and Tokyo, combined with a much less satisfactory settlement between their respective governments. This new settlement governed US-Japan relations until the crisis brought on by the Japanese invasion of Manchuria and the collapse of the international gold standard in late 1931 and early 1932.

After his visit to Tokyo in March, Thomas Lamont visited China and then returned to Tokyo in May. Lamont's efforts to re-create the prewar China consortium seemed at the time to be successful. In fact, the consortium was never recognized by China's new republican government. The Japanese government, represented in these negotiations by Bank of Japan governor Inoue Junnosuke, failed in its main political goals, which were to reserve Manchuria and eastern Inner Mongolia from the field envisioned for consortium lending and to gain de facto US recognition of Japan's "special" or "paramount" position there. Japanese authorities had to be content with the already existing reservation of the South Manchurian Railway zone itself. What the Japanese government did get from this settlement was direct access to the leading Wall Street bank, J. P. Morgan & Company, which was then approaching the historic apex of its national and international power and prestige. This connection would eventuate in several large loans between 1924 and 1930.

Lamont's entourage included his wife, two friends, a secretary, a maid, a doctor, and a consulting engineer, as well as Martin Egan of Morgan & Company and Jeremiah Smith Jr., a lawyer and close friend who would later serve as the League of Nations commissioner overseeing Hungarian finances. Lamont returned to New York well impressed with the cultured, internationally minded Japan represented by Inoue Junnosuke and the leaders of the great business groups. As a result of Lamont's and Inoue's initiative, Morgan & Company became the US bankers to the Japanese government after 1924. In 1922, Lamont himself became the leading partner at Morgan & Company, following the death of Morgan senior partner Henry P. Davison, who was the mentor of both Lamont and Strong and foster parent to Strong's children. Lamont's connection with Japan was of fateful significance; we discuss it less here because it is described in detail in the book *Lever of Empire*.[3]

Frank Vanderlip for his part led the largest American "VIP" mission to Japan yet conducted. They came on a lavish, all-expenses-paid tour, at the invitation of a "Welcome Association of Japan" directed by Shibusawa Eiichi, the grandfather of modern Japanese capitalism, and by Dan Takuma, chairman of Mitsui and Company.[4] Shibusawa's "Welcome Association" was an extraordinary assembly of Japan's elite. Indicative of their social and historiographical standing, its leading members have been the subject of multiple voluminous biographies in Japanese. Many of them hosted the American visitors as guests in their homes. These leading members, in order of formal precedence, were Prince Tokugawa Iesato, Viscount Kaneko Kentarō, Baron Shibusawa Eiichi, Baron Sakatani Yoshiro, Baron Megata Tanetarō, Mr. Inoue Junnosuke, and Mr. (later Baron) Dan Takuma.[5] Many of these names have appeared in the pages above. Presenting as they do a group portrait of Japan's internationally oriented elite, they deserve some further introduction.

The group was formally chaired by the aristocrat Tokugawa Iesato, who was president of the House of Peers and successor to the headship of the former shogunal house. The titles of nobility of the other group members were not inherited but awarded, reflecting their positions as Japan's highest civil officials and business leaders. Kaneko Kentarō was a former cabinet minister and member of the inner circles of the imperial government. It was Kaneko who directed the first, failed approach to Morgan & Company in 1898. Shibusawa Eiichi, now eighty years old, was the single most important entrepreneur in modern Japanese history. He was also the founder of the First National Bank (Dai-Ichi Bank) and of dozens (if not hundreds) of other enterprises. Shibusawa was Japan's leading advocate of international business diplomacy.[6] Sakatani Yoshiro was the former minister of finance and former mayor of Tokyo. Prior to that, as a high official in the Ministry of Finance, Sakatani had helped direct Japan's adoption of the gold standard in 1897. He was also Shibusawa's son-in-law. Sakatani's appointment in 1917 as financial adviser to the Chinese government helped provoke the US government response that led to the revival of the consortium project by Thomas Lamont. Megata Tanetarō was, like Kaneko, educated at Harvard University and was, like Sakatani, a top official of the Ministry of Finance, likewise closely involved in the adoption of the gold standard in 1897. In 1905–6 Megata directed Japan's monetary and financial annexation of Korea, then still ostensibly independent.[7] In 1917 Megata led a financial mission to the United States. It was Megata who conducted the negotiation for opening business relations between the Federal Reserve Bank of New York and the Bank of Japan. Inoue Junnosuke's role as governor of the Bank of Japan has already been described. Inoue would later serve twice as minister of finance. The second time, in 1929, Inoue, in consultation with Thomas Lamont, would direct the restoration of the gold standard, thereby inducing the deflationary crisis that helped to bring down Japan's liberal order. Dan Takuma, a graduate of MIT (and brother-in-law of Kaneko) headed the Mitsui group, the country's largest industrial, trading, and banking conglomerate. Inoue Junnosuke and Dan Takuma were in fact the senior active leaders of the "Welcome Association" that hosted Vanderlip's party. They both met repeatedly with Thomas Lamont during his visit. Inoue and Dan both died at the hands of the same band of ultranationalist assassins in 1932.

The membership of the "Welcome Association" was rounded out by an assemblage of company presidents, including the chief executives of Nippon Yūsen Kaisha (NYK, Japan's leading shipping company); Okura and Company, one of the largest trading companies; the Tokyo Chamber of Commerce; the Yokohama Specie Bank; the Oriental Steamship Company (Tōyō Kisen Kaisha); Mitsubishi Bank; Furukawa Mining Company; and Sumitomo Bank.[8] Two of these company presidents were also titled members of the House of Peers. Despite its ostensibly private nature, this was hardly a casual social gathering. In fact, its membership came close to encompassing the peak command structure of Japan's business and financial world. It also defined the intersection of that elite with the executive level of the Japanese state.

The American guests, with a few exceptions, were noticeably less highly placed in their own country's financial and governing elite than were their Japanese hosts, but evidently the Japanese organizers had tried to invite as influential a group as possible. Vanderlip himself was already known in Japan, and his ideas circulated there through Japanese translations of his books.[9] Joining Vanderlip was his old mentor Lyman J. Gage (1836–1927), former president of the American Bankers Association and secretary of the treasury in the Republican McKinley and Roosevelt administrations (1897–1902). As treasury secretary, Gage had overseen the formal enactment of the US gold standard in 1900. Other American members included Darwin P. Kingsley, president of the New York Life Insurance Company, and Henry W. Taft (younger brother of the former US president William H. Taft), a New York City attorney and Wall Street and political insider. Vanderlip and secondarily Kingsley were the leaders of the group, indicating that its financial character was its most significant aspect. Joining them was Jacob Gould Schurman, former president of Cornell University and president of the first Philippine Commission (which had established the US colonial government); Schurman was later the US ambassador to China (1921–25) and to Germany (1925–29). Other members were George Eastman of the Eastman Kodak Company and his physician; Seymour L. Cromwell of New York, who in 1921 became president of the New York Stock Exchange; Lewis L. Clarke, president of the American Exchange Bank of New York; and J. Lionberger Davis, a St. Louis attorney and banker who was a family friend and former student of Woodrow Wilson. During the war, under Wilson's presidential administration, Davis played a highly significant and unheralded role as managing director of the Office of Alien Property Custodian. He was thereafter also a friend and adviser of Franklin D. Roosevelt. Also present were the author Julian Street (whose son later married Vanderlip's daughter), and Harry E. Benedict, Vanderlip's secretary and protégé. Several of these men were joined by wives and daughters. Taft later wrote a verbose account of the trip.[10]

This friendship tour seems largely to have been a matter of big, lavish entertainments, and it is not clear that the Japanese side got their money's worth out of it. Strong disparaged it. He mentioned, writing home to the Federal Reserve Bank of New York, that he had met Vanderlip, Kingsley, and their associates soon after his arrival, and that they "were rushed about, saw only one limited class of Japanese, and were in official hands from start to finish." Strong contrasted his own superficial meeting with Vanderlip's group with the "fine visits" he had in Japan with Lamont, "who has done a splendid piece of work here in concluding the Consortium." Strong did note that Lamont and his party also remained "in official hands."[11]

Strong's own visit was supposed to be a strictly personal trip for rest and recuperation. After initiating the most severe deflation program in US history, as mentioned in the last chapter and discussed further in the next, Strong left the country before the effects of it really took hold. Probably he hoped to avoid the storm. Strong also said that he was interested in observing the situation in Japan, China, and other countries. During Strong's absence of almost one year, J. H. Case served as the acting governor of the FRBNY.

In fact, Strong and his Japanese hosts both worked hard to establish a closer relationship between their formally nongovernmental central banks. (The Bank of Japan was half owned by the government, and its governor was appointed by the minister of finance, but formally it was not part of the government.) As Strong noted, the opening of relations between the FRBNY and the Bank of Japan in January 1918 was reported in the Japanese newspapers, although when he visited in 1920, it seemed to him that "our understanding with them is not widely known."[12] In 1919, Strong had proposed to make the cooperative relationship between the FRBNY and the Bank of Japan concrete, by establishing a framework for receiving each other's deposits. This arrangement was negotiated in late 1919, after Inoue Junnosuke became BoJ governor. The contract was signed on March 5, 1920, shortly before Strong left for Japan, and on March 17, 1920, the BoJ deposited $20 million in Japanese government funds at the FRBNY. Shortly after Strong returned to New York, in February 1921, this amount was increased to $40 million under the terms of a supplemental contract.[13] As we saw in chapter 1, on the Japanese side there was an established precedent for this arrangement, in the BoJ's deposits with the Bank of England. The FRBNY itself had no deposits at the BoJ. Strong later attempted to make the relationship mutual by proposing to open an FRBNY account at the BoJ and investing in Japanese trade bills, but this initiative came to nothing. Despite these limitations, the authors of the Bank of Japan's official one-hundred-year history concluded that these arrangements established a "spiritual connection" (*seishinteki tsunagari*) between the two central banks.[14]

Strong was accompanied on his trip by his son Benjamin Strong Jr. and by Basil Miles, formerly of the US State Department, with whom Strong shared a house during the often extended periods when he was in Washington, DC. Both Strong and Miles were members of a kind of fraternity who called themselves "The Family," alluded to later by Strong: "As you know, Mr. Miles and I are members of a little group of men who live together in Washington and who are principally in the various government services." Members of this little-known group held several key posts in the new US administrative state at the time it was taking its modern centralized form.[15]

Strong arrived in Japan May 4. He stayed in Japan much longer than he had planned, until August 11. By his account, he spent

> most of the time in the country, on foot, horse-back, and boat, living in Japanese hotels and houses, eating their food and wearing their clothes. Have talked with workmen, school boys, college boys, teachers, fishermen, sailors, priests, and shopkeepers. Played games with them, travelled with them, made pilgrimages with them, lived in their temples with the priests.[16]

Because he extended his stay in Japan, Strong canceled the China leg of the trip. He thought in any case that the revolutionary turmoil in China made a trip there impossible. At the same time, Strong himself was not entirely out of official hands. He was in effect hosted during his trip by the Bank of Japan, "through [whose] courtesy, every arrangement has been made for our stay." Mr. Sasaki of the Bank of Japan was also, Strong reported, "assigned to me for general use as a secretary and general useful man." Strong also hired a Japanese guide.[17]

The Bank of Japan certainly understood Strong's visit as a matter of important state business. BoJ director Fukai Eigo, who would later become BoJ governor, met Strong's ship at Yokohama. So too did Finance Minister Takahashi's secretary Tsushima Juichi; Tsushima would later be the

Japanese government's overseas financial commissioner in London, and he served still later as minister of finance.[18] In the weeks after his arrival, Strong met in Tokyo with the directors of the Bank of Japan and with BoJ governor Inoue Junnosuke, for whom Strong formed a high regard. He subsequently visited Finance Minister Takahashi Korekiyo at his home, and was later hosted again by Inoue and by Baron Mitsui. He also had five or six additional lunch and dinner meetings at the Bank of Japan. Strong visited twice with Baron Shibusawa Eiichi ("who treats me like a son and is really a most wonderful and charming old man"). He visited once with Marquis Matsukata Masayoshi, the founder of the modern Japanese financial system, at Matsukata's seaside villa in Kamakura ("a most impressive old man [86 years old], keen, alert, frank, with a great fund of humor and a knowledge of world affairs that made me ashamed!").[19]

Strong largely avoided publicity, but on May 24 he did give a speech to the Tokyo Bank Club in which he presented a report on America's recent financial situation, as referred to already in chapter 2. It was here that Strong described the FRBNY's wartime controls to his Japanese counterparts and addressed the global problem of postwar adjustment. "You will appreciate that our problem was much the same as your own," as Strong told them.[20] In fact, Japan's extended "postwar adjustment" would ultimately be conceptualized by both American and Japanese financial leaders as something that was finally resolved only in 1930, with Japan's own restoration of the gold standard: the culmination of the cooperative process of the 1920s.

Benjamin Strong's Report on Japan

Japan made a powerful impression upon Strong. Japan also inspired Strong, as it inspires so many foreign visitors, to write out his own social and political analysis of the country. Strong retained this interest for a time, and after his return to New York purchased a subscription to the English-language newspaper the *Japan Advertiser*, to keep abreast of events there.

In the notes he composed during his trip, Strong began by saying that it was hard to fathom Japanese mental processes and motives. Japan "in a period of fifty years has adopted western things as one would put on a suit of clothes. The clothes are western, but the man inside is a Japanese and an oriental." In a like way, Japan "has adopted some of the forms of democracy, under the cover of which it has developed a highly organized bureaucracy." Strong also formed an impression similar to Thomas Lamont's, that there were actually "two Japans"—the liberal Japan of the businessmen whom he got to know during his stay, and the illiberal Japan of the militarists.[21] His more intimate introduction to the country also gave him a relatively more nuanced understanding of Japanese society. Strong's letters were also free of the references to "the Japs" that sometimes marred the personal comments even of such a friend of Japan as Thomas Lamont (Lamont seems to have reserved the term for the common people and did not use it, as some of his Wall Street colleagues did, to refer to the Japanese bankers).

As it seemed to Strong, the World War had occasioned a national overreaching for Japan. This was true of Japan's international political and military relations, and it was true of Japanese business. The setbacks that followed the war came as a healthy correction:

> Recent developments, —that is the Chinese boycott, the domestic economic collapse, the conclusion of the consortium by Lamont and Inouye, and world wide criticism of the Chinese-Siberian policy of the military party,— has taught these people a lot. They still have much to learn—they still have an "invisible" government, representative government and a responsible ministry is still something of a sham, —but with all that there is an undercurrent of popular thought among the middle classes, which is soundly and progressively liberal and sensible.[22]

Strong detailed the various fractions of the Japanese governing elite and concluded that the nation was "governed by a very small number of men, who are largely actuated either by materialistic aims or military ambitions." Strong may have been especially sensitive in perceiving the operation of an inner-circle "invisible government" given that he himself was seen by populist critics as a member of an invisible financial government. In Japan, Strong also saw feudalism underneath the Western garment. "The mass of the population still retains many of the characteristics of the serf of feudal times. The men of the governing class are almost a different race."[23] There were some honorable exceptions, he said. Here, he was surely thinking

of Inoue Junnosuke, BoJ director Fukai Eigo, and others of their cosmo-
politan type. Strong noted the tight, exclusive character of Japan's ruling
political-bureaucratic elite, ranked by a system of aristocratic titles, bound
by tight family, region, school, and professional clique ties, but also open to
new talent. Here too, Strong was a sensitive observer, having himself risen,
from somewhere beyond its fringes, into the inner circles of an American
ruling elite that was not as dissimilar to Japan's ruling elite as respective
national stereotypes might lead one to believe. Indeed, the web of family, region, school, and professional ties in the United States was especially
tight in the spheres of high finance and foreign policy. The social overlap-
ping of the Wall Street elite with the State Department of those days particularly reminds one of the ties linking the Japanese elite. As mentioned,
the Washington fraternity house where Strong and Miles lived reflected
this nexus. In this, the US "Eastern establishment" resembled England's
"gentlemanly capitalist" elites, upon whose behavior many of the Ameri-
cans consciously modeled their own.[24] We have seen how this kind of emulation also shaped Inoue and others of his milieu.

In 1920, the word *containment* was not yet part of the vocabulary of US
diplomatic policy. In fact, the thrust of US government policy was now to
build a multilateral framework to contain and constrain Japan. The US
troop dispatch to Siberia had that aspect, as did US policy in China. The
State Department's request to Lamont to revive the China consortium
represented the financial component of this strategy. Along this line, the
US government also began pressuring the British government to end the
Anglo-Japanese alliance, leading in 1922 to the institution of the multilateral "Washington system" in its place.[25] Such geostrategic concerns were
not so salient in Strong's own thinking on Japan, which evolved to include
a set of views on Japan's domestic social and economic development. Strong
did note Japan's new economic dependence on the United States. He also
indicated three directions where Japanese and US interests now clashed:[26]

1st, Our policy of exclusion of Japanese from settlement in the U.S. . . . . In
[this], we have undoubtedly hurt their pride, a much more serious matter than may be generally realized.[27]

2nd, Our resistance to their ambitions in China and Siberia.

3rd, Our determination to absorb a share of the trade, shipping and banking
of the Orient.

That is, because Japan and the United States both had commercial ambitions in China, "we directly conflict with their selfish interests." Strong concluded, "Even the best disposed Japanese believe that our methods of dealing with both immigration, and Chinese matters, are needlessly brusque and display lack of respect for a sensitive people, who regard themselves as our equals, and earnestly desire recognition of their claims to equality."[28] However, concerning the likelihood of a future war between Japan and the United States, Strong thought the chances very remote.

New York–Tokyo Cooperation

Personal and institutional connections developed out of Strong's visit, and from this point on, Strong maintained a regular correspondence with Inoue and Fukai. "I have formed the highest opinion of the officers of the Bank [of Japan], particularly Mr. Inouye, the Governor, and Mr. Fukai, one of the active directors," Strong reported to acting FRBNY governor J.H. Case. "Lamont and our Ambassador share my views." "It was Inouye," Strong wrote,

> who put through the Consortium, despite the military party and I have more than once heard him referred to as the coming man of Japan. He is a little over 50, rather quiet, dignified, polite, and hospitable to a degree. Mr. Fukai is quick, alert, and a gentleman all through. They have both had experience abroad and [are] widely informed and I regard them as men of exceptional ability. They have been frankness itself in discussing their own affairs, financial and political.

"My opinion," he concluded,

> is that the [B]ank [of Japan] is splendidly managed, that it stands for sound progressive ideas, without jingoism, and that our relations with them should be developed as experience justifies. Our chief concern should be to maintain stable exchange rates between the two countries. They are proud of our relationship and friendship and want it to be closer.[29]

There is something here to admire. In a world divided by violent national rivalries, this was a vision of rational, enlightened cooperation. We must also ask, what were the flaws in this type of highly personalized co-operation among top monetary authorities, which ended with such bad results?

After two months spent traveling around the Japanese countryside, Strong met Inoue and Fukai for a weekend at the hot-springs resort of Nikkō. Japan also did wonders for Strong's health. His tubercular cough had almost disappeared, he reported—though "of course one cannot put on weight out here, as the diet is not suitable, but that I can do when I reach the land of meat, butter and cream."[30]

In early August 1920, at a final long meeting with the officers of the Bank of Japan, Inoue and Fukai briefed Strong in detail about the Japanese government's intention to continue to carry large overseas balances until 1924 and then use them to repay the Russo-Japanese War bonds that would come due in that year.[31] "Overseas" in this case meant both London and New York. This matter involved central bank cooperation of the highest order. It appears, in fact, that Japanese financial authorities were seeking to replicate with the FRBNY the relationship they had maintained with the Bank of England, which, as described already, benefited by holding and making use of Japanese funds. In effect, the Bank of Japan was now offering New York, at least temporarily, the same consideration it had formerly offered London. Strong paid careful attention, and he immediately reported this information in detail back to the FRBNY.[32] The possibility of maintaining large Japanese balances in New York also answered the FRBNY's concern with the heavy gold outflows to Japan described in the previous chapter. These shipments were in 1919 and 1920 greater than those to any other country and in themselves were a source of pressure for higher US interest rates.

Three years later, in September 1923, the plan of carrying large Japanese balances in New York would be ruined by the great Tokyo-Yokohama earthquake and the enormous reconstruction expenses that followed it. In 1924, far from clearing off its overseas debts, the Japanese government therefore required another major British and American loan—one of the largest international loans of its time—in order to roll over existing debt and to help pay earthquake reconstruction expenses. New York became the primary center of Japanese long-term borrowing for the rest of the 1920s. From the standpoint of Japanese diplomacy, the wooing of

America's top financial leaders thus appeared an important success, amid the general picture of failure surrounding the nation's misadventures in China and Siberia.

Strong left Japan on August 11. He visited Java and then voyaged onward to Malaya, India, Ceylon, France, and England. By December he was in London with Montagu Norman. In January 1921 he was finally back at his post in New York.

6

Putting the Program into Action, 1920–1928

After leaving Japan I seemed to have been a bird of ill omen, for from
one place to the next I heard nothing but tales of losses and business
disaster. Literally my trip around the world seemed to be upon a wave of
depression, if such a thing exists, and I finally reached New York finding
much the same conditions here.

Benjamin Strong, writing to Fukai Eigo, January 1921

Knowing what he knew, Benjamin Strong may have felt ill-omened indeed. And the wave of depression indeed traveled right around the world.
This wave of depression was the first fruit of history's first truly globalized
monetary policy—and Strong probably knew more of its inside story than
anyone else.

"World Deflation Has Been Started"

The deflation and "adjustment" that Strong, Norman, and Inoue began
working to induce in the second half of 1919 appeared first in Japan, where
commercial and financial markets crashed in March 1920. The panic of
1920 was one of the greatest in Japanese history. "The decline in wholesale prices in the year [1920] has been more spectacular than in any other
country in the world," as the *Federal Reserve Bulletin* reported.[1] Wholesale
prices fell by 43 percent from March 1920 to December 1922, according to
the Bank of Japan index. (By contrast, the more recent deflation of Japan's

bubble economy after 1990 was a long-continued process more than a sudden collapse.)

In Japan itself, this crash was not seen as part of a global movement but rather as a specifically national reaction to a national speculative boom.[2] In fact, the panic of 1920 happened right across maritime Asia. In the US-occupied Philippines, where Strong's policies impinged most directly (and where he chose not to stop on his trip), prices also rose to a great peak in early 1920. The postwar inflationary boom collapsed in Manila after June 1920, as US colonial authorities adopted a deflation policy that reduced the money supply by 40 percent and caused a severe depression.[3] After Strong left Japan on August 11, he made his next extended stay in Java, where he was hosted in September by the Javasche Bank, the central bank of the Netherlands-occupied East Indies. Here the wartime and postwar booms were also especially great, facilitated by a great surge in Javasche Bank credit. The value of Java's exports more than tripled in 1919 and then fell back by almost 60 percent in 1921.[4] In Malaya, where Strong went in October, the postwar boom also gave way after March 1920 to a severe slump; the monetary value of Malayan exports fell by 60 percent from their high point in early 1920 to their low point in 1921.[5] In India, where Strong arrived in late October, the boom peaked in most sectors in April 1920. British colonial authorities adopted a severe deflationary program. In the Bombay financial markets, a speculative boom continued until October 1920, followed by a series of collapses and bankruptcies.[6] Indian exports fell by 29 percent from their 1919 peak level to a trough in 1922. The commercial depression of 1920–21 was thus widespread across the Asian region, though China and French Indochina, both on silver standards, were relatively mildly affected.[7]

In France, where Strong stopped in December, the postwar economic crisis was very severe. Strong arrived in London later in December 1920, where he was hosted by Montagu Norman (who had himself been promoted from vice-governor to governor of the Bank of England in March 1920). In Great Britain also the depression was severe. British wholesale prices fell 53 percent from their peak in April 1920 to a trough in July 1923. This appears to be the sharpest price deflation in the British historical record. Unemployment rates jumped from 1 percent to 23 percent—the onset of a new era of mass unemployment.[8] On December 22, Strong sent a telegram from the Bank of England to his New York bank: *"The Bank of England . . . consider general rate policy has so far been wonderfully success-ful . . . world deflation has been started.*"[9]

Privately, Strong was not so sanguine. In a pencil draft of the same tele-gram, which Strong refrained from sending out of deference to Norman's point of view, Strong worried openly about the "dangers from too great momentum" of the present rapid price reductions. Already, Strong feared that too much deflation, too fast, would cause businesses working on bor-rowed money to fail, would lead to European difficulties in repaying debts to America, and, finally, would cause unemployment and bring the danger of "legislative interference with our program." He turned out to be cor-rect on all points. Strong's final point, in this unsent draft: *"present depres-sion is world wide and seems to show no sign of cheer."* Five years later—and three years before his fatal illness completed its course—Strong evidently thought that his premonitions in December 1920 bore on his place in his-tory, for he had these handwritten notes filed at the FRBNY with the nota-tion, "these papers should be carefully preserved."[10]

World deflation had indeed been started, and worldwide depression with it. In the United States, wholesale prices fell by 45 percent from May 1920 to January 1922, and the economic dislocations were sudden and severe. A new period in economic history had begun.

Global Financial Governance: The London–New York Program

Chapter 4 surveyed the de facto alignment of central bank policy in late 1919 in the United States, Great Britain, and Japan. This informal pol-icy alignment was combined with more formal and multilateral efforts. In January 1920, an international meeting of bankers and financial ex-perts was held in Amsterdam. A second meeting was held in Brussels in September 1920. The Brussels Conference resolutions called explicitly for the universal establishment of central banks: "In countries where there is no central Bank of Issue, one should be established." The resolutions also specified that "if the assistance of foreign capital were required for the pro-motion of such a Bank some form of international control might be re-quired."[11] These September 1920 resolutions were the first formal public statement of the new multilateral central bank program.

In December 1920 and January 1921, when Strong was in London, he and Montagu Norman discussed central bank cooperation. Soon after, Norman drafted twelve principles of central banking, to be presented to other countries' central bankers as a common program. Calling it "my first attempt at an epitome on this subject," Norman sent his draft to Strong on February 17, 1921.

The first set of principles listed in Norman's draft "manifesto" were in the nature of protective prohibitions. The first principle was that "a Central Bank should not compete with other Banks for general business." Second, "a Central Bank should not take monies [deposits] at interest on its own account nor accept Bills of Exchange"—this business belonged to the commercial banks. Third, "a Central Bank should have no Branch outside its own country." Here, Norman's particular motivation was that all of the central banking relations of the British Empire should be channeled through the Bank of England.[12] And fourth, "a Central Bank should not engage in a general Exchange business on its own account with any other country." One immediate stimulus to Norman's thinking seems to have been the plan to establish an Imperial Bank of India, with ("to my disgust," Norman wrote) a branch office in London.[13]

The core of Norman's program was then discreetly outlined in points 5 through 12:

> 5. "A Central Bank should be independent but should do all its own Government's business—directly or indirectly—including Gold and Currency."

To say that a central bank should be independent meant that it should be independent of its own national government. And, to say that it should do its own government's business meant that it should have a monopoly of its government's monetary and banking business, including dealings in gold. The constitutional and political implications of this claim were obviously very far-reaching.

In relation to the banking sector of its own country, a central bank should take a "banking," or credit-creation role, as well as a regulatory role:

> 6. "A Central Bank should be the Banker of all other Banks in its own country and should assist them to develop its business and economic resources."

7. "A Central Bank should protect its own Traders from the rapacity of other Banks in its own country."

The final principles concerned the international relations among central banks.

8. "A Central Bank may have an Agency in another country."

Here was a critical point, which Norman spelled out in points 9 through 12. Using roundabout language, Norman indicated that the "Agency" could in fact be the other country's central bank—that central banks could serve as agencies for each other. But even if the agency were another central bank,

9. "That Agency (if not itself a Central Bank) should do all its banking and all kindred business with the Central Bank of the other country."
10. "And should co-operate in practice and principle with the Central Bank of the other country."
11. "And should receive the most favoured treatment and information from the Central Bank of the other country."
12. "And should do the Banking and kindred business of its Principal's Government in the other country."

In fact, this latter exclusive and indeed monopolistic part of Norman's vision did not interest other central bankers, many of whom had already established multiple international connections of their own.

To Norman's twelve points, Strong added three points of his own that were particularly relevant to the Federal Reserve System:[14]

"A Central Bank should act as the settling Agent for Clearing House balances arising between the Banks of its own country, and to the widest extent practicable."

"A Central Bank should handle domestic collections for its members and so regulate the domestic exchanges."

"A Central Bank should have the power to examine Banks which come to the Central Bank for credit and assistance."

As we have seen, this kind of regulatory authority had already been extended during the war, when the Federal Reserve Bank of New York was granted an extraordinary degree of administrative authority.

Subsequently, Norman summed up some of these points, in a more general and sweeping way, in the form of eight resolutions that he proposed for adoption by other central and reserve banks at meetings to be held at the Bank of England.[15] In summary form:

1. "Autonomy and freedom from political control are desirable for all Central and Reserve Banks."
2. "Subject to conformity with the above clause a policy of continuous co-operation is desirable among Central and Reserve Banks."
3. "Co-operation should include confidential exchange of information and opinions among such Banks with regard to such matters as rates of discount, the stability of exchanges and the movement of gold."
4. Central banks should recognize the importance of international as well as national interests.
5. Central banks should conduct their foreign banking operations with each other.
6. Central banks should extend facilities to each other, including the custody of gold, monies, and securities, and the discounting of approved bills of exchange, without undue regard for profit.
7. Central banks should ensure the absolute right to withdraw all gold, monies, and securities held on behalf of other central banks.
8. Each central bank should work to establish a free market in forward exchange in its own country.

Demands for "central bank independence" and "central bank cooperation" have been repeated so often that we forget how extraordinary these claims really were (and are), particularly in a country with aspirations to democracy. "Rather doctrinaire, undoubtedly somewhat utopian, perhaps even Machiavellian, [but] certainly possible!" was what Bank of France governor Émile Moreau thought when he learned the details of Norman's "work of the twentieth century."[16] Norman, as the head of a private, profitable bank, also had much more actual leeway and independence than almost any of his confreres. The Bank of England, always very profitable, was extraordinarily profitable during the period from 1916 to 1930. The depression year of 1921 was itself a year of record profits for the Bank of England—£9.2 million. This was a record for the entire period from 1890 to 1939; the bank also in 1921 set aside an additional £18 million as reserves.[17]

Not discussed in Norman's manifesto but at the core of his project were his efforts to establish British-linked central banks in countries that did not have central banks. This project began with the British Empire itself but in fact was significantly limited there by the balance of existing interests. As mentioned, the Imperial Bank of India was formed in 1921, out of a merger of the three presidency banks of Calcutta, Madras, and Bombay. The Imperial Bank of India continued to do business both as a commercial bank and as a bank of issue. A "proper" central bank would not be established in India until 1935—this was when the prospect of increasing Indian self-government prompted Norman and British government authorities to organize a central bank under Bank of England tutelage, precisely in order to "reserve" finance from the scope of the new constitutional arrangements.[18]

The British dominion of South Africa was the world's greatest source of newly mined gold: some three-quarters of British Empire gold production in the 1920s, which was half or more of world production. N. M. Rothschild & Sons had a dominant position in the handling of this business. Here a central bank was established in 1921 under the leadership of Norman's close ally Henry Strakosch.[19] The establishment of the South African Reserve Bank appeared to be a concession to the national demands of white South African elites who resented the monopoly marketing arrangements run from London. In fact, Norman was able to maintain close connections with the new reserve bank—"to which," he told Strong, "we have contributed a Governor."[20]

Australia, on the other hand, Norman described to Strong as having "a State Bank which in no sense acts as a Central Bank and which is doing more harm than good."[21] The Commonwealth Bank of Australia, a commercial and savings bank, did assume a monopoly of banknote issue in 1924. It later added other functions of a central bank, but in fact Australia had no central bank until 1959.[22] Australia would also be very early in leaving the gold standard, in 1929, and was consequently better able to weather the new phase of the world crisis that began at that time. Contra Norman, in terms of Australia's own interests, this looks more like a success than a failure.

The campaign to establish new "independent" central banks was most conspicuous in the cohort of newly independent republics that emerged in Central and Eastern Europe as a result of the war. After 1945, many of the same countries would serve as laboratories for Soviet economic forms. In the 1990s, they would be laboratories for "shock therapy" and austerity policies reminiscent of the 1920s. Here, there was more play for the workings of the new central bank program; accordingly, a core part of postwar monetary stabilization programs was to establish or reform central banks that would be legally independent of their national governments. These new central banks were not so independent of foreign financial institutions—in fact, they depended on them.[23] In the campaign to set up new central banks, US-British rivalry also entered the picture, as the American "money doctor" Edwin Kemmerer led a movement to establish "independent" central banks in the republics of South America and other countries in Asia and Africa.[24] Here, too, there is a substantial overlap with the geography of "structural adjustment" programs imposed by the IMF in the 1980s and 1990s. A large cohort of new central banks was thus founded in both colonies and independent states, as summarized in table 6.1.

TABLE 6.1.   Banks of issue organized, 1921–1931

Date	Bank	Notes
1921	South African Reserve Bank	Semicolonial bank; advised by Bank of England
1921	Imperial Bank of India	Colonial bank; merger of three Presidency Banks (Reserve Bank of India formed 1935)
1922	Bank of Lithuania	
1922	Austrian National Bank	Reorganized as independent central bank
1922	Bank of Latvia	
1922	Reserve Bank of Peru	
1923	State Bank of the USSR (Gosbank)	
1923	Bank of the Republic [of Colombia]	Result of Kemmerer mission
1924	Bank of Poland	
1924	National Bank of Hungary	Reorganized as independent central bank

(Continued)

TABLE 6.1   (Continued)

Date	Bank	Notes
1924	Bank of Syria and Great Lebanon	Colonial bank; based on the former Banque Impériale Ottomane
1925	Bank of Madagascar	Colonial bank
1925	Bank of Mexico	
1925	Bank of Mongolia	
1925	National Bank of Albania	
1926	National Bank of Czechoslovakia	
1926	Central Bank of Guatemala	Result of Kemmerer mission
1926	Central Bank of Chile	Result of Kemmerer mission
1926	Bank of Angola	Colonial bank
1927	Bank Melli Iran	Commercial bank with central bank functions
1927	Central Bank of Ecuador	Result of Kemmerer mission
1927	Bank of Estonia	Reorganized as independent central bank
1928	Central Bank of the Bolivian Nation	Result of Kemmerer mission
1928	Bank of Greece	
1928	Central Bank of China	
1931	Central Bank of the Republic of Turkey	Advisers: G. Vissering (1928); G. Volpi (1929)

Source: Central banks' websites and various sources.

A New Central-Bank Connection: New York and Tokyo

After Benjamin Strong returned from his world tour in early 1921, his communications with Governor Inoue and Director Fukai of the Bank of Japan focused on the questions of price deflation and the restoration of the gold standard. Concerning central bank cooperation, Strong wrote to Inoue, "very confidentially," in November 1921, "you know that I have long felt the need, as we so often discussed when I was in Tokyo, for a better understanding between the principal banks of issue." He informed Inoue that his friend Montagu Norman of the Bank of England had visited him in the summer of 1921; together with Sir Charles Addis, they had discussed central bank cooperation at length.[25] (Addis, in addition to being head of the Hongkong and Shanghai Bank, which itself conducted British state business in East Asia, was also a leading director at the Bank of England from 1918 to 1932, and a key backer of Norman. Addis had provided

Strong with letters of introduction to Japanese bankers before his 1920 trip.)[26] Norman, together with Strong's deputy Pierre Jay of the FRBNY, had also confidentially discussed central bank cooperation with Dr. Vissering, the former governor of the Javasche Bank and present governor of the Nederlandsche Bank in Amsterdam. They had spoken likewise with the president of the National Bank of Switzerland and with officers of the National Bank of Belgium.[27]

Connections between the BoJ and the FRBNY deepened when BoJ director Fukai Eigo visited the United States as Japanese financial attaché at the Washington naval disarmament conference of November 1921–February 1922. This was the conference that produced the "Washington system," which defined the status quo in East Asia and the international naval strategic balance of the 1920s. As part of this multilateral settlement, the Anglo-Japanese alliance was ended in 1922. Surviving documentary records also make it clear that US officials used their new financial leverage to press the British government to terminate the alliance.[28] Strong at this time invited Fukai to New York for a further discussion of central bank cooperation. Strong also wrote to Inoue, to tell him that he planned to go to Europe in the summer of 1922 and hoped Inoue could meet him there. He further tempted Inoue with the offer, "Would you care to be informed by cable of changes in our [discount] rates, and when possible (although this would not be very often) some warning in advance?"[29] This was the kind of inside information that Strong and Norman repeatedly exchanged; needless to say, such information would have been politically and commercially very valuable.

Fukai, an intellectual leader at the bank who often served as its international financial representative, shuttled back and forth to New York during the Washington conference and had repeated friendly discussions with Strong. This was probably the closest of Strong's Japanese connections. Strong introduced Fukai to members of the Federal Reserve Board and to numerous people in the US government. Fukai also met repeatedly with private New York bankers, including Paul Warburg and Charles Mitchell; Mitchell had succeeded Frank Vanderlip as president of National City Bank.[30] Strong now proposed that the FRBNY establish an account at the BoJ and begin to deal in Japanese trade bills, but the Japanese authorities discovered objections to this, and it did not happen. In early 1923, the Bank of Japan and the Federal Reserve Bank of New York also concluded an agreement to establish correspondent (*koruresu*) relations, to arrange for holding "earmarked" gold for each other, and to exchange information about conditions in their respective financial markets.[31] All of this indicates a high level of informational cooperation, and a degree of operational coordination as well. Fukai himself later became BoJ governor, in 1935–1937; had those times been more peaceful, he would likely have continued Inoue's international cooperation line, but by then the political winds were blowing in another direction.

The "exchange of views" also continued. One question on Strong's mind was the question of how much deflation was enough. By the summer of 1921, US wholesale prices had fallen 44 percent from their peak levels of early 1920. The postwar depression had not lifted. Nonetheless, Strong thought that a more thorough deflation was still needed. In his communications with Norman, Strong described deflation as the product of a successful central bank policy, though he also expressed the fear that excessive deflation would provoke a political backlash and lead to intervention by the US Congress. Norman likewise saw deflation as a success but worried that America was out-deflating Britain. In Britain there were coal strikes, provoked by wage cuts that were now running ahead of declines in the cost of living.[32] Writing to Inoue in August 1921, Strong explained that deflationary "adjustment" was continuing in America—but "we cannot yet say that a new price level has been definitely established and stabilized." Wages in particular still had to come down, he thought. Strong also acknowledged the resistance to his program: "We have had considerable agitation in this country by agricultural classes of a character that is inimical to the Federal Reserve system."[33]

This agrarian "agitation" in fact signified a historic reinvigoration of the populist movement that had been so active during the long price deflation of 1873–1896 and had faded during the more prosperous decades since then. This opposition between agrarian and creditor interests was a classic one. In Japan, the deflation policy would make this tension manifest in a severe way. One future consequence of the deflation policy in Japan: it was an ultranationalist "agrarianist" group that plotted and executed the assassination of Inoue Junnosuke in early 1932, during the final phase of the deflation crisis.

Strong himself shifted his stance toward deflation in 1922, at a time when the Japanese government was actually reintensifying its own deflation policy in order to prepare for a return to the gold standard. "In a general way you are dealing with a situation which presents many points of resemblance to our own," Strong wrote to Inoue in December 1922, saying he understood the Japanese government's steps to reduce the circulation of currency in order to promote further deflation. But now he criticized the effort to force prices down to the prewar "normal":

> I have sometimes wondered whether any program looking to a contraction of credit as distinguished from a stabilizing of credit may not have its source in a latent and possibly unrecognized feeling that we should get back to something which we consider to be normal, and at times are too liable to consider that "normal" is a credit situation and a price level such as prevailed before the war.[34]

This view of a lost prewar "normalcy" was then general in the financial world. As Bank of England historian R. S. Sayers wrote, "The men of 1919 believed that the best possible monetary system was that of 1913."[35] Sayers means especially the male elites who directed the worlds of banking and business, and these men tended likewise to believe that a profitable and normal level of prices and wages was that of 1913. This view was reflected also in the common statistical practice of using 1913 as a base year in order to compute price indices and thereby to convey the extent of wartime and postwar inflation. But Strong now gently tried to dissuade Inoue from such a view. Although it was "a subject of much discussion here," he concluded, "there is no such thing as a pre-war normal." Efforts to return to "a corrected 1913 normal" would actually do injustice to one or another class. Strong again invoked the problem of agricultural depression, and he even acknowledged implicitly that it was the "agricultural classes" who paid for price deflation. One can surmise his concern to forestall a political reaction "inimical" to the central bank, for an agriculturally oriented populist movement was growing even within the Republican Party.[36]

Tokyo and London: Coordinating the Return to the Gold Standard

After the conclusion of the Washington conference, Fukai Eigo went next to Europe, where he represented the Bank of Japan at the Genoa

Conference in May 1922. The international economic conference in Genoa was the culmination of the series of personal meetings and international bankers' conferences of 1919–21. It concluded with the enunciation of two new principles originally championed by Montagu Norman; these were now agreed by the representatives of twenty-nine governments (including Great Britain and Japan but not including the United States). The first principle was general restoration of currency convertibility, to be based on the *gold exchange standard* rather than the prewar gold specie standard. That is, gold-backed currencies, meaning US dollars (and prospectively, British pounds) would be able to serve in place of gold in other countries' central-bank reserves as the basis for the issue of domestic paper money. This meant a kind of double-leveraging of gold. In Norman's mind, this prospective enlargement of sterling's place in other countries' currency reserves opened the way for restoring an international pound-sterling standard. Historian Harold James has called this technique "a generalization of the prewar Japanese or Indian practice."[37] That is, a generalization of prewar Japanese or Indian practice *in London*, as the Bank of Japan, like the colonial government of India, had before the war maintained large overseas funds in the Bank of England; and the Bank of Japan had counted these overseas sterling balances as part of its own reserve against note issue, as noted in chapter 1. On this point there was a gap between US and British plans, and this international leveraging of sterling's position was the part of Norman's program that Benjamin Strong resisted.

The second principle that the assembled representatives agreed to at Genoa was a recognition of the desirability of the independence and "continuous cooperation" of central banks. Both these principles would be realized increasingly in practice during the remainder of the 1920s.[38]

After the Genoa Conference, Fukai Eigo toured depressed postwar Europe, meeting with central bankers. Fukai now became friendly with Norman as well. In frank and detailed discussions with Fukai, Norman averred that the Bank of Japan had an important international position, and he sought to bring the Japanese into his project of central bank cooperation. Norman also gave Fukai an updated version of his central banking manifesto. Fukai and Inoue responded positively to Norman's proposal for a central bankers' meeting. Other central bankers did not, however, and the meeting never happened.[39]

In his memoirs, published in November 1941, Fukai refrained from describing the content of his 1922 conversations with Norman "because they had no results," beyond the establishment of direct telegraphic communications. In fact, these discussions concerned a question of profound significance for both countries (and 1941 might not have been a good time to delve into such things). In fact, in 1922, the Japanese government planned, as Fukai told both Norman and Strong, *that Japan would return to the gold standard simultaneously with England.* "When I discussed currency problems of the world with you and Mr. Norman in 1922," Fukai later wrote to Strong, "it appeared Japan would be in a position to take a concerted action with Great Britain if and when the latter should decide to resume gold payments." Fukai confirmed this point in his memoirs.[40] Had the Japanese been able to fulfill this intention, Japan would have returned to the gold standard when Britain did, in April 1925. More than a dozen other countries actually did directly follow the British government's action.[41]

If Japan had joined this movement and restored the yen's gold convertibility at its prewar par value in 1925, Japan would also have taken part in a deflationary "stabilization crisis" at that time. In Britain itself, the renewal of deflation, industrial recession, and wage cuts had severe effects, as reflected in the great General Strike of 1926. This deflation policy, the second radical deflation since 1920, was the occasion for Keynes's famous essay, "The Economic Consequences of Mr. Churchill," which pinned the blame on the politician then serving as chancellor of the exchequer.[42] Keynes could better have titled his essay "The Economic Consequences of Mr. Norman." Privately, Churchill himself had doubts about the deflation policy, saying that he "would rather see Finance less proud and Industry more content." He was forced along by pressure from the Treasury and the Bank of England, as Montagu Norman warned Churchill that Britain's failure to return promptly to the gold standard would mean that "the world centre would shift permanently and completely from London to New York."[43] Moreover, an American gold-standard mission led by Edwin Kemmerer and cochaired by Dutch central banker Gerard Vissering had already persuaded the South African government to opt for a unilateral return to the gold standard. This wedged an opening that could have jeopardized London's financial primacy within its own empire and could further have jeopardized the position of London as the world's gold market.[44]

Japan, however, could not return to the gold standard in 1925. As Fukai reminded Strong in June 1925, "Our situation . . . underwent a great change because of the [earthquake] disaster of 1923."[45] Fukai himself was back in Tokyo when the great Kantō earthquake happened on September 1, 1923. He, with Inoue Junnosuke, helped lead the firefighting efforts at the Bank of Japan building. It was then that much of the bank's historical archive was lost, though the main vaults were saved. In the aftermath of the burning of most of central Tokyo, and during the immense reconstruction effort that followed, the balance of international payments again turned heavily against Japan, interrupting fiscal retrenchment and preparations for the return to the gold standard. Japan's own "stabilization crisis" would be deferred until 1929–31, when it coincided with the world crisis. The Japanese government, under the pro-British cabinet led by Katō Takaaki, did return to a more modest deflation program in 1925–27, maintaining an alignment with British policy. The Ministry of Finance, by simultaneously licensing some gold shipments, thus followed a policy that functioned as a kind of shadow gold standard after 1925.[46]

Altogether, however, financial relations between Tokyo and London became less close after the war, and the grounds of the Anglo-Japan financial relationship changed.[47] Japanese surpluses trapped in London during the war were repatriated, and the Bank of Japan no longer kept large balances in London. The termination of the Anglo-Japanese alliance as part of the Washington system contributed to this distancing. Japan's total overseas "gold" reserves (which were actually gold plus foreign-exchange reserves) reached a peak of ¥1,343 million in 1919. They were then drawn down to ¥258 million in 1925.[48] British overseas lending was greatly diminished after the war, but careful negotiations did lead to the issuance of Japanese corporate loans on the London financial market. The Tokyo Electric Light Company (the present TEPCO) floated bonds worth £3 million in June 1923. The parastatal South Manchurian Railway Company floated bonds worth £4 million in July 1923. Critical here was the British government's long-standing recognition of what were called Japan's "special rights and interests" in South Manchuria and eastern Inner Mongolia.[49] At the same time, the US State Department consistently intervened to prevent American banks from lending to the South Manchurian Railway Company.

After the great Kantō earthquake of September 1, 1923, however, the Bank of England seemed intent on refusing Japanese requests for new loans, at a time when the Japanese government was desperate to secure for-eign-exchange funds for reconstruction. Montagu Norman now had grave doubts about Japan's financial situation, and he seems to have offended Japan's overseas financial commissioner, Mori Kengo, with his insinua-tions. As both Tokyo and London maneuvered to protect and restore their gold reserves and return to their prewar gold standards, the Bank of En-gland's confidential insistence that the Bank of Japan deposit "special secu-rity" or "security reserves" in London became a sticking point.[50]

The Washington system did enable Japanese borrowing in New York. Postwar Japanese efforts to borrow in New York began in 1921, before the Washington Conference, when the Oriental Development Company, a parastatal colonial corporation with large landholdings in Korea and interests in Manchuria, negotiated with National City Bank to arrange an overseas bond issue. Again, National City Bank played a trail-blazing role. The US State Department nixed the loan because it could have been taken to imply US recognition for a Japanese sphere of influ-ence in Manchuria. For both sides, the political aspects of this loan ini-tiative were clear. In February 1922, the Nine-Power Treaty was signed in Washington, leading to a withdrawal of Japanese military forces from Shandong and signifying a strategic rapprochement between the US and Japanese governments. In December 1922, National City Bank renewed its effort to arrange a bond issue for the Oriental Development Company. A deal was put together in 1923, for a total of $19.9 million. National City Bank also tried to arrange a loan for the parastatal South Manchu-rian Railway Company. For the US Department of State, this again went too far toward recognizing Japanese claims in Manchuria, and they again prevented it.[51] From these beginnings, NCB's business with Japan grew greatly, as described further in chapter 8.

This was the context of the giant "earthquake loan" negotiated by the Japanese government with Morgan & Company of New York in 1924. Morgan henceforth became Japan's chief foreign banker. Much of the loan proceeds went not for reconstruction but instead to roll over the for-mer Russo-Japanese War loans. These funds also replenished the Bank of Japan's gold reserve held in London.[52] The Japanese government bond issue was followed later in the year by the even larger Morgan-brokered Dawes Plan loan to Germany. Together, these signified a new stage in the shift of the world financial center from London to New York. Notably, as a destination of US long-term lending during the 1920s, Japan was the third-largest borrower, after Canada and Germany.

Burying Gold: Strong and Norman

Despite Benjamin Strong's concern to moderate the deflation policy after 1922, he continued to fear that large gold inflows to the United States would cause renewed inflation. These gold inflows commenced in 1921, as foreign governments and financial institutions settled some of their debts by means of gold shipments. Although prices had fallen greatly since 1920, Strong continued to speak of rapid price increases, of workers' wages being too high, and of the possible need to increase interest rates. To prevent a gold-based inflation, he therefore acted to "sterilize" gold inflows, excluding increased US gold reserves from the monetary base.

This violation of the "rules" of the gold-standard game has often been condemned by scholars as a cause for the ultimate breakdown of the international gold standard after 1931. Under idealized gold-standard rules, the accumulation of gold in the United States should have increased the US monetary base and caused the US price level to increase; higher US prices would then have hampered US trade competitiveness and increased the competitive strength of other countries, allowing them to repair their trade deficits with the United States. This was the equilibrium model of specie-flow adjustment as described by David Hume. Strong did not see things that way. *"Our great economic problem is dealing with the continued addition to our mass of gold,"* he told Fukai in March 1924—a time when Japan had the opposite problem. Strong continued:

> We cannot keep it out but must absorb it and put it away temporarily until the world comes to its senses and readjusts its monetary systems. It is a menace to us in presenting the possibility of inflation.[53]

A bit more US dollar inflation, after the severe deflation of 1920, would in fact have gone far to alleviate the debts that burdened American farmers. It would also have lightened the debts that burdened the external financial balances of countries around the world. On the other hand, under a gold standard system in which gold as monetary "base" was leveraged into a great "skyscraper" of purchasing power, large unregulated gold flows could have enormously magnified effects in the world of credit. American bankers, having created a great stock of inflation-inducing credits during and shortly after the war, now held large portfolios of debt claims. Their financial interests now seemed to run in the direction of deflation rather than inflation. Thus, the world's gold was dug out of the ground only to be reinterred in American depositories.[54] And we can note again that more than two-thirds of that gold was being dug up in lands belonging to the British Empire.

Strong's "sterilization" of gold inflows was publicly known and was apparent on the face of the published statistics. Montagu Norman appears also to have sterilized gold inflows to Britain in pursuit of his own deflation policy. He conducted these operations secretly through the agency of Strong's Federal Reserve Bank of New York, and the story that the Bank of England reported to the public is the version of events that has come down to us in the history books. In this construction, Britain in the 1920s suffered from a shortage of gold; monetary authorities were therefore compelled, like it or not, to contract the currency and bring on deflation. A statistical reconstruction by John R. Garrett suggests instead that Norman engaged in systematic deception, understating the size of BoE gold reserves and misreporting gold flows, sometimes to the extent of even misreporting their direction. It also seems that Norman's policy from 1925 to mid-1928 was radically more deflationary than it appeared to be in the reported statistics.[55] Deflation, more than being a means to an end for Norman, appears itself to have been the goal. Keynes publicly declared his own suspicions of the bank in June 1928: "We do not want to be governed by masked men in false beards muttering Mumbo Jumbo." The Bank of England's real reasons and motives, he said, were "like its profits and its statistics, secret and unavowed."[56]

There is, in fact, a long history of tension between Bank of England secrecy concerning its reserves and the demands for accountability of its various publics. An early instance appears in public criticism of the bank's "cabalistical numbers" and "mystical scale" during the deflation of the early nineteenth century.[57] A century on, gold reserves were much more highly leveraged, and additions to and subtractions from these reserves could be highly destabilizing. Garrett suggests that there was a multiple of ten times between the gold reserves and the larger money supply (including bank balances).[58] Norman's manipulation of gold reserves could not be traced, because they were carried out in the New York money markets, by the Federal Reserve Bank of New York, which acted as agent for its brother bank. The Bank of England did not list its holdings of US Treasury bills in its published accounts but rather included them under "other securities." In effect, Norman operated a bank within the bank, known only to himself and a few key confidants. The conclusion seems inescapable: for the foremost advocate and practitioner of the policy of restoring the international gold standard, the supposed "rules" of the gold-standard game were an elaborate charade.[59] Garrett thus concludes that Norman developed false reporting of reserves into a regular tool of monetary policy. His goal appears to have been to keep the reported reserves continually on the edge, so that it was easy to make things appear to swing either way. As mentioned in chapter 8, Norman also appears to have hidden the facts when the Bank of England in fact did begin to lose gold in late 1928. Benjamin Strong died in office on October 16, 1928. One can speculate that with his passing, Norman lost an enormous scope for quiet maneuvering.

For Benjamin Strong, one solution to the problem of "too much gold" was to reexport the incoming funds. Briefly, Japan had experienced the same potential problem during its wartime boom, when the country's large international credit balances likewise threatened to exacerbate inflation. Inoue Junnosuke had then counseled the same response: that Japan invest much of its wartime credit balances overseas in the bonds of the Allied countries. This too would have served to sterilize gold inflows.[60] But by 1924, Japan's wartime loans to Russia and China were in default, and its windfall financial surpluses were gone. Far from repaying old foreign loans, Japan was taking out new ones. In the United States, banks did begin to "reexport" money in a big way in 1924. In that year alone, some $1,250 million in foreign loans were placed on the US market, as Strong informed Fukai Eigo in January 1925. As both of them well knew, $150 million of this new lending was accounted for by the massive Morgan-led loan to the Japanese government in February 1924. Another $190 million was accounted for by the great Morgan-led loan to the German government in September 1924, to support the reestablishment of the German mark on a gold-standard basis.[61]

Thus, following the first great wave of US overseas lending during the world war, the large loans to Japan and Germany in 1924 initiated a follow-on wave of lending, which powerfully reoriented international financial relations in the second half of the 1920s. Temporarily it seemed a virtuous circle all around. As Strong explained in January 1925, this overseas lending "facilitated the export of our surplus farm produce" and eased the pressure on US agriculture. The first phase of this new wave of US international lending coincided with an international recovery in 1924–25. International agricultural prices were also temporarily high in 1924–25. Both international cooperation and postwar recovery seemed for a time to be working. This overseas lending also meant that the United States was now actually exporting gold—$102 million in 1925—removing the pressure for domestic inflation.[62]

As a negative aspect to this virtuous circle, Strong did mention the revival of speculation in the stock market.[63] The Wall Street stock-market bubble of the late 1920s thus began in the broadly deflationary international circumstances that followed Britain's restoration of the gold standard in April 1925. This is another historical case of the phenomenon of asset bubbles arising in the context of price deflation: new credit creation was no longer going into broad-based industrial investment but rather was feeding into a cycle of asset bubbling, whereby bank lending for the purpose of purchasing company shares further boosted share prices, promoting still more share purchasing on credit. The same broad set of circumstances— credit bubbling within an incipiently deflationary environment—would characterize Japan's great bubble at the end of the 1980s.

There were self-generating limits to the apparent international recovery of the late 1920s. The surge of US lending in 1924–27 increased still further the volume of dollar debts owed by the rest of the world to US institutions. By 1930, it would be manifest that this surge of credit creation, much of it to refinance war debts, had ultimately worsened rather than alleviated global credit-debt imbalances. The cycle of repaying old debt by creating new debt could continue for a time, but when this wave of international lending halted after 1928, a world debt-default crisis was at hand.[64]

The Central Banking Family

Strong, like Norman, was usually scrupulous in avoiding official contact with foreign governments. Central banks might provide credits to each other, but the business of dealing with and providing credits to foreign governments instead belonged to private bankers. When Inoue Junnosuke resigned from the Bank of Japan in order to join the government as minister of finance after the September 1923 earthquake, Strong therefore expressed his disappointment:

> Of course, I think you will readily understand that the news of the honor which you have received in being made Minister of Finance was not received entirely with pleasure, greatly as I appreciate your qualifications for the office and the need that your country has for your services. In some ways I felt that it might interrupt our contact, although I am sure it can in no way affect the deep friendship which I feel we have had ever since my visit to Japan.[65]

In actuality, Strong was very close to the private bankers who lent to foreign governments, above all to his friend and senior colleague Thomas Lamont of Morgan & Company. And despite his scruples, Strong seems to have played a key role in helping arrange the giant 1924 bond issue for the Japanese government. When the Japanese government's overseas financial commissioners, Mori Kengo and Tsushima Juichi, traveled to New York in January 1924 to negotiate the loan, it was Strong himself who broached the business, in a luncheon meeting he hosted at the cafeteria of the FRBNY. The loan was managed by Thomas Lamont of Morgan & Company. It was therefore more than a diplomatic nicety when Inoue thanked Strong for his help "re formation of longwishedfor powerful and influential group," in a wireless telegram Inoue sent the day he departed from Japan for Europe in January 1924.[66] This powerful and influential group was the "New York Group" led by Morgan & Company and including National City Bank of New York, First National Bank of New York, and Kuhn Loeb. Their issue of $150 million in Japanese government bonds in February 1924 was done jointly with a £25 million bond issue in London. The same New York–London group would later back Japan's return to the gold standard in 1930.[67]

Inoue ended his first tenure as finance minister in January 1924, just in advance of these loan negotiations. Extended sojourns in London were a regular, even annual practice for American financiers like J. P. Morgan Jr., Thomas W. Lamont, and Benjamin Strong. Inoue now made his own round-the-world tour, featuring an extended visit to London. There, later in 1924, Inoue met Norman. Though they had often corresponded, they had not met in person. Inoue later recalled that he had imagined Norman as a typically red-faced English businessman, but instead found him to be more a continental and scholarly type. They talked for an hour, and then Norman with a smile told Inoue, "There is someone in this building who is very eager to meet you. Can you guess who it is?" Inoue said he could not. Norman led him into another room, and Inoue was surprised to see Benjamin Strong standing there. He would never forget, he recalled, the happiness of Norman and Strong, who had not seen each other for some time, as they gripped each other's hands. This was a secret meeting, but Inoue did not find this secrecy strange, considering all the attention paid by the newspapers to the Anglo-American financial negotiations in anticipation of Britain's return to the gold standard. As Inoue learned, "the two heads of the international financial world" would use false names and disguises to avoid being detected when they traveled back and forth between New York and London, and Strong would spend his stays quietly at Norman's house. The ensuing conversation between Inoue, Norman, and Strong mainly concerned the preparation for Britain's return to the gold standard, which was scheduled to follow a year later.[68]

Inoue, now retired from the Bank of Japan, was thinking of entering politics. While in London, he discussed this idea "with a friend who was a director of a certain large New York bank," as he discreetly put it in a later memoir. The friend, presumably Strong, told him that a banker had best remain a banker. Inoue unfortunately ignored the advice. In London, Inoue also met Thomas Lamont, who was then in town. Inoue returned home via America, again visiting Strong in New York City. These visits with fellow international bankers were a high point of Inoue's trip.

In April and May of 1927, Tokyo experienced its greatest banking crisis. The crisis was brought on by the Wakatsuki cabinet's policy of deflation, at a time when Japanese banks were carrying large amounts of bad debt, much of it going back to the crash of 1920 and to the earthquake of 1923.[69] In May 1927, in response to the financial emergency, Inoue reluctantly returned to serve a one-year tenure as Bank of Japan governor, in order to manage the great banking reorganization and bailout that followed. Strong sent him a one-sentence cable at the Bank of Japan: "*Hearty congratulations and welcome back into the family.*"[70] The entry of Inoue, and his country, into membership in this exclusive "family"—and the fear of losing this hard-won status—was a powerful incentive in Inoue's restoration of the gold standard at the old par in 1930. It is impossible to measure the effects of this membership for Inoue's own self-identity and for his policy thought and vision of Japan's place in the world, but such intangible factors are vitally important in understanding the pro-Western era in Japanese politics. They are also important in understanding how it ended in the 1930s.

More Cooperation, More Debt, More Deflation

"The Norman conquest of $4.86"—the return of the pound sterling to gold convertibility at the old par—was attained in April 1925.[71] The support of Strong's Federal Reserve Bank of New York was critical in this undertaking. This support was visibly demonstrated with an FRBNY credit of $200 million to the Bank of England. This credit from one central bank to another was paired with a credit of $100 million by Morgan & Company for the British government. As we have seen, before the First World War, India, Japan, and other countries had quietly supported Britain's financial position. The Bank of England kept this support "in house" as much as possible; these arrangements were also quite systematic rather than case by case and ad hoc. In these connections, we see some of the ambiguities of Britain's status as the world's great creditor. More than being the international "lender of last resort," Britain was becoming the "borrower of last resort," in Ramaa Vasudevan's phrase—as the United States would later become in the 1980s.[72] By 1925, however, external support for sterling had become a matter of formal, open lending, and Britain appeared openly as the debtor country. This was an immense historical turnaround.

The Bank of Japan provided more modest support for the Bank of England's position. In April 1924, shortly after the Japanese government had received the large US-British loan ($150 million issued in New York plus £25 million issued in London), Norman asked the Bank of Japan to join with several other central banks in providing a credit to the German Reichsbank. The purpose of this multilateral central-bank credit was to capitalize the new German Gold Discount Bank (Golddiskontobank), which was to do business in British pounds, thus supporting Norman's ambitions to restore and advance the international position of sterling.

This operation was part of the long process of stabilizing the German currency and restoring it to gold convertibility in the wake of the hyper-inflation of 1922–23. The Bank of Japan's legal charter ruled out direct BoJ participation in a foreign loan. It was therefore worked out that the Bank of Japan would deposit its share of the credit, £500,000, in a Bank of England account for the Reichsbank, in effect lending that amount to the Reichsbank. This contribution might also be considered an unofficial service charge attached by the British to their portion of the big Japanese government loan of 1924. In effect, Japan was again being asked to main-tain a "special reserve" or "compensating balance" at the Bank of England.

At the end of the one-year term of this credit, in April 1925, when it was Britain's turn to restore the gold standard, this balance was withdrawn from the Reichsbank's account at the Bank of England and credited to the BoJ's own account at the Bank of England.[73] Because accounts at the Bank of England did not pay interest, this latter deposit could also be considered a de facto loan and as de facto support for Britain's own return to the gold standard. This method of working through the Bank of England estab-lished the formula used in later BoJ credits to help support the restoration of gold convertibility in Belgium in 1926 and in Italy at the beginning of 1928, as described below.

The year of Britain's return to gold, 1925, was also the peak of the international economic recovery of the mid-1920s. As we have seen, world prices for agricultural and other primary commodities had fallen drasti-cally in 1920–21. Commodity prices then recovered strongly in 1924–25. From this high point, commodity prices again began to slide. The British pound, restored to its prewar gold par, was now significantly overvalued relative to the actualities of British trade. This overvaluation became a source of constant economic pressure in Britain. Simultaneously, Norman apparently hoped to reduce prices below the levels prevailing in the United States, or at least not fall behind, and the Bank of England tried to main-tain its bank rate at a level higher than interest rates in New York in order to keep funds in London.

Strong's backing continued to be critical to keeping the pound on the gold standard. In Thomas Lamont's estimation, "the establishment and maintenance of the gold standard in Great Britain and in the leading coun-tries on the continent of Europe" was only possible owing to the "active and constant" cooperation of the Federal Reserve Bank of New York.[74]

These words sound like politic praise, but they are also almost certainly correct. And if they are correct, they point to overreaching on both sides.

After Britain's return to the gold standard in April 1925, Strong again asked BoJ director Fukai Eigo where Japan stood on the matter of restoring gold convertibility. Fukai explained that, following the depreciation of the yen after the September 1923 earthquake, the gold embargo had become a subject of bitter public controversy in Japan. Many argued for an immediate lifting of the gold export embargo, but to do so threatened to bring on severe deflation. The majority view was that the balance of payments had first to be improved and the yen brought back up to near its old par. Fukai reported that there were also "a few inflationists who see a boon in a depreciating currency and falling exchanges as a stimulus to trade and industry." (In fact, the yen's depreciation did stimulate trade and industry, and its return to the old par in 1929–30 would bring on a depression.) These "inflationists," Fukai said, were joined by "nominalist doctrinaires who are impatient with the trammels of a metallic standard and dream of an ideal 'managed currency.'" These ideas were not very influential, Fukai said. Advocates of currency depreciation had formerly found support in the example of the depreciation of the pound sterling in the early 1920s, but when Britain returned to gold it knocked the legs from under their argument: "Now that the gold standard prevailed in America and the British Empire, it must be the goal of all self-respecting countries, whether it be ideal or not." Thus, Fukai reassured Strong, "the Japanese nation, as a whole, will henceforth strive with the single aim for the resumption of an effective gold standard."[75]

With the progress of the movement to restore the gold standard in Europe, the vision of an *internationale* of cooperating central banks also came closer to realization. The restoration of the gold standard in Belgium in 1926 involved central bank cooperation of unprecedentedly wide scope, as the central banks of nine countries, including the Bank of Japan, jointly provided a one-year credit to the Belgian national bank. As with the credit for Germany's Gold Discount Bank, the Bank of Japan's share of the credit of October 1926 was £500,000, or about ¥5 million. Again, it was a case of the Bank of England in effect using BoJ funds. On the Bank of England's advice, the BoJ again made a sterling deposit with the Bank of England, and the Bank of England itself then made the loan, in sterling, to the Belgian national bank. The same method was used again for the BoJ portion of the multilateral central bank credit provided to the Italian central bank in January 1928.[76] One might say that the Bank of Japan provided the funds, and Montagu Norman got the credit.

Kenneth Mouré, bringing in the standpoint of Paris, identifies 1927 as the "high tide" of interwar central bank cooperation.[77] It was after July 1926 that the Bank of France actively entered into the process of central bank cooperation, although French-English rivalry complicated that cooperation. Other strains also appeared. Facing an alarming drawdown of Japanese foreign-exchange reserves, the Bank of Japan chose not to take part in multilateral credits for the returns to the gold standard of Poland in June 1928 and Romania in July 1928.[78] These latter credits were organized not by the Bank of England but, respectively, by the FRBNY and the Bank of France. By 1927, British finance itself was already becoming overextended internationally: only two years after returning to the gold standard, the Bank of England appeared to be facing a renewed sterling crisis.

This slowly building pressure on the revived gold-standard system became the occasion for one of the high points of central bank policy coordination. This was the famous and elaborately orchestrated secret meeting of central bankers on Long Island, New York, in July 1927. Norman of the Bank of England, Charles Rist of the Bank of France, and Hjalmar Schacht of the German Reichsbank urgently requested Strong to cut US interest rates, so that investment funds would not be sucked into the United States from Europe. They also requested that the United States retain gold on deposit in London banks, in order to ease the pressure on the European banks. After the fact, many people have seen Strong's agreement to cooperate in cutting interest rates as the great mistake that pumped up the New York stock-market bubble and led to the crash of 1929. This meeting also had an air of comic opera, as Norman and the others attempted to travel to New York in disguise (their names were not on the ship's manifests, and their luggage was unmarked) but were found out by news reporters.[79] The meeting thus became known, but its significance was only partially disclosed. Inoue Junnosuke, despite his "welcome back" to the bank governors' family, was not informed in advance of the historic interest rate cuts in New York. In fact, he got no explanation from Strong until he made his own inquiries.[80]

In his representations to his own national government in Washington, DC, Strong insisted that domestic and international policy were in

Figure 6.1. The governors (*left to right*): Reichsbank president Schacht, FRBNY governor Strong, Bank of England governor Norman, Bank of France deputy governor Rist. Taken in New York City, July 1927. Courtesy of the Archives of the Federal Reserve Bank of New York.

harmony. Facing accusations to the contrary, he never admitted that international considerations had overridden domestic ones. Some historians have taken these professions too much at face value.[81] To Inoue, however, Strong expressed the policy tension frankly. "As your representative in New York has made a personal inquiry on the subject," Strong wrote to Inoue, he would like to explain:

> *Under ordinary circumstances* at this [late summer] season of the year when demands upon us for crop moving and other business purposes are generally rather heavy, *we would not have reduced the rate, and certainly not in the face of a very active speculation in securities* which is taking place in New York and which is employing a very large amount of credit.

It is this latter point—the bubbling up of the stock market under the stimulus of low interest rates—that has gotten so much attention. But "outweighing these arguments," Strong explained, were the two principal [arguments] of the need for easing the movement of the crop this year with as moderate credit change as possible, *and more especially the need for easing the strain which seems to have been developing upon European exchanges* which, if allowed to continue through the fall and early winter when heavy payments have to be made to us for our exports, might have imposed a very heavy strain upon European Bank reserves and been accompanied by a very heavy movement of gold to this country.

Better to let speculators in the stock market profit now, Strong wrote—they would likely pay it back later—and to develop instead a helpful relationship between money rates in the United States and Europe.[82] Strong's remark on crop movements appears as a non sequitur, and the primacy of international central banking concerns seems clear. Commentators at the time described Strong's pretended agrarian motivations, supposedly demonstrated by letting the Kansas City Federal Reserve Bank act first in cutting rates, as "camouflage" and "the bunk." Indeed, Strong privately confided at the time that lowering interest rates was itself "a good alibi," to counter charges that the Federal Reserve was pushing a deflation policy.[83]

But was Strong himself also being manipulated by Norman?[84] In any case, this high point in central bank cooperation was oddly lacking in actual multilateral discussion but seems instead to have consisted of a series of one-on-one meetings. Strong, for his part, did not like the possibility of being confronted by a potential united front of debtor-country representatives, while Norman preferred to pursue his own personalized balancing act. Strong thus continued trying to prevent an excess, inflationary inflow of gold into the United States. Simultaneously he worked to support the revived European gold standards, above all the British. These twin concerns now seemed powerfully congruent, and they outweighed his fear of contributing to a stock-market bubble.[85]

In fact, lower US interest rates did not reduce the flow of funds from London to New York. Before the Federal Reserve's 1927 reduction in the discount rate from 4 to 3.5 percent, higher US interest rates had indeed pulled in British and other overseas funds. But when Strong lowered interest rates, the profits to be made in the billowing stock-market bubble on Wall Street continued to attract British and other funds. The collapse of stock prices twenty-seven months later then set into motion, by stages, the collapse of the whole gold-based international monetary order.

We can return here to a larger set of questions. American historians of the Great Depression of 1929 routinely point to mistakes in Federal Reserve policy as the cause of the crisis. Some have more or less blamed the Federal Reserve for the entire world crisis. This blame is assigned for some conflicting reasons. One idea has just been mentioned—that the Federal Reserve's rate cuts in 1927, in defense of the British gold standard, generated a stock-market bubble in New York. This idea, which we could call the "misdirected cooperation" view, goes back to the time of the Great Depression. It has a significant historical resonance with the run-up of the Japanese bubble of the late 1980s, and with the argument that the Japanese bailout of US finances following the New York stock-market crash of October 1987, and particularly the BoJ's reduction of interest rates, led to Tokyo's bubble of 1988–89.[86]

In another view of the 1929 crisis, argued most prominently by Charles Kindleberger and to a degree by Barry Eichengreen, it was rather an insufficiency of international financial cooperation that was to blame, as the Federal Reserve failed to follow the rules of the international gold standard by refusing to monetize the gold inflows that attended America's big export surpluses of the decade. That is, had the Federal Reserve allowed the incoming gold to expand the US monetary base and push up US prices, American demand for foreign goods and reduced pressure from American competition would have enabled European industry to recover; Europe could have then repaid its war debts to America, and the international imbalances of the decade would have been rectified. However, Strong argued that the gold inflows were only temporary, and so he blocked this classic form of "Humean" adjustment. Alternatively, it has been argued that it was Strong's death in 1928 and the absence of his leadership that caused international cooperation to lapse and aggravated the depression.[87] These are all arguments about what might have happened. What is especially interesting here is that Benjamin Strong's policies are in any case at the center of the story.

The autumn of 1927 also brought a renewal of American interest in Japan. At the invitation of the Japanese government, Thomas Lamont led a second mission to Japan in October 1927, with Benjamin Strong's backing. Lamont advised Inoue, Fukai, and Mori Kengo of the Ministry of Finance that the Japanese government should cut its spending, complete the process of economic liquidation and "adjustment," and restore the gold standard.[88] Morgan & Company also advised the Japanese government that the Bank of Japan should be made independent of the government. This particular Anglo-American idea would be acted on—partially—only seventy years later, with the revised Bank of Japan law of 1997. But the Japanese government did move, immediately after the cabinet change of July 1929, to align itself with the Anglo-American monetary program. Its restoration of the yen to gold convertibility and allowance of free gold exports in January 1930 was backed by international credits provided by the Morgan-led "New York Group," which included National City Bank, First National Bank, and Kuhn Loeb.

Strong himself did not live to see these plans come to fruition. In June 1928, Inoue Junnosuke resigned as BoJ governor for the second time. Strong, ill and with only two months left to live, wrote his last letter to Inoue in August. He repeated his expectations that Japan would return to the gold standard. Strong was also disappointed that, as it seemed to him then, Inoue would not be the one to do the job:

> Now that France has followed the orthodox procedure in adopting a plan of stabilisation for their currency, it does seem to me that the outlook in Europe has been greatly improved. . . . I hope that in due time your own country will realize its ambition in this respect, and I am only regretful that your own hand has now been removed from the tiller, for I had rather counted on your experience and wisdom being applied to this important task.[89]

Strong's hope was realized after his death. In July 1929, Inoue was reappointed as finance minister and had his hand back on the tiller, guiding Japan's return to the gold standard at the old par. It may also be just as well that Strong did not live to see the bitter results of the "orthodox procedure" in which he had placed so much faith, as Inoue, rationally and cooperatively, but following the wrong map, piloted his country into the maelstrom.

When Japan returned to the gold standard on January 11, 1930, national money was freely convertible into gold in Tokyo, as it was in New York, as in London, as in Vienna, Berlin, and Paris. But for whom was it convertible, and what were the actualities of the international market for gold, which had its center as much as ever in London?

Making a Market

London and Gold in the 1920s

> There was in the world of prewar capitalism one gold market which in importance and accessibility overshadowed all others.... The gold market, toward which, with the partial exception of the production of the United States and Russia, practically all newly produced gold gravitated, was located in the same country and controlled by the same financial organism that also controlled the international short-loan fund.... As far as the Bank of England controlled the domestic open market, it may, therefore, be said to have controlled international gold movements and to have—indirectly— acted as the bankers' bank of bankers' banks.
>
> Joseph Schumpeter, *Business Cycles*, 1939

At this point, we step back to consider the world's central gold market itself. As Inoue Junnosuke had seen it in 1917, a free market in gold was vital to London's international financial centrality.[1] The de facto closure of London gold trading during the war threatened this position, and to reestablish it was an imperative of postwar financial policy. The Bank of England had long controlled major gold movements in Britain, and in 1919, it asked Rothschilds to establish a gold market.[2]

Gold, as a monetary base and standard, has historically been a peculiar commodity. London's new "free" market was peculiar as well, its exclusive and theatrical nature symbolized by the gathering of five anonymous brokers at Rothschilds' London New Court offices each weekday morning to raise and lower Union Jacks as they "fixed" the price of gold. Far from being a public agora at the hub of a naturally self-balancing system, the London gold market was a closed and secretive institution, a place of mysterious ways and means, shaped and reshaped by national prerogatives. The involvement of the world's premier central bank and the world's most famous banking dynasty heightened its mystique.[3] Although many writers refer to this market, its actual history and role remain obscure, and details, including basic statistical information, remain difficult to come by. The picture offered here, drawn mainly from the documentary archives of the Bank of England and N. M. Rothschild & Sons, offers a fuller view and helps clarify its international position.

The London gold market described here consisted of five participants meeting in one room, and yet it had global influence. The annual volume of world gold production in the 1920s, valued in gold-standard US dollars, ranged from $320 million to nearly $400 million, or some £80 million to £90 million British pounds (table 7.1). At the time, $400 million was equivalent to about nineteen million troy ounces, or roughly six hundred thousand kilograms. Half or more of the world's gold was then produced in South Africa alone. If we add in production from Australia, Canada, India, Northern and Southern Rhodesia, and other British territories, British Empire gold production came to more than two-thirds of the world total.[4] London handled the refining and onward sale of this gold, the largest part of which was actually destined for the United States.

Beginning in 1920, there was also a great increase in the purchasing power of gold, under the influence of the combined central bank policies already discussed. In 1920–21 alone, the power of gold to command labor and resources (as measured in British pounds) increased by some 58 percent. By 1930, the purchasing power of gold was double the historically low level reached in 1919. By 1935, the purchasing power of gold was nearly four times greater than the level of 1919, touching the highest levels since the sixteenth century.[5] (Measuring in pounds sterling, the price of gold itself had almost doubled—meaning that the British pound also experienced a great appreciation vis-à-vis the prices of labor and resources.) The restoration of gold-based monetary systems contributed to this great appreciation of gold. As we will see in chapter 8, the re-creation of a world of "freely flowing" gold in all three centers, New York, London, and Tokyo, completed as of January 1930, set the stage for a rush for gold, and this rush for gold brought the whole system crashing down.

The Bank of England as London's Gold Market before 1919

London's place as a market for precious metals can be traced back many centuries. The Mocatta bullion brokerage firm, Britain's oldest extant gold market agent, was founded in 1671, and by the time the Bank of England was established in 1694, large amounts of gold bullion and specie were finding their way to London. Given the Bank of England's need to guarantee the convertibility of its paper notes by maintaining an adequate gold reserve, the Bank of England emerged as the leading player in the London gold market. The Bank of England consolidated its financial hegemony by redeeming the notes of its competitor banks in silver or gold.[6] In 1717, Sir Isaac Newton, in his capacity as master of the royal mint, set the mint price of gold at 3 pounds (*l*) 17 shillings (*s*) 10.5 pence (*d*) per ounce at the standard 22-carat (91.6%) purity, equivalent to £3.89 in decimal notation.[7] Thus key parameters of the gold market's operations were set. The great French economic historian Marc Bloch called this "a major turning point in the economic history of Europe."[8] Amazingly, Newton's official mint price remained unchanged for two centuries, with wartime interruptions, until the formation of a "free" gold market in 1919.

Many historians have looked back upon Newton's action in 1717 as marking the origin of the British gold standard. Newton did not intend to establish a gold standard; but in fact a system of credit based on gold-backed banknotes was taking shape, operated by England's precociously modern central bank. It was still very far from a unitary gold standard. British monetary circulation remained disorganized and chaotic in the eighteenth century, but gold "sovereign" coins and gold-convertible Bank of England notes became the mainstay as high-value money. Silver was demonetized after 1774. In 1797, during the wars of the French Revolution, the Bank of England suspended specie payments—as would happen again in the First World War. With the postwar restoration of gold payments in 1821, the gold standard was also established as a comprehensive and integrated monetary system. Subsidiary silver and bronze coins were now tokens, denominated in terms of gold, and a monometallic standard was established in theory and in fact. The Bank Act of 1844 cemented the Bank of England's gold standard system, by providing the bank with the monopoly of note issue.

The Bank of England itself served as London's gold market. The bank was legally obliged to sell gold—that is, to redeem Bank of England notes—at 77 shillings 10½ pence per ounce standard ("77/10½," as it was written), at a 22-carat purity of 916 parts per thousand, or 91.6 percent pure gold. This is equivalent in decimal terms to £3.89 per common ounce. The BoE was to purchase all gold received at "77/9" (3*l* 17*s* 9*d*), equivalent to £3.87. The difference between these two points, the sale and purchase prices, represented the costs associated with minting. Up until August 1914, therefore, there was no need to allocate a designated space or building as a gold market, or to convene a regular gathering of brokers or traders for the buying and selling of gold bullion or specie in London. That is, *there was no gold market* as we might understand it in present-day terms. In general, all the requirements of buyers and sellers were "freely met" by the Bank of England, which acted as the ultimate buyer and seller of gold. As a matter of course, the larger commercial banks accumulated their own gold reserves; bullion brokers, goldsmiths, and jewelers held their own gold stocks, and a large amount of gold was carried by everyday people in the form of gold coin.[9] The values of all gold transactions in London were expressed using "pound sterling," supporting the Bank of England's monopoly issue of gold-convertible paper notes.

How do we account for the Bank of England's unrivaled success in attracting gold to its own market? Put bluntly, the scientific might of British technology, the commercial might of the city's capitalism, and the political economy of British colonialism and imperialism ensured that a significant proportion of Australian and Canadian unrefined gold, and practically the entire output of African and Indian mines, were channeled to London for refining, where it could purportedly *realize* its best obtainable price. Gold's refining and "realization," that is, its prompt processing and sale, was vital to the Bank of England's maintenance of the gold standard. The outflow of capital from Britain, as David Williams explained, "was accommodated partly by a countervailing inflow of capital but also by *sales of gold produced within the empire, sold in London for sterling, and then, in large part, re-exported.*"[10] Over time, branches of the Royal Mint in London were established with the same rights, duties, privileges, and responsibilities to the Crown as their parent mint, in the separate Australian colonial capitals of Sydney (1855), Melbourne (1872), and Perth (1899), and in the Canadian capital of Ottawa (1908). Indian and South African mining companies were also keen to establish their own refineries and mints, but their requests were largely ignored until the outbreak of the First World War.

Thus, most of the world's unrefined gold found its way to London in the nineteenth and early twentieth centuries. The British government leased the Royal Mint Refinery to Anthony de Rothschild in 1852, and it was controlled by N. M. Rothschild & Sons from 1896. It was the empire's premier refinery and treated the bulk of all gold ores shipped to England. The remaining share was handled by the other officially appointed refiners to the Bank of England, Johnson Matthey & Company, H. L. Raphael's Refinery, and Browne & Wingrove. These refiners paid an advance according to the approximate value of the unrefined gold on its "acceptance" or receipt. Later they settled their accounts with the mining companies through their appointed bank—most often N. M. Rothschild & Sons—with sales showing the net proceeds of the gold's "realization," or sale, after deduction of refining, transport, and other charges. In 1913, for example, the Royal Mint Refinery refined 6.1 million ounces standard, and Johnson Matthey & Company some 4 million. The newly minted gold's actual "realization" typically consisted of its transport for sale to the Bank of England's Bullion Office. There were, however, instances where the refiners satisfied trade or other private demands before they delivered the bulk of the gold to the Bank of England for purchase. Such private purchases incurred a premium over and above the statutory purchase price. Any such premiums were credited to the refiners, not the miners, but these negotiated purchases were less expensive than buying from the Bank of England. For example, Rothschilds' Royal Mint Refinery charged a premium of one farthing (one-quarter of a penny) per ounce standard. That is, buyers could, on negotiation, purchase gold direct from the Royal Mint Refinery at 77s 9.25d, instead of paying 77s 10.5d per ounce standard at the Bank of England. Rothschilds thought that Johnson Matthey & Company was able to charge much higher premiums when selling in this manner, "particularly as they would sell in certain cases in semi-manufactured forms."[11] Nevertheless, gold traded between the Bank of England's sale and purchase prices was restricted to official gold brokers and London's premier banking houses, and was ultimately overseen by the Bank of England itself.[12]

Gold Afloat

More than two-thirds of world gold production in the 1920s took place within the British Empire, as shown in table 7.1. Accordingly, the largest part of international gold flows in the 1920s were actually internal to the British Empire. Gold was not only critical as a means of international settlements and as a foundation of national monetary systems; as a mineral commodity, gold was also critical to Great Britain's international balance of payments. Indeed, if we put together the numbers for gold mined in the empire and coal mined in Britain itself, Britain's balance of payments was being sustained by the exports of two strategic mineral commodities.

Within the British Empire gold trade, it was London's connection with South Africa that was most important. Gold production itself was far from free of cost—gold mining in the Witwatersrand (the Rand) was a massive industrial undertaking, requiring the excavation from deep mines, crushing, and crude refining of tons of rock containing a low gold content. The mining companies enjoyed the near-unique circumstances of having

TABLE 7.1.   Estimated gold production by countries and areas, highlighting British Empire production, 1919–1930 (in millions of US dollars)

Year	World total	South Africa (A)	Rhodesia (B)	India (C)	Canada (D)	Australia (E)	USA	A+B+C+D+E (% of total)
1919	358.4	172.2	12.3	10.5	15.9	22.0	60.3	65.0
1920	333.8	168.7	11.4	10.3	15.9	19.8	51.2	67.7
1921	330.7	168.0	12.1	8.9	19.1	15.7	50.0	67.7
1922	320.3	145.1	13.5	9.0	26.1	15.6	48.8	65.3
1923	368.9	189.1	13.4	8.7	25.3	14.7	51.7	68.1
1924	384.9	197.9	13.0	8.2	31.5	14.0	52.3	68.7
1925	384.0	198.4	12.0	8.1	35.9	11.6	49.9	69.3
1926	395.2	206.0	12.3	7.9	36.3	10.7	48.3	69.1
1927	394.0	209.3	12.0	7.9	38.3	10.4	45.4	70.5
1928	390.4	214	11.9	7.8	39.0	9.5	46.2	72.3
1929	397.2	215.2	11.6	7.5	39.9	8.8	45.7	71.2
1930	432.1	221.5	11.5	6.8	43.6	9.6	47.2	67.8

Source: Federal Reserve System, *Banking and Monetary Statistics* (1943), 542–543.
Note: The dollar price of gold was then fixed at $20.67 per troy ounce (≈31.1 grams). Under the gold-standard parities restored in April 1925, one US dollar was worth £0.2054.

a guaranteed market and a guaranteed price. Otherwise, their volume of production was determined by their costs of production. If the purchasing power of gold fell, as it did during the war, they tended to reduce their production. If the purchasing power of gold increased relative to the costs of production, as it did after 1920, then gold mining companies tended to increase their production using lower-quality (higher cost) ores.[13] This was, moreover, production under highly racialized social conditions, with a divided workforce of relatively privileged European workers and relatively exploited African workers. It was no "magic mountain." For one institution, however, the price of gold did have a kind of magical quality, for the Bank of England could purchase solid gold with paper banknotes or by crediting bank balances of its own creation, and the basic legal premise for its creation of such monies was that the amount was tied to corresponding gold reserves.

Here, it is also important to note the central place of the United States in the world economy of gold during the interwar period. Seen from within the United States, most gold actually came from New York City during the 1920s, and the single largest share of that gold came in turn from London. In fact, annual US imports of gold from London were about twice the total produced by US gold mines. Table 7.2 gives the net figures during the period when the "free" London gold market was operating from 1919

TABLE 7.2. Reported gold flows from the United Kingdom to the United States, 1919–1925 (imports to and exports from the United States, in millions of US dollars)

Year	US gold imports from UK (net)	Net total of all US gold imports (+) and exports (−)	Notes
1919	+2.0	−291.6	Massive net US gold exports, incl. gold exports to Japan of $94.1 m.
1920	+280.7	+95.0	Cf. US gold exports to Japan of $101.3 m.
1921	+202.1	+667.4	
1922	+121.9	+238.3	
1923	+149.5	+294.1	
1924	+118.6	+258.1	
1925	+43.1	−134.4	US gold exports reflect large int'l gold loans; UK return to gold std. April 1925

Source: Federal Reserve System 1943, 539–540.
Note: Gold valued at $20.67 per troy ounce (≈31.1 grams).

to 1925. We will return in the next chapter to the question of international gold flows in the context of the Great Depression, and to the question of gold flows involving Japan.[14]

The successive reorganizations of the London gold market in 1919, 1925, and 1931 were conditioned by the British government's decisions to suspend, return to, and then resuspend the gold standard. As we will see in chapter 8, viewing this history in terms of gold flows offers an unusual view of the Great Depression, which brought a great boom in the gold trade.

The Founding of London's "Free" Gold Market in 1919

The legislative underpinnings of the gold market—the Royal Mint's statutory gold price set in 1717 and the Bank Charter Act of 1844—remained legally in force during the First World War. The two major refiners, Rothschilds' Royal Mint Refinery and Johnson Matthey & Company, continued to deal with shipments of unrefined gold, all of which was sold at the Bank of England "on behalf of His Majesty's Government" at 77/9 per common ounce (at 22-carat purity). That is, formally, the British gold standard was not suspended during the war. However, the war began with a run on gold, and the Defence of the Realm Act of August 8, 1914, prohibited the private export of gold. The government issued low-denomination (one-pound and half-pound) Treasury notes in place of specie, and according to Rothschilds "practically the whole of the gold in circulation was called in." The forces at work here were those of patriotic moral suasion and occasional threats of state control rather than harsh laws. British gold was collected and transferred through the commercial banks to the Bank of England in London, where it was exchanged for BoE banknotes. It also appears, however, that the big national banks continued to hoard stocks of gold sovereigns.[15] Thus, in 1914, the gold standard was in practice abandoned.

As the war was coming to an end, South African and Indian politicians, backed by their respective mining companies, called for the establishment of their own national refineries and mints.[16] These demands became louder after March 21, 1919, when the British government freed the sterling-dollar rate from control, and the pound sterling began to depreciate against the US dollar. Thus ended the post-1717 era of the "77/10.5" (or £3.89) gold price. (Here again, in a long view of world history, the spring of 1919 was a turning point.) In essence, the South African and Indian mining companies were selling unrefined gold at undervalued prewar prices in London. Hence the mining companies demanded to be able to sell gold in New York or elsewhere. The notion that British authorities allowed gold to move freely was clearly a fiction. Facing these challenges, the Bank of England, apparently at the insistence of the government, attempted to do everything in its powers to keep the refining and sale (or "realization") of gold centered in London. To that end, the Bank of England even built its own, short-lived gold refinery, St. Luke's Refinery, which extraordinarily offered to "refine at cost" in order to neuter the growing calls for a national South African mint and counteract the mining companies' long-standing complaints of high refinery costs in London. Almost unknown, St. Luke's Refinery operated from November 1920 to March 1923, producing fifty-one thousand gold bars for the Bank of England.[17] The Royal Mint did establish branches in Bombay in 1918 and in Pretoria in 1923; however, the Bombay operations closed after only a year.[18]

As described in chapter 4, the US government's lifting of its embargo on gold exports, on June 26, 1919, released a surge of gold shipments out of the United States. From the standpoint of London, it also threatened to turn New York into the center of the international gold trade. Against this backdrop, the British government decided to permit the export of gold under license from September 12, 1919. Furthermore, these licenses would be "freely given in respect of newly mined gold from the Empire."[19] Although, on one hand, gold exports were now re-enabled, this export-licensing system itself represented the formal suspension of the gold standard by the British government. The private joint-stock banks now purportedly agreed to hand over all gold bullion and specie they had in their vaults to the government, in exchange for Bank of England banknotes. These gold reserves were to be held at the Bank of England in a special Treasury account. Ironically, the Bank of England thus obtained, for the first time in its history, almost complete control of the nation's gold reserves, just as Great Britain formally left the gold standard.[20] The central bank alone was now concerned with holding gold reserves, as Paul Warburg had described the function of the "central reservoir" in 1914, but its own banknotes were no longer "so much gold."

Simultaneously, the Bank of England made arrangements with N. M. Rothschild & Sons for the immediate formation of a free gold market in London, also on September 12, 1919. The Bank of England indicated its wish that N. M. Rothschild & Sons preside at and manage the market to ensure there was only one official price for gold on any given day, and that quotation of forward gold prices be avoided.[21] As the Bank of England conceived it, the new gold market would provide an international benchmark, at a published price, and facilitate a narrow dealing spread (that is, close sale and purchase points). Any quantity could be traded, and all transactions would be anonymous—only the brokers would know whom they represented. Along with Rothschilds, four bullion brokers were enlisted as founding members: Mocatta & Goldsmid, Samuel Montagu & Company, Pixley & Abell, and Sharp & Wilkins.[22]

The participants transmitted the first few results of "gold fixing" (price setting) through telephone bids, but Rothschilds quickly decided to formalize the procedures. Representatives from the four bullion brokers would gather each weekday morning at the N. M. Rothschild & Sons New Court headquarters for the formal eleven o'clock meeting. They arrived already having "married" (that is, counterbalanced) their respective buying and selling orders from banking and other clients.[23] All gold available for sale on any given day had to be delivered by the refiners to Rothschilds by this time. Advances were paid to the producers of the gold at the old mint price (£3.87 per ounce standard) with settlement following after the gold's sale. Rothschilds would then decide, with reference to international market prices, the best sterling price that gold could obtain, or *realize*, in any part of the world. The head of Rothschilds' Bullion Department, Clement J. G. Cooper, or occasionally one of the Rothschilds partners, would announce the gold fix price to those assembled. The brokers and, on occasion, "responsible persons who desire to give their view, including intending buyers," were invited to comment upon the proposed fix price. In practice the day's fix price remained unaltered.[24] The London Dollar Exchange (the exchange rate of British pounds in US dollars) was then quoted for sellers, and the exact sterling equivalent was calculated minus deductions made for the costs of "(a) freight to U.S.A.; (b) insurance; (c) interest; and (d) certain charges in the U.S.A."[25]

Once the price of gold had been fixed in pounds, the four brokers were given the opportunity to bid, customarily at 11:15 a.m. If their bid equaled

or exceeded the realization price fixed by Rothschilds, they would success-
fully obtain their requirements. In practice, almost all gold sales took place
at this time of day—11:15 a.m. None of the bullion brokers was allowed to
return to the meeting once its representative had left the room. Additional
purchases, therefore, would require new bids on the next market day.[26]
Initially, the brokers arrived with their own orders, and communication
with their offices or their clients was prohibited while the price of gold
was being fixed, but after a representative of the refiner Johnson Matthey &
Company was admitted to the meeting, participants were permitted to
keep in touch with their offices during the proceedings by telephone.
Representatives would raise small Union Jacks to indicate their wish to
interrupt proceedings and use the telephone to check with their offices,
lowering their flags having received confirmation or new instructions.[27] If
there were no bidders in the market or when there was an unsold quantity
of gold, Rothschilds would send that portion for which it was the agent
(for example, gold refined from South African and West African mines)
on to New York, where it was sold in exchange for US dollars.[28]

The Free Gold Market during the Years of the Floating Pound, 1919–1925

From the establishment of the Rothschilds-administered gold market on
September 12, 1919, until Great Britain's return to the gold standard on
April 29, 1925, the market operated according to the above described practices of fixing, bidding, and selling. The New York exchange provided the
de facto standard for the price of gold, as the US government enforced its
statutory price of $20.67183 per troy ounce fine 995. Thus, the American
usage of the troy ounce at 995 parts per thousand or 99.5 percent purity
was adopted, and the British tradition of quoting gold's value in common
ounces at the 22-carat (91.6%) purity was abandoned. In effect, then, the
sterling price of gold for sellers was the US statutory dollar price divided by
the New York exchange rate, with deductions made for the costs of shipping gold from London to New York and other related charges.[29] The first
fix in the new London market was £4.96 on September 12, 1919. This price
represented a 17 percent increase on the Bank of England's long-standing

purchase price, which had been equivalent to £4.25 per troy ounce fine (995). For the next five years and seven months, the London gold price in sterling would fluctuate essentially according to the fluctuations of the pound sterling vis-à-vis the US dollar.[30]

Altogether, during the five years and seven months of the free gold market's operation, Rothschilds shipped 25.7 million troy ounces of fine gold to New York for sale. Valued at $20.67 per fine troy ounce, this was worth $531 million. This compares to total shipments of gold from Britain to America of $918 million for the years 1919–25, according to official US statistics.[31]

Only part of the gold Rothschilds sent for sale to New York was on its own account. In fact, the entire sale and management of South Africa's refined gold was put in Rothschilds' hands by the South African mining companies, as Rothschilds had, in its own words, "long experience of the bullion market and would no doubt obtain the greatest profit."[32] The mining companies came to terms on June 11, 1920, with some reluctance. A formal agreement was then put in place, with the approval of the Bank of England, whereby Rothschilds "undertook to sell the gold as it becomes available in fine form at the best price obtainable throughout the world, giving the London market and the bullion brokers an opportunity to bid."[33] Explicitly, any gold mining company could join the South African gold producers' pool (or cartel), utilizing its agreement with Rothschilds. Rothschilds thus collected all proceeds of sale on behalf of some fifty-four gold mining companies. It deposited these earnings, in the "African Gold Realisation Account" at its own bank in London, for redistribution to member companies of the producers' pool. Finally, Rothschilds' longtime business associates in New York, the German-Jewish-American banking house of Kuhn, Loeb & Company, handled all shipments in New York for ¼ percent (0.25%) commission in cooperation with Rothschilds "in Rothschilds own accounts."[34] Kuhn Loeb, we can recall, had arranged the big Japanese war bond issues in 1904–5 and served as the US fiscal agent of the Japanese government, until Morgan & Company took over that role in 1924. Kuhn Loeb's German financial connections were ruined by the war, while Morgan & Company prospered as never before. In its business with Rothschilds, Kuhn Loeb thus saw an opportunity to build new connections with London and Paris.

"Second to None": Kuhn Loeb and Rothschilds

The decision of Abraham Kuhn and Solomon Loeb to relocate from Cincinnati, Ohio, to New York City in 1867, and to transform their merchandising business into a merchant bank, led to the remarkable rise of Kuhn, Loeb & Company. Riding the investment boom of the railroad era, and under the dynamic leadership of Jacob Schiff, Kuhn Loeb was driven at such a pace that by the close of the nineteenth century it had emerged as a powerful American investment bank, second only to J.P. Morgan & Company. On a personal level, Jacob Schiff was the only acknowledged rival of J.P. Morgan among America's private, or merchant, bankers. Prior to the First World War, Kuhn Loeb enjoyed a long association—albeit, at times, as somewhat "poorer cousins"—with Rothschilds, who shared Kuhn Loeb's German-Jewish heritage.[35]

As discussed in chapter 2, the First World War damaged the standing of Kuhn Loeb, particularly vis-à-vis Morgan & Company and its friends. In January 1921, near the depth of the postwar depression and at the same time that Montagu Norman was hosting Benjamin Strong in London, Kuhn Loeb received Samuel Stephany, Rothschilds' general manager, in New York. Kuhn Loeb audaciously proposed to him the formation of a "consortium for financial operations, which would be second to none," between itself and the Rothschilds in both London and Paris. The question of being "second," of course, could not fail to invoke the current primacy of the Morgan & Company network.

According to Stephany's memorandum, Kuhn Loeb was interested in reviving the exchange of market intelligence and "all kinds of information," as in the days when Sir Ernest "Windsor" Cassel was active.[36] There were undoubtedly obstacles. For example, Kuhn Loeb asked, was Rothschilds prepared "to take part in issuing operations in conjunction with Morgan and Barings," its erstwhile rivals, in order to assist with Kuhn Loeb's obligations in New York? The potential shared opportunities, however, were immense, ranging from the financial reorganization of Vickers (the armament and engineering conglomerate) in Britain to the financing of loans in South America. In short, Kuhn Loeb argued that the London and Paris Rothschilds "should consider taking up this business" with its friends in New York because "much power" and prestige would be given to the three-party combination if their consortium was "generally and publicly known." Kuhn Loeb concluded by stating boldly that it "would always co-operate with R. group in preference to Morgan's, the latter very rich but most incompetent." Kuhn Loeb then qualified its proposal with an exit clause: "Refusals upon either side not to be taken seriously, but only as evidence that market or investment conditions on either side would not permit of success."[37]

Kuhn Loeb seemed confident that Rothschilds would be interested. They urged that either "Mr. Lionel or Mr. Anthony should pay an early visit" to New York. On February 1, 1921, they wrote more formally to Rothschilds in London, inviting a senior partner to visit and concluding, "most receptive to any suggestions to develop still further our business relations with your goodselves . . . glad to do anything we can to accomplish the result which we both desire."[38] On February 17, 1921, Rothschilds replied, somewhat tardily, by agreeing to an unconditional exchange of information. In regard to joint issuing operations with Barings and J. P. Morgan, however, Rothschilds would not pledge participation in advance, although, of course, they were "very ready to consider any proposal." Regarding the establishment of a "consortium for financial operations," the London Rothschilds expressed interest but then poured cold water on the idea by saying that owing to the "present state of business in Paris and the restrictions that still exist there we do not think it either possible or advisable to commence the formation of such a group just now." They likewise noted Kuhn Loeb's interest in Vickers but asked them to understand that the Vickers matter was "not easy." Regarding the request that Kuhn Loeb be publicly associated with the Rothschild banking houses of London and Paris, Rothschilds equivocated by saying that wider publicity could be given to their business connections in the future; but owing to "the somewhat delicate situation that exists for the moment," it should be refrained from for the time being.

So what was Rothschilds' position? "We should be very pleased to make offers of business as they come along and we hope that we may considerably develop our relations in the near future. On the other hand, it must be remembered that our Market is at present a very difficult one and with but little business coming on."[39] Unmistakably, Rothschilds was turning down a wide-ranging commercial opportunity in the New York market, at a time when its traditional European markets were moribund. In effect, Kuhn Loeb was bidding to establish a new New York–London connection that would have rivaled the existing Morgan/FRBNY–Bank of England axis. Perhaps the London Rothschilds also understood the impossibility of such a venture from the start.

In reply to this refusal, the exasperated partners at Kuhn, Loeb & Company could only reiterate that "we, on our part, shall be pleased to do all we can to establish the most intimate business relations with your goodselves." With regard to the Paris Rothschilds, "we would of course welcome their cooperation, when conditions permit." Kuhn Loeb continued to see an opportunity with Vickers: "If a reorganization became necessary and predictable, it could be done under the auspices of yourselves and ourselves." They added, "it would at all times interest us . . . to make American co-operation desirable and feasible." Finally, Kuhn Loeb assured Rothschilds that they understood the delicate nature of Rothschild's relations with New York and had no desire "to force this situation in any way."[40]

In January 1921, Kuhn Loeb's bold vision of a new association with Rothschilds, anchored across continents in New York, London, and Paris, appeared to have enormous potential. After the First World War, however, Rothschilds' New Court offices "remained a closed shop," and any influence it held over its French cousins had waned. Certainly, Kuhn Loeb was correct in identifying the cousins Lionel de Rothschild and Anthony de Rothschild as key personnel. Indeed, the two took over leadership of Rothschilds from the phlegmatic Charles de Rothschild in 1923 but seem to have performed the task with little enthusiasm.[41] After nearly a century of being Britain's largest bank, the position of N. M. Rothschild & Sons was in eclipse. Furthermore, Kuhn Loeb's view seems to have been clouded by a competitive and personal bias, as evidenced by its disparaging remarks about the "very rich but most incompetent" J. P. Morgan & Company. Had not Morgan & Company effectively taken over Rothschild's role as the linchpin of war finance, thus highlighting Rothschilds' failure in not establishing a presence on the other side of the Atlantic?[42]

The sense of rivalry was on both sides. Morgan & Company views often carried an edge of anti-Semitism. Strong and Norman were unquestionably closer to the Morgan network, and Norman, writing confidentially to Strong, warned against working with Rothschilds and Kuhn Loeb: "If you are in their [Rothschilds' and Kuhn Loeb's] hands they will somehow wangle the price against you: therefore again I believe you had better employ, for the purpose of purchasing the gold and so of deciding the price, some such independent concern as the [National] City Bank."[43]

Kuhn Loeb thus sought to position itself as the New York vertex in a new London–Paris triangle. The existing business between Rothschilds and Kuhn Loeb was relatively simple at its core, as Kuhn Loeb handled all Rothschilds gold shipments to New York, earning a standard 0.25 percent commission on sales. Kuhn Loeb's view of Rothschilds' financial strength reflected the weekly gold deliveries it received from Rothschilds, and in the immediate postwar years, Rothschilds was sending Kuhn Loeb unprecedented amounts of mainly South African gold. With the end of wartime production bottlenecks, Rothschilds' Royal Mint Refinery refined a record amount of gold bullion, ready for sale on the London gold market and thus for international trade. In 1919, for example, its London refinery refined and minted 10.4 million ounces of gold, worth some £52 million.[44] A large part of Rothschilds' merchant banking actually revolved around the business of gold—its exploration, mining, refining, assaying, minting, pricing, shipping, delivery, sale, and storage. Underestimating this dependence, Kuhn Loeb perhaps failed to appreciate the magnitude of the financial and economic problems facing the Rothschilds in the interwar years. In any case, N. M. Rothschild & Sons was in danger of becoming unstuck from its position in the gold market as well.

1925: The Central Banks Take Control

The British government's formal return to the gold standard on April 29, 1925, reestablished the sterling price of gold at £3.89 per common ounce (at 22-carat purity), or £4.25 per troy ounce fine (995). If we call this a gold standard, there must be one great qualification: the minimum amount of gold one could purchase was now four hundred troy ounces—that is, one "London Good Delivery" bar. Britain's classical gold specie standard, whereby all Bank of England banknotes were in theory convertible to gold coin, was thus replaced by a gold bullion standard. A minimum of £1,700 in Bank of England notes would be needed to purchase gold. In practice, the limit was higher than that, as gold for export was usually purchased in "export boxes," with each box containing four "London Good Delivery" bars, costing £6,800 (or $33,048 in 1925 dollars), which was then a very large sum.[45] (At 2014 prices of roughly $1,600 per ounce, an export box would sell for more than $2.5 million in today's dollars.) In effect, Britain had reintroduced a gold standard for financial institutions only.

The revived British gold standard was part of a general shift toward "a new kind of gold standard," described by E. A. Goldenweiser (1929) as a "gold reserve standard." Paper money was no longer truly convertible into gold for ordinary people. The operation of these postwar gold standards, even in the system's core gold-center countries, thus resembled the gold-exchange standards that Great Britain, the United States, France, and Japan had operated in their colonies before the First World War.[46] In this regard, as in others, colonial territories served as laboratories for working out new technocratically administered forms of governance. Compared to the "classical" gold standard before 1914, the highly managed gold standards of the 1920s thus conformed much better to the central bankers' ideal that gold should be removed from ordinary monetary circulation and concentrated in a "central reservoir" at a central bank.

The changes accompanying the restoration of the gold standard led also to the termination of Rothschilds' administration of the African Gold Realisation Account, which had been held by them, at their bank, on behalf of gold producers. South African gold mining companies had long resented London's control of the gold market, and over Rothschilds' opposition they had sought to win greater commercial freedom in the sale of their gold.[47] The establishment of the Rand Refinery by the South African Chamber of Mines in December 1920, the establishment of South Africa's central bank, the South African Reserve Bank, on June 30, 1921, and the founding of a branch of the Royal Mint in Pretoria on October 3, 1923, meant that their demands would have to be accommodated.[48]

Under the revised gold standard of 1925, all proceeds from the "realization" of gold in London were now paid directly to the South African Reserve Bank by the Bank of England. Beginning on September 19, 1925, gold bullion from the Rand Refinery was officially accepted by the Bank of England for sale in London, alongside bullion from Rothschilds' Royal Mint Refinery and Johnson Matthey & Company.[49] Unmistakably, the Bank of England's granting its approval of Rand Refinery bullion was yet another blow to Rothschilds' operations, not just in South Africa but also in London. A rival refinery was effectively whittling away the exclusive production rights and privileges of Rothschilds' Royal Mint Refinery in

London. From its side, the South African Reserve Bank ("to which we have contributed a Governor," as Norman had told Strong) supported the Bank of England in the same way that the Bank of Japan and other central banks had done, by lifting its minimum balance at the Bank of England to £150,000 and maintaining a further £100,000 as a floating reserve. The South African Reserve Bank's assurances with regard to the maintenance of a large balance, or "special security," at the Bank of England tightened the connections between the two central banks, and the Bank of England (which may well have instigated the South African bank's proposal) was quick to accept the proposal with gratitude.[50] In July 1926, the South African gold mining companies formally agreed to let their new reserve bank negotiate gold sales on their behalf with the Bank of England, thus altogether removing Rothschilds from their "realization" transactions.[51]

After April 1925, the operation of the London gold market was again dominated by direct Bank of England operations as it had been during the years of the classical gold standard. International gold flows were undiminished, but the gold now passed mainly through central bank channels. The private trade of the London gold market was thus at historically low levels during the years of the gold standard's restoration (1925–1931). Rothschilds' internal memoranda characterize this era as a "dull period" for the London gold market. These were also the years when Montagu Norman apparently engaged in the extraordinary manipulations of gold reserves discussed in the previous chapter.

Altogether, there had been a historic shift. Rothschilds had been effectively dealt out of the refining and sale of South African gold in London. Moreover, the South African Reserve Bank was involved in exporting direct, large-scale shipments of bullion from Durban for sale in Bombay. The much diminished London gold market was in danger of losing its largest producer—and it was now losing a large consumer in India.[52] What is more, the South African proposal to establish a special gold depot in Cairo, supplied exclusively with South African gold by regular air service between Cape Town and Cairo, threatened to erode one of the London gold market's last remaining advantages: namely, the "free" (of cost) delivery of gold sent to it.[53] The "automatic replenishment" of the Bank of England's gold reserves could no longer be assumed. Still, unrefined gold arrived weekly, each Tuesday by custom, from Rhodesian, South African, and West African mines for handling by

Rothschilds on behalf of the London gold market.[54] In addition, promising new suppliers of gold ores were sourced, most remarkably from the Soviet Union. Many hurdles confronted Anglo-Soviet trade, not the least of which was the enormity of outstanding debts owed to the City's financiers by previous Russian governments. And yet, for a brief period in the mid-1920s, almost the entire output of the Lena goldfields in northeast Siberia was being refined in London.[55] Thus, a large but shrinking proportion of the world's gold ores continued to be refined and sold on the London gold market. "Any balance not absorbed by the market at a price above the Bank of England's buying price was taken by the Bank of England at this price."[56] As the 1920s came to a close, the "free" gold market was still in place, if not in full use.

Channeling Free Gold

There was an "unquestioned tradition" of secrecy and intrigue associated with the London gold market.[57] Theoretically, anyone was free to trade on the London gold market, providing they employed a broker. At the market's most diverse, however, just five appointed brokers handled all the gold transactions in a few tense minutes each business day. Moreover, building a commercial relationship with one of these London brokers was notoriously difficult, often requiring elaborate introductions, made on the understanding that there were no conflicting, prior relations with one of the other brokers. Likewise, while there was a plethora of gold mining companies, only bullion from the Bank of England's officially appointed assayers and refiners (later defined by the Good Delivery List) was accepted for trade on the London market.[58] In the period from 1919 to 1939, there were just two large refiners: the Royal Mint Refinery and Johnson Matthey & Company, although bullion from the Rand Refinery was accepted by the Bank of England after September 19, 1925. Moreover, all gold coin for the British Empire and Commonwealth was minted by the Royal Mint in London or at one of its six international branches.

The buying and selling of gold in the London gold market was dominated by the transactions of a single player, the Bank of England, with the exception of the two periods from 1919 to 1925 and 1931 to 1939, when the market was chaired by N. M. Rothschild & Sons. (The 1930s period is discussed in the next chapter.) From 1954, when the London gold market was reopened, it was again chaired by N. M. Rothschild & Sons, who continued in that role until 2004. Rothschilds continued to cooperate closely with the Bank of England and often acted as its formal agent. The London gold market did provide a gold trade–price mechanism, but as a market it was highly exclusive and carefully managed. Indeed, if we think of a market as an open, public place with many buyers and sellers, then to use the term *market* in connection with gold is a misnomer. Moreover, under the gold standard, gold was the one commodity whose price in national currency was eternally fixed. The London gold market was indeed a peculiar market.

Consistently, Rothschilds and the Bank of England worked to channel the largest possible amount of gold to London for sale on the London market. The demand of the United States and other foreign countries for gold, purchased from London, played a crucial role in curbing their balance-of-payment surpluses with Britain. Even when the establishment of refineries and mints became politically necessary in Britain's colonies and former colonies, the refineries often sent their bullion to London, and the mints continued to coin gold specie (typically sovereign coins) denominated in pounds sterling, identical to those minted at the Royal Mint in London. The operations of the London gold market thus backed the operation of the gold standard, not only in Britain but in many other countries, and supported the standing of London as a world financial center and of sterling as a world currency. Indeed, London's centrality was enhanced during the world depression of the 1930s, which began with another series of sudden gold movements. These gold rushes were sufficient to knock down the world's gold-based monetary systems, while simultaneously bringing a great boom to the London gold market.

8

The Rush for Gold

One lesson to be learnt from the experience of the last few years is the
survival of the old-established position of London as an international credit
centre. . . . If we take a broad view of the gold situation both in 1929 and
in the years of depression that followed, the outstanding fact is that it was
through *London* that the abnormal demand for gold made itself felt.

R. G. Hawtrey, *The Art of Central Banking*, 1932

The world depression that began in 1929 was a compound crisis affecting almost all fields of economic, social, and political activity. At an underlying level, the depression was an immense and nearly worldwide debt-destruction crisis, happening simultaneously at the levels of national and local governments, banking systems, business enterprises, trading networks, and agricultural households.[1] And when we consider questions of debt and overindebtedness, it returns the inquiry immediately to the processes of credit creation.

Government purchasing during the Great War of 1914–18 was funded by an enormous creation of new credits. So too was the further business activity stimulated by government purchasing. Bankers created new means of payment, "almost with a note of joy," as Benjamin Strong had said, by writing new debt contracts and making new entries in the asset columns of their accounting books. Central banks backed them up, and made sure that these new credit operations had as little to do with actual gold as possible. Governments in turn backed the central banks, whose holdings of government debt substituted for gold. Prices soared. Given the enormous increase in means of payment, an insoluble problem was thus created when final payments were expected in gold. Debtor countries could postpone the problem by taking out new loans in order to pay existing debts. This is what they did, and these stopgap loans meant still more credit creation, above all by Wall Street banks.

War debts thus contributed to the international monetary contradictions of the 1920s, but they were far from the whole story.[2] Two interconnected aspects are especially significant. First was the great appreciation, in terms of real commodities, of gold and of gold-linked currencies. This appreciation in the value of gold-standard money—alternatively called price deflation—increased the real burden of debt. Thus, Irving Fisher defined the problem in 1933 as "*over-indebtedness* to start with and *deflation* following soon after."[3] A farmer's debt that was equivalent, say, to one thousand bushels of grain in the spring of 1920 would require roughly two thousand bushels to repay in 1922. The abstractions of monetary policy thus became very real, very quickly. And that was only the first phase of gold appreciation. The purchasing power of gold began to rise further when Great Britain and a large cohort of other countries returned to the gold standard in 1925, and in 1929 it began to rise still further. Even had the gold standard as a monetary framework proved to be sustainable, an enormous volume of actual debts denominated in gold would not have been.

This chapter highlights a second related aspect of the world crisis: the rush for gold. As the volume of actual gold appeared less and less able to sustain the volume of claims said to be convertible into gold, there commenced a movement to cash in paper claims for physical gold, which mounted into a series of runs on gold-backed currencies. Viewed now from a sufficient distance in time, the events of 1930–33 appear as a single globalized run on central-bank gold reserves. This run on gold reserves was largely conducted by the private banks. There was thus a strangely recursive and elastic aspect to this movement also, as banks created new credits to fund the speculative attacks on other banks' reserves. In the end, gold itself was nationalized, converted by mandatory state directives into a strategic commodity to be held only in national treasuries and central banks. Central banks themselves were brought under closer state control. It was from this time that we can speak of a movement of radical deglobalization of finance as well as of commerce and industry.

New York: An Inflated Inverted Pyramid

On March 7, 1929, Paul Warburg outlined the shape of what would shortly be an open crisis:

> From the economic lessons taught by the aftermath of the Great War, we learned that the excessive creation of money or bank credit without an equivalent production of [real, productive] assets spells inflation. Yet the public mind does not appear to realize *that the creation of an inflated purchasing power is not a monopoly enjoyed by governments.*[4]

Warburg was speaking at the International Acceptance Bank, which he had founded. What he meant was that there had been an excessive creation of private bank credit, especially in New York City. As Warburg indicated, much of this newly created purchasing power was not balanced, on the real side of the social ledger, by being invested into the creation of new productive resources. Although stock-market values had doubled since 1927, these gains were mostly "quite unrelated to respective increases in plant, property, or earning power," Warburg explained. Rather, inflated stock prices were "sustained by a colossal volume of loans" from the banks. Real-estate values had been inflated in the same way. As for "the banking structure carrying this inflated inverted pyramid," it rested "on a basis of Federal Reserve credit." And this Federal Reserve credit had itself had been greatly extended.

Another example is offered by the business of bankers' acceptances, which was at the center of Warburg's long-term plan to make New York an international credit center. In the years 1927–29, the volume of acceptances nearly doubled. In 1928, the volume of acceptances regained the heights reached when the first acceptance credit bubble peaked in 1920, and then rose to a new peak of $1.7 billion in December 1929. However, this increase did not correspond to an actual boom in US trade, the volume of which did not change greatly during those years. More than a third of this total consisted of "foreign" dollar acceptances, to finance trade between other countries not involving the United States. The acceptance business was dominated by the New York banks.[5] New York had indeed opened up a new field of international dollar-based credit creation and was now doing a profitable business that London had formerly done. This meant more international competition in the business of trade financing, and lower profit margins for London financial institutions. And again, Federal Reserve credit supported this movement: "the Federal Reserve Banks played a key role by reducing the risk borne by private dealers," as J. Peter Ferderer concluded.[6] In fact, these private risks had become socialized, while the systemic risk was augmented. As in 1920, this new credit proved to be a speculative taking of claims. In 1931–32, the inflated volume of dollar acceptances collapsed to a level about half that of 1929–30. Twenty years later, it was only a third of the 1929 peak.

Warburg's own conclusion in March 1929: "Conditions such as these recall to our minds the painful events of the years 1919–21." But, he noted, unlike the inflationary boom of 1919, there was no inflation of *commodity* prices in 1929—rather the opposite; there was a tendency toward deflation. Thus, Warburg said, people did not realize the problem.[7] Again, one might think of Tokyo during the great bubble of 1989, when the valuation of assets such as real estate and company shares surged, at a time when Japanese wholesale (but not retail) prices had actually shown a tendency to decline. Or one might think of the bubble that came to a peak in New York and London in 2007.

The "huge skyscraper based on a comparatively small foundation of gold" that Warburg had described with admiration when he advocated for the new Federal Reserve System in 1914 had thus become an "inflated inverted pyramid."[8] This was the situation in New York City, which commanded the world's largest store of gold. In other countries, including Japan, Germany, and Britain, the supposed foundation material of this huge financial superstructure would now, in a rush, be cashed in by banks that held large paper claims, to be packed into crates and shipped across oceans. In this rush for gold, gold indeed "flowed" freely, as advocates of the revived gold standard said it naturally ought to do. We see again in these images a radical mixing of metaphors—of a solid "foundation" and of liquid "flow." These contradictory images suggest the nature of the crisis itself. A monetary system premised upon a substantive, "hard" conception of money was showing itself to be something else entirely. One can think also of how the structural foundations of a building are affected by soil liquefaction during an earthquake.

A World Central Bank?

At this moment of impending crisis, bank-led globalization advanced to a new level. As we have seen, an international network of central banks developed during the First World War as an initiative of the Bank of England. This was a major turn for the Bank of England itself. John Clapham, as cited above, reported only two countries of the British Empire and only four foreign countries ("all of secondary importance") whose banks had accounts at the Bank of England before the First World War. Of these six countries, Japan held by far the largest balances. "But by 1930," Clapham wrote, "the Bank of England held seventeen central bank accounts, and from all the leading countries. They might not be active but they served as connecting wires."[9] In the meantime, the administrative power of the Bank of England had also grown. The bank had one thousand staff members in 1914. By 1930, its staff was close to four thousand.[10] That year, 1930, also saw the establishment of the Bank for International Settlements (BIS) in Basel, organized by the leading central banks as an international bank of banks. Thus the project of central bank cooperation gained lasting institutional form.

The BIS project appears to have come together very quickly. Discussions for organizing the bank arose out of the Young Committee meetings in the first part of 1929, where they were energized by the prospect of managing Germany's giant reparations payments in a "de-politicized" and "commercialized" way. They were doubly energized by the prospect of American involvement. Plans for the BIS were outlined in a meeting at The Hague in August 1929. They were finalized at a second meeting at The Hague in January 1930 and a meeting in Rome in February. The meeting in Rome was the largest group meeting yet of central bank governors.[11] The BIS began operations in May 1930. The project for a central bankers' central bank thus happened at the moment Japan opened its monetary doors and the moment the gold outrush began, as described further below.

On the model of the US Federal Reserve System, the Bank for International Settlements was owned and capitalized by its member banks. The original members were a prototypical "Group of Seven," consisting of the central banks of Belgium, France, Germany, Italy, Japan, and the UK, joined by a US banking group led by Morgan & Company. The BIS directors directly represented their countries' central banks. On the model of the League of Nations, the BIS was hosted by Switzerland. On paper, this looked like a great step toward the realization of the Comte de Saint-Simon's 1820s vision of uniting the banks of the world into a unitary governing structure.[12]

The US Federal Reserve itself could not formally participate in the BIS project, so the United States was instead represented by a group of private bankers led by Morgan & Company. In actuality, the Federal Reserve Bank of New York was very close to the process. Gates W. McGarrah, who was chairman of the FRBNY, resigned in order to serve as US representative, president, and chairman of the board of the BIS in Basel. Frank Costigliola therefore interpreted the establishment of the BIS not only as an effort to institutionalize the process of central bank cooperation, but also as a move to Americanize it.[13] Montagu Norman was a key mover in the project—the key mover, perhaps—though operating well behind the scenes.[14] Also notable was the inclusion of the German Reichsbank, which had been excluded from the first phase of central bank cooperation earlier in the decade.

The Bank of Japan was projected to be one of the BIS founding members. As usual in the "executive level" diplomacy of the era, Japan was the single country not belonging to the circle of racially European and religiously Christian powers. This geography of power persisted well into the second half of the twentieth century; we can note the likeness to the "Group of Seven" formed in 1976—the only difference in membership being the absence of Belgium and presence of Canada in the latter group. In 1929, however, there was also a threat that Japan would be excluded from this core "G7" group, on the grounds that the yen, as the currency of a country that had not returned to the gold standard, would be ineligible for deposit in the bank. This potential national humiliation became another source of pressure for the Japanese government to return quickly to the gold standard.

In Japan as in the United States, legal restrictions seemed to bar the formal entry of the Bank of Japan. Therefore, a group of Japanese banks led by the parastatal Industrial Bank of Japan and the Yokohama Specie Bank provided the Japanese share of the capital in the BIS, "in place of the Bank of Japan."[15] The Bank of Japan was in fact represented on the BIS board by the manager of its London agency and by the manager of the Yokohama Specie Bank's London branch.

Sixteen other European central banks joined the BIS by the end of its first business year.[16] Historians of the BIS note that one of its most important functions was social, to act as a club for central bankers, who could discreetly meet at one of Western Europe's most convenient rail junctions. Here, Montagu Norman particularly met privately with other central bankers, outside the observation of the press or of governments, including his own. One might say that Norman's preference for incognito excursions and clubby surroundings had been institutionalized.

In the meantime, however, the runs on individual countries' gold reserves had already begun. An era of world history was about to close.

The Endgame Begins

The postwar decade began and ended with enormous international movements of gold. These movements were especially clearly delineated in Japan, as shown in figure 8.2. The great run on gold-backed currencies also began with Japan, in 1930. This story is missed in Europe- and America-centered accounts of the depression.

As described in chapter 4, the First World War was followed by a great rush of gold out of the United States. Japan was the single largest recipient. In the 1920s, Japan's wartime export surpluses vanished, and its trade reverted to a deficit position. However, gold exports were restricted by the Ministry of Finance, and gold outflows were modest. If we divide this period according to the movement of gold to and from Japan, we see the following phases (the numbers given are net totals):[17]

1919–20–21	Heavy gold flow into Japan, totaling ¥881.3 million (US$439 million)
1922–23–24	Modest gold inflow, totaling ¥14.7 million
1925–26–27	Gold outflow of ¥76.5 million under a "shadow" gold standard
1928–29	Gold inflow of ¥9.6 million
1930–31–32	Heavy gold outflow of ¥738.7 million (US$368 million) under restored gold standard

These flows and ebbs were aligned with the alternation in power of Japan's two established conservative parties, which followed opposed policies

Figure 8.1. Taken to be the foundation: gold bars stored in an auxiliary vault at the Federal Reserve Bank of New York. Courtesy of the Archives of the Federal Reserve Bank of New York.

vis-à-vis gold. In 1918–21, 1927–29, and again after December 1931, cabinets led by the Rikken Seiyūkai (the Constitutional Society of Political Friends, described as the "Conservative party" in the British press) followed a more nationalist policy. Little or no gold was shipped from Japan under their tenure. The cabinets led by their rivals, the more pro-British Kenseikai (Constitutional Government Society, known as the "Liberal party"), allowed limited gold exports from the spring of 1925 to the spring of 1927. This interval of gold outflow was one of monetary contraction and price deflation. This, too, was a case of informal international policy alignment, for the period after April 1925 was a time of deflation internationally, in the wake of Britain's restoration of a gold standard. The same years also marked a high point of central bank cooperation, exemplified by the Bank of Japan's provision of funds to support the Bank of England's monetary diplomacy in Europe, described in chapter 6.

The liberal cabinet's deflation policy in 1925–26 helped bring on the great banking panic of spring 1927. That crisis caused a cabinet change and reversal of policy. There was another reversal in July 1929, when the Kenseikai's successor party, the Minseitō (Popular Government Party), carried the Western-aligned policy to its conclusion by restoring the gold standard. Inoue Junnosuke served as finance minister. Tensions surrounding Anglo-American-style financial globalization were thus reflected directly in domestic politics.[18]

In the autumn of 1929, following intense negotiations in New York and London, the Japanese government arranged a joint credit from the private banks of the New York and London groups, $25 million in New York and £5 million in London. This deal was finalized on November 20, at a moment when "monetary conditions were still unsettled and uncomfortable" on Wall Street, in the wake of the "Black Thursday" panic of October 24.[19] Having awaited the signal from New York, Finance Minister Inoue announced on November 21 that the Japanese government would lift the embargo on gold exports as of January 11, 1930. The FRBNY and the Bank of England declared their "moral support." This phrase was code for the fact that they were not providing actual monetary credits. This holding back on the part of the New York and London central banks revealed one limit to cooperation—in this case, they would not provide a credit because the Bank of Japan did not want to open its books concerning its extensive and controversial "special accommodation" bailout lending to Japanese banks in distress. The foreign central banks therefore did not provide Japan with the cooperative central bank credit that typically accompanied a country's return to the gold standard—and that the Bank of Japan had itself taken part in providing to European central banks.

The great run on gold commenced from this point. If we look at the pattern of international gold movements, the numbers tell their own story, and they clarify some basic dynamics of the depression itself. Already in 1928, gold was being pulled from the commodity-producing peripheral countries—the restored gold-standard system was beginning to fray around its edges. This was barely three years after the supposedly successful restoration of the gold standard in the British Empire and the many countries that followed Britain's lead. The Bank of France exercised an enormous attractive force following the restoration of the French gold standard in 1926–28. The United States also continued to pull in gold. The Bank of England on the other hand experienced large gold losses in 1929. John Garrett indicates that actual gold losses were even larger than reported; had this fact been known, he speculates, Britain would have been forced off the gold standard in 1929.[20] In other words, Britain might have been forced off gold when Australia was. Here again, it seems that an institutional culture of secrecy, combined with the facility of secret arrangements with other central banks, created opportunities for false reporting by the Bank of England. Lacking accurate informational feedback, the public remained befuddled, and policy makers made enormous mistakes.

Australia, which did not have a central bank under direct Bank of England influence, went off gold in a de facto way in December 1929. This move helped Australian financial authorities manage a burgeoning debt-deflation crisis with relative success. Argentina and Uruguay both left the gold standard in December 1929.[21] In retrospect, the action of these commodity exporters appears as the beginning of a global movement.

Ignoring these signs, the Japanese government moved in the opposite direction. On January 11, 1930, the Ministry of Finance lifted its gold export controls. Western banks were free now to present their paper Bank of Japan notes for redemption in gold, and free to ship that gold out of the country. They hastened to do so.

As shown in figure 8.2, Japan's massive gold losses in 1930–32 were almost a mirror image of the gold inflows of 1919–21.

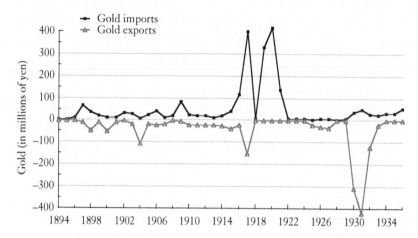

Figure 8.2. Great boom, great depression: reported Japanese gold imports and exports, 1894–1936. Japan's gold-standard era ran from 1897 to 1931, with a partial suspension from 1917 through 1929. Data from Nihon Ginkō Tōkeikyoku 1966, 298–299; table A.1 in the appendix to this book.

As was emphasized in chapter 7, the largest part of whole-world gold flows from the 1890s into the 1930s normally consisted of gold shipments internal to the British Empire. Of these, the flow of gold from South Africa to London was by far the largest. Gold flows internal to Japan's own overseas empire in northeast Asia were minor by comparison but were significant for Japan's own overall balance of gold inflows and outflows. Following the Japanese annexation of Korea in 1910, gold bullion worth millions of yen annually was shipped from Korea to Japan. The total of these shipments added up to nearly ¥100 million by 1919. By 1931, Japan had imported another ¥100 million in gold from Korea. These amounts were small compared to Japan's massive gold imports in 1916–21 or its massive gold losses of 1930–32. During "normal" years, however, Japan's small positive gold balance was practically identical with the gold delivered from Korea (see appendix table A.3). Korea was in fact the largest gold producer in Asia (excluding the Soviet Union), surpassing Indian gold production after 1925.[22]

When the Japanese government lifted its gold export embargo in January 1930, it was National City Bank of New York that led the movement to cash in Japanese yen for gold. National City Bank did an active business in Japan, and the Japanese government was one of its clients. Altogether, NCB had a share in eight Japanese bond issues from 1923 to 1931 and directly issued three Japanese corporate debentures. These loans totaled some $350 million. Japan was also a good source of ordinary banking business for National City Bank. By 1930, National City Bank had the most extensive international branch network of any bank, with ninety-eight branches in twenty-three countries. Among all these branches, NCB's local business in Japan was exceeded only by the business it did locally in Havana, Shanghai, and London. During the era of the floating yen exchange in the 1920s, speculation on the Japanese yen in Shanghai was also an important source of the bank's earnings.[23] Most to the point, National City Bank, as part of the New York Group, had taken part in the November 1929 credit to the Japanese government; the purpose of this credit was to demonstrate the support of New York and London finance for the supposed stabilization of the yen on the basis of gold.

None of this stopped National City Bank from cashing in yen and shipping out ¥100 million ($50 million) in gold. This total was far more than that taken by any other bank. It also reveals the great amount of yen that National City Bank had purchased at a depreciated price in the expectation of cashing in when Japan returned to the gold standard.[24] As NCB and other foreign banks took their profits, the Japanese Ministry of Finance, after some delay, allowed the big Japanese banks, Mitsui, Mitsubishi, and Sumitomo, to do the same. The running down of Japan's gold reserves thus looked like a premeditated looting, and it became notorious as the "dollar buying scandal." Coming amid severe deflation and depression, it also discredited internationalist liberalism as a force in Japanese politics. Radical Japanese nationalists blamed American and British financiers, and more than that, concluded that their own top financiers were traitors.

The outrush of gold in 1930–32 was very large compared to the Japanese monetary base. On the eve of the lifting of the gold embargo, in December 1929, the Bank of Japan reported a gold reserve against banknote issue of ¥1,072 million (about US$500 million). By late 1930, this reserve had fallen to the ¥800 million level. It fell to ¥469 million in December 1931, when Takahashi Korekiyo, now seventy-seven years old, succeeded Inoue Junnosuke as finance minister and immediately re-embargoed gold exports. By the time all contractually agreed-upon shipments of gold were concluded in 1932, the Bank of Japan's gold reserve was only ¥425 million. This represented a loss of ¥647 million, or 60 percent, relative to December 1929.

The effect of this shrinkage of the gold reserve was highly deflationary, though significantly, the Bank of Japan banknote issue declined by less than gold-standard rules would seem to have demanded. The BoJ note issue had reached a peak already in late 1928, at the ¥1.7 billion level, meaning a gold cover of about 60 percent. By early 1932, when the gold outrush ended, the note issue was down to the ¥1.1 billion level. The gold cover thus fell to less than 40 percent, though gold convertibility was no longer allowed. Japan's wholesale price index slid by 36 percent from December 1928 to June 1932, roughly matching the ratio of reduction in BoJ notes in circulation.[25]

Altogether, ¥850 million in gold (approximately $425 million) was shipped out of Japan in 1930–32. More than 95 percent of these Japanese gold exports appear to have gone to the United States. Gold shipments to Japan for the same period were ¥112 million, most of which came from Korea.[26]

Japan was a substantially industrialized country in 1930, but raw silk for the American market still had a large place in its exports. Vis-à-vis the United States, Japan therefore remained to a significant extent a commodity-exporting country (just as, vis-à-vis Korea, it was an industrial country). Raw silk prices were especially vulnerable to the world economic downturn, and for this reason also the profile of gold flows from Japan to the United States resembles those of "peripheral" commodity-producing countries. This image is confirmed by a survey of gold flows to the United States in 1930, when the largest gold inflows came from Japan ($157 million), Brazil ($88 million), Mexico ($20 million), and Argentina ($20 million). Again in 1931, the largest gold flows to the United States came from Japan ($191 million) and Argentina ($141 million), followed now by Canada ($81 million) and Germany ($36 million). Notably, both Japan and Argentina had built up large export surpluses during the First World War, and they received the largest volumes of gold from the United States in 1919–21.[27] In this view also, the rush of gold back to the United States in 1930–31 was the trough in a great wavelike movement initiated by the Great War. Seen from the side of the United States, Japan was therefore not only the greatest destination of gold shipments in 1919–20 but also the greatest source of gold in 1930 and 1931. (These latter inflows were more than counterbalanced by a great outflow of gold from the United States to France.)[28]

The rush of private banks to cash in Japanese yen for gold was the beginning of a cascade. If one looks at more recent history, these runs on national gold reserves resemble nothing so much as the runs staged by Western hedge funds and banks on the currencies of Thailand, Malaysia, Indonesia, South Korea, Russia, Brazil, and other countries in the so-called Asian financial crisis of 1997–98. As in 1931, the big speculators in the dollar rush of 1997–98 were largely the international banks themselves, whose behavior was enabled and supported by a network of multilateral financial institutions ultimately backed by the treasuries and central banks of the United States and other money-center countries. Also reminiscent of the 1920s, austerity and economic depression were greeted by spokespeople of these latter institutions as a healthful restoration of good order and discipline.[29]

The movement to cash in Japanese yen for gold was only the beginning. Viewed from a worldwide level, the critical phase in the run on the revived gold standard system began in May 1931, with the run on Austria. After the World War, Austria had been an early test case for internationally coordinated monetary-stabilization policies, backed by the Bank of England and by Morgan & Company. Now, banking and monetary crises were conjoined there. There was an effort to stem the crisis by means of international central bank loans organized by the Bank for International Settlements and the Bank of England, to little effect. The crisis in Vienna spread at once to Hungary and then to Germany, where the run on the gold-backed reichsmark began in June. The debt/gold crisis had now reached the largest industrial economy in Europe. On the eve of the run on Germany, at the end of May 1931, the Reichsbank had gold reserves of Rm 2.4 billion (about US$570 million). The Reichsbank then lost almost a billion reichsmarks in gold in the month of June alone. By June 1932, its gold reserve was down to the Rm 800 million level (about $190 million).[30]

The British pound was the next big target. At the beginning of July 1931, the Bank of England reported more than £160 million in gold reserves. In the second half of July the bank paid out more than £30 million ($146 million), equivalent to more than seventeen thousand "London Good Delivery" gold bars. Norman became ill at this point and took a leave from his post, for a rest across the Atlantic. Robert Boyce argues that Norman had excellent reasons for escaping, as he was responsible even to the extent of working to intensify the crisis in pursuit of his own ends.[31] Giant loans from the US Federal Reserve System and from the Bank of France did not end the run on sterling. On Monday, September 21, 1931, the British government suspended the gold convertibility of the pound, effective as of Friday, September 18, according to the Gold Standard Amendment Act of 1931.[32] A large cohort of countries followed Britain in leaving the gold standard, and the world of gold-convertible currencies suddenly contracted. There was a renewed run on the Japanese yen. September 18, 1931 also happened to be the day that local Japanese military commanders staged a fake act of sabotage on the South Manchurian Railway, as a pretext for launching a carefully planned invasion of the whole Manchurian region. The war in Manchuria added to the sense that the "Washington order" of the 1920s had broken down. The final run on BoJ gold reserves ended when Takahashi Korekiyo took office as finance minister and immediately re-embargoed gold exports on December 13, 1931.[33] Meanwhile, there was also a great rush of gold out of India and out of the United States. By this time, we can begin to speak of a run on the US dollar itself.

Boom Times in the London Gold Market

After the British government resuspended the gold standard on September 21, 1931, the operation of a free gold market in London again became a matter of importance. In fact, the London gold market boomed. Again, the British pound was floating against the US dollar, which remained on a gold basis until April 1933. The gold-pricing ("fixing") arrangements of 1919–25 were reinstated, and until the spring of 1933 the US dollar exchange rate of the British pound was again the main variable and determinant of the gold fix.

Compared to the functioning of the gold market in the 1920s, however, there was a crucial difference: South African gold now reached the London market only via the Bank of England. N. M. Rothschild & Sons, in their own description, were no longer "at once president of the gold market and the largest seller." They became instead "president and agent for the largest seller (the Bank of England through the South African Reserve Bank)."[34] The influence of central banks on the purchase and sale of gold thus "increased enormously," in Rothschilds' estimation, and Rothschilds and the other four members of the gold market now tended to act "purely in the capacity of brokers."[35] At the same time, the Bank of England itself came under greater control by the government, and in 1931 the Bank of England's gold and foreign-exchange reserves were transferred to the keeping of the Treasury.[36]

Effective December 1931, the Bank of England also renegotiated its relationship with Rothschilds. The Bank of England had been discontented with Rothschilds' practice of charging double commissions on foreign gold sales. Typically, Rothschilds earned a ¼ percent (0.25%) commission when shipping gold for sale in New York or Paris. Rothschilds' own agents, Kuhn, Loeb & Company in New York, and their cousins M. M. de Rothschild Frères in Paris, likewise charged a 0.25 percent commission. The Bank of England no longer accepted this arrangement and threatened to ship gold itself if no accommodation was forthcoming from Rothschilds. The Bank of England then reduced Rothschilds' commission charges for handling gold transactions on the Bank of England's account by more than half. Reflecting their dependence on the Bank of England, Rothschilds, through Clement J. G. Cooper, nevertheless "expressed themselves quite satisfied with this arrangement."[37]

Notwithstanding these changes, Rothschilds continued to handle a large share of the gold trade. In the heady days of the last quarter of 1932 alone, while the US gold standard system was entering its terminal crisis, Rothschilds handled Bank of England transactions involving almost three million ounces of gold worth some £18 million (or roughly US$62 million, at the then statutory price of $20.67 per ounce).[38] The great appreciation of gold that had begun in the spring of 1920 continued, not only vis-à-vis commodities in general but now also vis-à-vis the pound sterling itself. After Britain went off the gold standard on September 21, 1931, the sterling price of gold jumped from the old mint price of £4.25 per troy ounce to a range between £5.50 and £6.34 per ounce. This appreciation of gold catalyzed frenzied gold sales and a boom in gold mining. Amid the general spectacle of a world in depression, the South African economy experienced a significant economic recovery.[39] As the price of gold rose, members of the British public sold gold specie, principally "hoarded" £1 sovereign coins, and gold jewelry in unprecedented quantities. Higher gold prices also spurred huge gold exports from India, under the combined pressures of depression and efforts by Indians to realize profits on gold sales. Some 343 million rupees (or approximately £25 million) worth of gold went to Britain in the last three months of 1931. During 1932, Indian gold exports to Britain were worth £50 million, or US$220 million. The Bank of England deliberately contributed to these exports, by covertly buying gold in India via the Hongkong and Shanghai Bank.[40] For Britain, India was thus momentarily a second South Africa, leaving Britain with a substantial net gold gain for the year, despite shipping nearly $300 million to France.[41] The press called it the "Gold Rush of 1932."[42]

In 1932, the greatest gold flow of all came out of the United States, $446 million, mostly in one great surge in May and June. This gold went mainly to France, Switzerland, the Netherlands, and Belgium, which all remained on the gold standard.[43] During the final period of the US gold standard between December 1932 and March 1933, foreign speculation against the dollar was centered in London. The Bank of England itself appears to have taken a leading role, actively buying dollars and selling them for gold in the London market. Bank of England gold reserves jumped by more than 40 percent in these three months.[44] Simultaneously in the winter of 1932–33, a tremendous series of bank runs spread across the United States. By the end of February, most US state governments were either restricting withdrawals or had imposed total banking moratoriums. Immediately upon taking office as president on March 4, 1933, Franklin D. Roosevelt invoked special powers under the Trading with the Enemy Act of 1917 and ordered a national bank moratorium. Again, the moment has the appearance of a globally systemic crisis, for it was at the same critical point, March 5, that Hitler began to govern by decree in Germany.[45] On March 7, Roosevelt ordered an extraordinary "gold moratorium." On April 5, 1933, the US government enforced a full embargo on gold exports. Still more extraordinarily, the US government nationalized the supply of gold, as US citizens were required by law to deliver all gold specie, bullion, or gold certificates to the Federal Reserve by May 1, 1933, at the statutory price of $20.67183 per ounce. This nationalization of gold ownership was the kind of measure one might expect from a country involved in a total war, and it reveals the depth of the monetary crisis. The US government formally abandoned its adherence to the gold standard on June 5, 1933. The private ownership of gold specie, bullion, or gold certificates in the United States would not be fully re-legalized until January 1974.

Further legislative changes between 1933 and 1935 deliberately reduced the independent authority of the Federal Reserve Bank of New York. In particular, the FRBNY was prohibited from negotiating with foreign central banks. In 1935, the head of the FRBNY also lost the title of "governor," becoming simply a bank president.[46] The chief US agent of central bank cooperation was thus prevented from continuing in that role—and that program itself was now widely understood to have gone disastrously wrong. Looking at these events from the standpoint of the present, it is therefore all the more striking to see the way the FRBNY took the lead in the international banking system bailouts after 2008, a point we reflect upon in the final chapter.

After April 1933, the international gold standard system included only France, Belgium, the Netherlands, and Switzerland. Accordingly, prices in the London gold market now followed the exchange rate between the British pound and the French franc.[47] London remained the world's leading gold market. Japan, China, Canada, and South American countries all used the London market. They used it overwhelmingly to sell; the Bank of England purchased gold worth nearly £71 million during 1933.[48] After Britain abandoned the gold standard, its financial and economic position had improved considerably, largely owing to the formation of the sterling bloc, which provided a consistent source of purchasing power in an increasingly disintegrated world economy.

In September 1933, the US government began an extraordinary period of experimenting with the gold price, decided on the basis of conversations between Treasury Secretary Henry Morgenthau and President Roosevelt. A new statutory price was finally fixed on January 31, 1934, at $35 per troy ounce fine for all gold tendered to the US Assay Office (with a 0.25% deduction for commission and minting charges). With this increase in the gold price, the dollar value of the Federal Reserve's gold assets jumped by 59 percent over their former level.[49] The direction of international gold flows now reversed again, as higher US gold prices began to pull in unprecedentedly large shipments of gold from across the Atlantic. Net gold shipments from the UK to the United States, given in millions of dollars at $35 per ounce, were as follows:[50]

1934: $501.6
1935: $315.5
1936: $174.1
1937: $891.5
1938: $1,208.7
1939: $1,826.4

There were likewise massive French shipments of gold to the United States in 1934–35. This was the final run on national gold reserves, now focused on the franc. France too finally ended gold convertibility in September 1936.[51]

The world's gold—perhaps 70 percent of it—became concentrated in the United States. As for the gold that remained in Europe, it was estimated that during the heyday of the London gold market in the mid-1930s, up to two-thirds of Europe's privately owned gold was physically held in the vaults of London's gold brokers. With the abandonment of the gold standard, gold was not suddenly unimportant—more the opposite. Gold became all the more important as faith in fiat paper banknotes withered in the lead-up to war. By April 1937, however, with gold export controls now generally in place, the daily trade in the London gold market itself was very quiet. The Bank of England was "practically the only buyer." Rothschilds and the other four brokers continued to meet and fix the price of gold, but the Bank of England now worked outside this channel, by directly negotiating with sellers, to fix the gold price for themselves.[52]

The second-largest shipper of gold to the United States in 1937 and 1938, after Great Britain, was Japan. These shipments were now driven by military imperatives, as the Japanese government used gold to purchase war supplies in the United States for the invasion of China it had begun in July 1937. Japanese gold shipments to the United States had been nil in 1935–36. In 1937, to settle its large trade deficits, Japan shipped $246 million in gold to the United States, and then $169 million in 1938. Compared to London, the United States was now a better market for Japanese gold sales. In 1939, Japan shipped another $166 million in gold. With war looming in Europe, these shipments were now smaller than the volume of gold coming to the United States from the Netherlands and Belgium. (These statistics include shipments of gold that remained under foreign ownership and was earmarked as such, to be held chiefly at the Federal Reserve Bank of New York.) Even in 1940, Japanese gold shipments to the United States were large at $112 million.[53] In total, Japan exported a massive $693 million worth of gold to the United States from 1937 to 1940, equivalent to ¥3 billion in terms of the dollar–yen exchange rate prevailing on the eve of the war.

The London gold market's final gold fix of the interwar period was set at £8.05 per ounce on September 3, 1939, the day Britain declared war on Germany. Compared to the first 1919 gold fix of £4.96, this price represented a 61 percent increase. After that, the London gold market would not reopen for almost fifteen years.[54]

De-globalization in the 1930s

The panorama of the years from the 1890s to the 1930s, portrayed as a history of *world orders*, appears as a triptych of scenes. In the first panel, from the late 1890s to 1914, we see the classical gold standard in its final, most world-encompassing phase. The City of London is at the center of the picture. Then in the middle panel we see the 1920s, when the gold standard was revived. Wall Street appears as an international financial center; New York and London are joined in a relationship of cooperation and rivalry. In the history books, it is the rivalry that is conspicuous. On an actual day-to-day level, cooperation had never been more extensive or continuous. In the third and final panel is the harsh new world of the 1930s. Here we see the appearance of various regional "new orders," each organizing financially around its own center: a sterling bloc centered on London, a dollar bloc with its center in New York, the reemergence of Berlin with a hinterland in Central Europe, and in East Asia the extension of a yen bloc centered on Tokyo. The two hinges between these panels are the World War of 1914–18, and the world depression of 1929–33.

The First World War itself was less a lull in globalization than a storm of globalization. The war induced enormous international and transoceanic movements, of soldiers and war workers, of goods, and of new political ideas.[55] The war also induced enormous transoceanic transfers of claims to wealth. The wave of financial globalization that followed in the 1920s involved new centers of activity, above all New York. It also involved new organizational networks—conspicuously including a new network of central banks. This movement also involved new ideologies, of central bank independence and central bank cooperation, framed within a new language of technocratic internationalism. To those who lived through the period, this transformation was evident—"the world of the twenties had become economically unified as never before," as Bank of England historian John Clapham (1873–1946) experienced it.[56]

It is also important to remember that for both Britain and Japan—quite unlike the United States—economic times were by and large better in the

1930s, after the initial phase of crisis, than they had been during the 1920s. Japan in particular experienced a new phase of export growth and industrial revolution after 1932. During the era of slow growth in the 1920s, the Japanese national economy was roughly the same size as the British national economy (though with a larger population), and the two national economies grew at roughly the same pace. Both economies grew faster in the 1930s, but the Japanese economy now pulled ahead rapidly, although Japanese national income per person still remained much lower.[57]

The international lending boom of the late 1920s was followed by the international debt-default crisis of the 1930s. The global geography of the crisis of the 1930s is itself evidence of how far globalization had gone.

Currency depreciation was part of this process of debt destruction. When British authorities abandoned the gold standard in September 1931 and allowed the British pound to depreciate—by about 30 percent by the end of the year—they did not describe it as a debt default. In effect, however, it was a massive partial default on sterling claims held by foreigners, whose holdings suddenly lost 30 percent of their value. Those who held the largest stocks of sterling claims had the greatest volume of losses. Foreign central banks such as the Bank of France were among the largest losers, and foreign governments did consider the British action a kind of default. In fact, the Bank of England did indemnify one bank for its losses on sterling's depreciation. This was the Bank for International Settlements, which was treated "as a special case."[58] We might also compare the great depreciation of the pound sterling in 1931 to the great depreciation of the US dollar in 1985–86, which then fell by some 40 percent against the Japanese yen (although in this case the foreign financial authorities represented at the Plaza conference of September 1985 had actually agreed to some reduction in the value of their own countries' claims).[59]

In the early 1930s (as in the 1980s), these partial defaults via depreciation, involving the world's pivotal currencies, happened simultaneously with a wave of open international debt defaults, mainly involving countries on the periphery of the world financial system. Few metropolitan observers cared to equate these phenomena. By 1933, twenty-five countries were in default on their international debts—this was more than one-third of the sovereign countries of the world.[60] There were also domestic banking collapses in many countries, including Austria and Germany in the spring and summer of 1931, and the United States in 1932 and early 1933.

With these systemic collapses, the international financial system became radically more disintegrated, and the ability of central banks to cooperate was radically diminished.[61] Trade barriers, which had been put up after the First World War by many of the newly independent republics of Central and Eastern Europe, were now raised further by the United States and other countries. The volume of world trade diminished sharply. In these circumstances, the discounting of trade acceptances by the Federal Reserve banks also fell to a low level. Finally, in March 1939 the FRBNY gave up on the effort, initiated by Benjamin Strong, to establish a London-style discount market.[62] With all these changes, one can truly speak of a phase of radical economic de-globalization.

Japan, in this three-phase story of globalization and reaction, acted as a "swing" power.[63] In the first period, from 1896 to 1914, Japan was an important backer of London's central place. In the second period, the 1920s, Japan cooperated with both London and New York. Finally, through a series of back-and-forth movements in the 1930s, Japan moved into a position of enmity vis-à-vis the Anglo-American international order.

When one incorporates Japan into the international financial history of these decades, another curious fact emerges. In every truly major international financial panic of the era—1907, 1920, 1929—the crisis seems to have come early to Tokyo, appearing some three to six months before it did in New York and London.[64] The same tendency toward early manifestation of systemic crisis can be seen again in the run on world gold reserves, which began for Japan in 1930.

In the first instance, in 1907, Japan experienced an especially great boom-bust cycle, connected to a wave of credit inflation leading to debt deflation during and after the Russo-Japanese War of 1904–5. A speculative postwar boom peaked in January 1907. As it seemed in Japan, the panic of 1907 thus began as a domestic reaction to a domestic bubble, whose effects were then compounded by the panic in New York in October.[65] In fact, the Russo-Japanese War itself, by reason of the immense British and American loans that funded it, was also a factor in the international boom-bust cycle. This factor has probably been underrated by historians. Here it is relevant to remember that the Japanese war loans of 1904–5 were the largest foreign loans yet raised in New York.

In the inflationary boom of 1919 and the deflationary crash of 1920, the effects on both the upside and the downside were again especially great in Japan. The collapse of the postwar speculative boom also came first in Japan, in March 1920. If one looks closely at the timing of this boom-bust cycle, the flow of gold from the United States to Japan after June 1919 was highly significant. So too was the Bank of Japan's role as first mover in raising interest rates in October 1919.

Finally, in 1929, deflation and depression began in Japan three months in advance of the New York stock market crash, as a result of the decision taken by Japan's liberal party cabinet in July 1929 to prepare for a restoration of the gold standard. Japan thus had the misfortune of combining its own gold-restoration depression with the world crisis. The big runs on gold-standard currencies also began first in Japan, immediately upon the yen's return to gold convertibility in January 1930. Japan was subsequently the first country to adopt "Keynesian"-style policies under the leadership of Takahashi Korekiyo after December 1931, and it was the first country to recover from the world depression, in 1932.[66]

As we evaluate the 1930s, should we also use the word *globalization* to describe the new worldwide fashion for ultranationalist ideologies? In the 1990s, *globalization* often implied the spread of a globalized corporate capitalism, and the word was frequently used programmatically to refer to a particular set of neoliberal policies. If we use the word simply to mean the globalized circulation of social practices, and beyond that, a heightening of global synchronicity, then the 1930s was a critical "globalizing" moment in its own right. But whether we describe it as a new style of fascist globalization or as a reversal of liberal globalization, Japan in any case appears as a first mover. This is true when it came to adopting the new imperialism, the new militarism, and the new bloc economics of the era. We can date that movement from September 18, 1931, when Japanese Kwantung Army forces launched their conquest of northeast China. Their secretly planned campaign had a strong domestic political aspect, being in many ways a local coup d'état directed against the authority of the pro-Western "gold standard" cabinet in Tokyo. As we have noted, the Kwantung Army's action came on the same weekend that the British government ended the gold convertibility of the pound sterling. In retrospect, this was the end of an era. Four months later, at the end of January 1932, Japanese naval forces attacked the Chinese section of Shanghai, which was not only China's commercial and financial capital but was also adjacent to Shanghai's International Settlement, which was the semicolonial headquarters of Western capital in China. On February 9, 1932, a member of an ultra-nationalist group assassinated former finance minister Inoue Junnosuke. Inoue's murder was one of a series of political assassinations and coup plots in Tokyo. Japan's civilian government thereafter realigned itself with military goals, and in February 1933, Japan's representatives walked out of the League of Nations.

Japan's break with the Western world order came at the same historical moment that Chancellor Hitler, from the peak of the state apparatus in Germany, was directing his own "top-down" coup. Hjalmar Schacht returned to office in March 1933 as Hitler's central bank governor and was Hitler's overall economic czar from 1934, with the mission of establishing a Berlin-centered regional economic order. In East Asia, Tokyo began to function more than ever as the financial capital of an imperial economic bloc. Japan's network of parastatal "special banks" had by the beginning of the 1940s expanded to some 185 branches and offices, 160 of which were in Asia. The Yokohama Specie Bank alone had 76 branches, of which 61 were international.[67] Japan's trade was settled in yen drafts as much as possible, and gold was reserved for the strategic purchase of supplies from other economic blocs such as the British Empire and the United States. In this Orwellian world, the Bank of Japan itself was reorganized in 1940 along the lines of the Nazi Reichsbank, and it took on the role of a "Greater East Asian" central bank during the war.[68] With movements for national or imperial autarky happening on all sides, economic de-globalization was now truly a global current in thought and policy.[69]

Conclusion

PRIVATE NETWORKS AND THE PUBLIC INTEREST

> I remember well his [Benjamin Strong's] telling me two startling things.
> First, that the power that he and his colleagues had was so great that he
> shuddered to think of how it could be abused and how it could really be
> prevented from being abused.
>
> Second, that he did not want to have any legislative guidance for fear that in
> exercising the powers he and his colleagues might not be able to measure up
> to the requirements of law.
>
> IRVING FISHER to Clark Warburton, 1946

The previous chapter offered some conclusions concerning the rhythm of
financial globalization, which attained a historic peak in the 1920s, and
concerning the scramble for gold, the possession of which became so concentrated that it could no longer serve its former monetary role. In this
final chapter we return to the questions of our three "capitals of capital"
and of the banks that were at their centers. These metageographies of capital are as much virtual and communicative as tangible and real.[1] Despite
the intangibility of these operations, however, they have been persistently
rooted in particular places. Tokyo, New York, and London, and their central banks, have also in recent decades been the center of credit bubbles
of historically unprecedented magnitude. We see here some extraordinary
departures and some unexpected continuities, and we see, again, the quiet
but surprisingly central place of Japan. Especially notable is the way that
Japan has been an involuntary pioneer in the new world of post-bubble
economics.

Hierarchical Markets

Markets are places where people meet to buy and sell. In the present book, we have dealt with the making and managing of *meta-markets*, where people buy and sell the means to purchase in other markets. Many social scientists treat markets and hierarchies as opposites. At the apex of the market economy, however, markets themselves become less marketlike. Operations at these peak levels involve just a few organizations, which are often modestly staffed. State agencies and private agencies often blend together at these levels. These operations are also framed by elaborate, ideologically dense social codes that need the attention of anthropologists as well as economists, sociologists, and historians.

The language used in these exchanges already begins to suggest their strangeness as markets. For example, in the market for bonds (one kind of promise to pay), the products on sale were said to be "issued" and "floated," then "taken" or "carried," to be later "redeemed" or "dishonored." The market for gold—on the face of things an elemental, tangible commodity—was especially strange. Gold was not said to be sold in this market but rather was "accepted" and "realized" (that is, as money). Having had its price "fixed," it was "married," and frequently "sterilized" after that. The business of handling gold was also a primary business of central banks—in fact, handling gold was one of the few substantially physical operations that central banks engaged in. Central banks were entrusted with the collection, marketization, transport, and storage of gold, and payments imbalances between nations were ultimately settled by gold being moved from one to another of these central banks. Central banks were accordingly much more than "guardians"—they were fixers and brokers who facilitated the very largest of international financial transactions. Indeed, the first great age of central bank influence ended with the withdrawal from circulation and de-commodification of gold in the United States in 1933. The working of the gold standard was typically presented at the time, and has often been presented since, as the automatic effect of quasi-natural forces—a system in which the proper institutional framework, once set into place, would enable and indeed force proper system functioning. There was always a large element of mythmaking and mystification in this naturalistic account, and one of our tasks has been to identify actors and understand their agency in the framing and operation of this system.

Prior to August 1914, direct connections between central banks were episodic and relatively rare. The secret arrangements between the Bank of England and the Bank of Japan were thus an early development in the history of regularized central bank cooperation. The 1902 Anglo-Japanese alliance was also a significant departure, for both countries. For Britain, it meant abandoning the nineteenth-century policy of "isolation." These facts are well known to diplomatic historians but deserve reemphasis: Britain's historic reengagement in the international military alliance system—lighting the "long fuse" that led to the explosion of 1914—began outside Europe, with the Anglo-Japanese alliance.[2] For Japan, allying with Britain meant joining the European imperial-state system at the height of the age of "Great Powers," and it cleared the way for building an empire on the Asian mainland.

Secrecy was intrinsic to many of these relations. Concerning the intelligence-sharing dimensions of the Anglo-Japanese alliance, John Chapman has written that Japan and Britain both had extremely secretive governments, but "their collaboration as allies was attended by dimensions of secrecy considerably greater than the sum of the individual publicly admitted parts."[3] The same appears to be true of the financial relations between their central banks. Tight-knit national elites facilitated this style of quiet international understanding; we see it again, along a North Atlantic axis, in the Norman-Strong connection. Although central banks took on a wide range of governing functions and shared in state authority, most central banks remained privately owned and jealous of their private prerogatives.[4] This private character was very strongly marked in the Bank of England and was replicated in some of its key features in the Federal Reserve Bank of New York. Cooperation between central banks thus arose in the context of the international cooperation of private banks, which has a much longer history, while central bankers themselves were largely drawn from these wider banking circles.

In the 1920s, central banks enjoyed an influence without prior historical parallel, and they cooperated with each other in an unprecedented way. This was the first great age of central banks, and the first great age of central bankers. Individual central bank governors exercised an authority within their national economies and in the wider world economy that they would not have again until the 1980s and 1990s. The context of this influence was created by the First World War, and more than that, by the projects of price deflation and international monetary reconstruction that followed the war. In their execution of these programs, central bankers practiced a private diplomacy of their own, on a newly opened "central bank" track. They worked in partnership with leading private bankers, while private bankers themselves, preeminently Thomas W. Lamont of J.P. Morgan & Company, played a quasi-public role in the reorganization of national monetary and financial arrangements.

Beginning with the US restoration of the gold standard in June 1919 and driven forward by the British restoration of the gold standard in April 1925, fifty countries either restored gold-standard systems or adopted them for the first time.[5] These monetary operations were often combined with the establishing of new or reorganized central banks. The movement to restore and extend the gold standard culminated with Japan's return to the gold standard in January 1930. The US dollar, British pound, and Japanese yen were thus restored to their prewar gold pars. All this contributed to a great increase in the purchasing power of gold. On an enormously larger scale, it also increased the purchasing power of debt instruments linked to gold. Those holding debt claims were enriched, while those owing debts were more heavily burdened. In support of the American, then British, then Japanese restorations of the gold standard, financial authorities in the three countries conducted severe deflation policies first in 1920–21, then in 1925–26, and finally in 1929–30. Prices in all three countries were thereby pushed down nearly to the "normal" levels that prevailed before the war.

Central bank cooperation, as a new feature of the international politics of the 1920s, has been viewed by many scholars as something akin to the League of Nations—a hopeful but failed experiment. This system of cooperation was indeed the financial counterpart of the League of Nations system, and the two were directly linked.[6] And international communication and cooperation are certainly good things in general. The problems appear when we consider which institutions and whose concerns were included in this supranational governance network, and which were excluded, and when we consider the actual details of "common doctrine" and "sound policies." The central and private bankers introduced in the present book all believed in the civilizing force of what is now called financial globalization. Modern believers in the same idea might be reassured if we could conclude that rational, enlightened economic cooperation was developing in a wholesome way in the 1920s but then was cut short by "exogenous"

factors in the form of brutal and irrational nationalist rivalries. This is
how the story was told afterward by Thomas Lamont and others.[7] It is
also how the story is told, more or less, in many of the history books. The
problem with this version of events is that the internationalist financial
order of the 1920s ultimately failed for reasons *internal* to that order. The
conclusion of the foregoing chapters should therefore be repeated: in its
own time, in its own terms, the policy results of the London–New York
consensus looked like a great success, notwithstanding the feeling among
British male elites that their "restoration" efforts fell short of the world of
1913. In May 1919, when the "restoration" effort was getting under way,
no country's currency was freely convertible into gold. Ten years later,
in late 1929, when the new Japanese cabinet was implementing its own
preparations for a return to the gold standard, almost all countries were
on some form of gold standard or gold-exchange standard. The only independent countries that lacked gold or gold-exchange standards, according
to a survey by the gold-standard consultant Dr. Edwin Kemmerer, were
China, Spain, Turkey, and the USSR.[8] (In fact, the Soviet Union adopted
a gold ruble as part of its own currency stabilization in 1924, though it was
not part of the international gold-standard system.) These monetary operations all involved international cooperation, and usually financial credits,
often conducted through central-bank channels. These operations were
also done at international insistence, as informal metropolitan bank cartels
made gold convertibility a condition for the issuance of international loans.
In May 1919, central banks were rarely found outside of Europe. Just ten
years later, however, twenty new central banks had been chartered around
the globe, mostly with foreign assistance. And finally in the spring of 1930,
shortly after Japan completed its own return to the gold standard, central
bankers opened their own central bank, the Bank for International Settlements, owned by its member central banks and serving as an international
depository for gold and as a meeting place for central bank governors. In
line with the new London–New York vision, physical gold holdings had
indeed been concentrated mainly in a few "central reservoirs," above all in
New York, London, and now again Paris. The use of gold coins as a means
of daily exchange was a thing of the past. For international banks, however,
borders were now generally open, meaning that large claims held in the
form of national currencies could be converted into gold, and gold could
be freely exported. *Never in history had there been anything approaching this*

level of conscious coordination of international monetary and financial affairs.
But to what end, and in whose interest? The program had succeeded, but
the program itself was the problem.[9]

One can therefore take the argument we have presented concerning
the timing of financial globalization a step further: it was less the deficien-
cies of financial globalization in the 1920s and more its excesses that led
to the unprecedentedly globalized depression of the 1930s. In both Japan
and Germany, the self-inflicted collapse of financially oriented liberalism
in 1930–31 preceded the victory of fascism; the reaction against financial
globalization became politically potent only after the collapse of the global
debt bubble in 1929–33. Could fascist ideas and practices have gained
political hegemony in any case? We cannot know, but we do know that
economic depression and attendant social stresses created the conditions
for fascism to flourish. In all these connections, the issues at stake in "global
financial governance" were enormous, just as they are today.

"Capitals of Capital"

"Capitals of capital"—this is the apt description of Youssef Cassis.[10] The
present investigation has focused on the connections of the three "capital
cities" of Tokyo, London, and New York. This trilateral geography has
been analyzed by several writers in reference to developments late in the
twentieth century. Saskia Sassen's influential account described these three
cities as "command and control" centers of international capital. As a heu-
ristic device, we have found it useful, even unexpectedly useful for thinking about the early part of the twentieth century. It is more useful still in
thinking about recent developments.

If we view Britain and its empire, the United States, and Japan terri-
torially as nations or even as imperial systems, they may appear relatively
incommensurable. If we focus on their financial capitals, another set of
features comes into view. It is first of all interesting to note that over the
course of the past two or three centuries these three megacities have succeeded each other as the world's largest city—in fact, as the largest cities
in world history. London was the world's most populous city, by far, in
the nineteenth century, growing from about one million in 1800 to over
seven million in 1914. London's population has remained roughly around

the seven or eight million level since then. New York surpassed London as the world's most populous metropolitan area in the first third of the twentieth century, reaching the fifteen million level in the 1950s. The Tokyo metropolitan area then overtook New York as the world's largest city in the 1960s, ultimately surpassing the thirty million level. This was not the first time for Tokyo to be in this position. Around the year 1700, Edo, as the city was formerly called, was probably also the world's largest city, with a population of around one million.[11] London around 1700 was already Europe's greatest metropolis, with a population of more than half a million. We are evidently talking about much more than finance when we approach modern history from the standpoint of these three cities.

Tokyo at the beginning of the twentieth century was a fast-growing national financial center. Even then, however, it had not completely displaced Osaka in this role.[12] Vis-à-vis London, Tokyo was then a center for receiving capital. At the same time, at a micro level—a hidden and highly strategic one—the Bank of Japan began to make some of its own borrowed funds available for the Bank of England's various market operations.

The relationship between the Bank of Japan and the Bank of England highlights another fact: the primacy of the pound sterling was itself mainly an extra-European phenomenon. Within Europe, the international usage of the French franc and that of the German mark were both roughly on a level with that of the British pound. It was outside Europe that the British pound predominated as an international currency, as appears in Peter Lindert's picture of world currency reserves in 1913.[13] Japan in 1913 held the largest sterling reserves of any country, while Japan and India between them held three-quarters of official sterling reserves. Britain's financing of American trade and industry, Britain's informal economic predominance in South America, its formal empire in Africa, and its formal and informal empires in Asia were other aspects of this world picture.[14] In Europe, Britain was a power among powers. The popular conception of British hegemony, if it applies anywhere, refers to the world outside Europe.

New York City began the twentieth century as a great national financial center and as the main conduit for British capital coming into the United States. The First World War brought a surge of credit creation and international lending by New York City banks; the roles of the world's financial capitals shifted.[15] In Tokyo, neither Inoue Junnosuke's "London of the East" initiative nor the wartime surge of Japanese international lending had the intended results. In London, American-oriented financial elites began to imagine that their way forward lay in serving as the receiving end of a channel of capital flowing from the United States to the Old World, in a new Atlantic age. In Japan, in parallel, American-oriented elites began to envision a new Pacific age. These were both images of a dawning American age. Although London's international financial position declined relative to New York's after 1914, London remained the most infrastructurally central and internationalized of world financial centers. London's place in the gold trade was central to this position, for when it came to gold, it was London that supplied other centers. London thus remained a leading international center for "processing" capital and for making decisions about its investment, well after the rise of New York.

If we focus on the financial connections between international financial centers, the greatest fact is the emergence of "the New York–London axis."[16] J. P. Morgan & Company had a peak role in regard to the management of this capital connection already in the late nineteenth century, when it was mainly a matter of organizing British investment into the United States. The First World War, and the deepened connection of the New York and London central banks, turned the New York–London connection into the central axis of the world financial system as a whole. Again, financial alliance prepared the way for military alliance. The Second World War, meaning the creation of a standing US-British military alliance as a permanent feature of the new international order, supported this relationship in the strongest way, and it was institutionalized in the Bretton Woods order.[17] At the same time, the Japanese war against the US and British positions in Asia and the Pacific temporarily shut down the relatively newly established links between Tokyo–London and Tokyo–New York. In view of the war's ferocity, what is most surprising is how quickly these connections were restored after 1952.

In 1991, when Saskia Sassen's account of "the global city" was published, part of its novelty was to emphasize the *addition* of Tokyo to the London–New York financial axis, and the way the three cities combined to form the apexes of an integrated global hierarchical system. At that time, about 80 percent of world stock-market "capitalization" was listed in the stock markets of these three world cities (measured by the current prices of the shares of listed firms). As it seemed then, Tokyo had become the main center for the "export" of credit-capital. London was the main center for "processing" credit-capital. And New York was the main receiver (borrower) of credit-capital, and the center for decisions concerning its actual investment. Enabled by new information and communication technologies, the three cities merged into an interlinked twenty-four-hour financial marketplace.[18] That was something new at the time. It was around this time that Japan became the world's largest net creditor country. This movement was associated with the great appreciation of the yen, which rose from a rate of ¥360 per dollar in the fixed-rate era of 1949–71 to about ¥125 per dollar at the end of 1991.

The year 1991 was also when Tokyo's "bubble economy" was entering its long deflationary descent into the so-called "lost decade" (or decades—for one measure of the bubble's significance is how long the post-bubble deflation has continued). Since then, among analysts who don't know Japan very well, there has been a tendency to forget about Tokyo entirely. Simultaneously, international financial centers have multiplied. Continental European centers disrupted by twentieth-century wars have recovered their former positions; the historic restoration of France and Germany as capital centers has itself been remarkable. The really new thing has been the development of Asian financial centers—Tokyo's rise was the beginning but obviously far from the end of this movement. Hong Kong, Shanghai, and Singapore have become international financial centers. (There are continuities here as well—two of these capitals of capital were British colonial entrepôts, while the third originated as an international treaty port, another British initiative.) China's central financial institutions have surpassed even Japan's in their holdings of US Treasury securities ($1.25 trillion in October 2015, against $1.15 trillion for Japan), although according to the most recent comprehensive report available, Japanese holdings of all categories of US government debt were still the largest of any country, at $1.92 trillion in mid 2014.[19] In net overall terms, Japan appears so far to remain the world's largest creditor country. The state-owned Chinese banks have surged to the top of the world's debt-claim tables, in much the way that the big Japanese banks did at the end of the 1980s. To what extent this represents a great Chinese bubble remains to be seen. In any case, bubbles and their effects also pass, and a long view suggests that we are nearer the beginning than the end of China's financial rise. The emergence of new centers has created a manifestly multipolar financial geography in East Asia, parallel to the multipolar geography that has reemerged in Europe. Historically, this kind of multipolar finance appears to be a normal state of affairs.

In the face of these changes, it is also remarkable to see London's ongoing position as global financial center, a role now out of all proportion to the radically diminished position of British commerce and industry. London's repeated reinvention as a financial center has been well analyzed by historians.[20] It is Tokyo's place in this geography that needs reemphasis.

Capital City Bubbles

In the years since 1989, first Tokyo and then, eighteen years later, New York and London jointly have been at the center of what have been, each in their turn, the largest bubbles in international financial history. The three central banks have also set new records for the bailouts of their countries' private banking systems. The bailouts themselves are ongoing, and seem, for now, to have taken on a quasi-permanent structural aspect.[21] Their full implications remain to be known. Researchers have only begun to outline the nature and dimensions of the transformations involved; it will likely take decades to begin to grasp their real historical significance.

Tokyo's great bubble reached its peak in 1990. The "bad loans" (*furyō saiken*) underlying the bubble may have come to ¥200 trillion, or roughly $2 trillion. Japan in the quarter century since then has seen the first sustained price deflation anywhere in the world since the 1920s and 1930s. Indeed, back-and-forth swings between stimulus and austerity policies in the Japan of the 1990s were surprisingly similar to those of the 1920s.[22] In this context, Japanese financial officials conducted deregulatory (or re-regulatory) reforms modeled on London's "big bang." The Bank of Japan also initiated such historic departures as the "zero interest-rate policy" (ZIRP) and "quantitative easing" (QE).[23] Under the quantitative easing policy, the Bank of Japan increased its account balances for private banks from the level of ¥5 trillion (roughly $50 billion) in early 2001 to around ¥30–35 trillion in 2004–5. The Bank of Japan then sharply curtailed this immense surge of credit creation in 2006.[24] Quantitative easing and near-zero interbank interest rates also promoted the international yen "carry trade," as Japanese banks created credits for foreign banks to deploy abroad. In the early 2000s, the yen carry trade (which does not appear in statistics concerning the yen's international use) appears to have played an important but little-documented role in the buildup of the international bubble that had its greatest centers in New York and London.[25]

The New York–London financial bubble came to its own peak in 2007. In a striking way, the bubble was jointly produced in both New York and London; this aspect of synchronized coproduction needs further study.[26] Also in need of examination are the connections, or lack of connections, to developments in Tokyo. Japan itself largely stood aside from the international bubble, instead experiencing an unusually long and slow recovery during the early 2000s.[27] The deflating of the Anglo-American bubble after 2008 then brought a great reverse flow of funds to Japan, causing the yen's exchange rate to surge. The international crisis had its great impact on Japan's export trade, which suffered an enormous sudden decline in 2008. Japanese exports of financial capital, however, again began to surge.

Events in New York and London since the collapses of 2008 indicate both radical changes and deep continuities. The central banks have been more than ever at the center of things, making a series of extraordinary purchases of the questionable debt claims held by the private banks. The magnitude of these "asset" purchases is not easily grasped. Following the September 2008 "Lehman shock" (as it was called in Japan), the consolidated balance sheet of the Federal Reserve banks doubled in only four months, to reach $2.2 trillion.[28] And if one looks at what were euphemistically called "policy assets," one sees not a doubling but rather an increase of more than 4,000 percent. Much of this lending happened through the quick creation of entirely new lending instruments. Considerable secrecy surrounded these operations. One result noted by Peter Stella in 2009: "by some measures the Fed is now the largest bank in the United States."[29] Simultaneously, the biggest private banks were themselves consolidated and enlarged—as Japan's megabanks already had been a few years earlier.[30] More than six years after the bailouts began, the Federal Reserve System in 2014 was continuing to buy unwanted "mortgage-backed securities" from the private banks at the rate of billions per month; the Fed's balance sheet now surpassed $4 trillion.[31] By this measure, the US Federal Reserve had become *the largest bank in the world*. In effect, the Federal Reserve banks bought the bubble, or at least a large part of it, from the big private banks, thus socializing their debts across the whole economy. This too echoes Japanese experience. However, it happened on a scale more than ten times greater, and in an even more sudden, irreversible, and seemingly haphazard way. In an indirect sense, via its purchase of mortgage-backed securities, the Federal Reserve System had also become one of the world's largest landlords. None of this has a place in central-banking theory; and narrow theorizing about central-banking practice cannot begin to capture the wider socioeconomic effects and implications of these changes.

In the context of the present study, two points are especially noteworthy. First, a significant part of these new Federal Reserve credits went to other central banks and was used by them to help bail out private banks in their own countries. This was central bank cooperation on an entirely new scale. The Federal Reserve thus acted as a global central bank, providing dollar credits, as in Montagu Norman's 1921 vision, via the agency of foreign central banks. This movement began in December 2007 with Fed credits to the European Central Bank (ECB) and the Swiss National Bank (SNB). In October 2008, the ECB, the SNB, the Bank of England, and the Bank of Japan were designated to receive "unlimited" credit facilities from the US Federal Reserve. Ten other countries' central banks received credit facilities of either $15 billion or $30 billion each. By the end of 2008, these banks had actually drawn on credits totaling nearly $600 billion, with the biggest shares going to the ECB, the BoJ, and the BoE.[32] (The participation of the Bank of Japan may have been a kind of window dressing, as it probably had no need of additional credit facilities.) As in Norman's international operations in the 1920s, these operations were highly secret, mysterious, and suspiciously opaque.[33]

The second notable point, also harking back to the era of Benjamin Strong, is the way in which the Federal Reserve Bank of New York led this movement. As of April 2009, the FRBNY accounted for 50 percent of total Federal Reserve Bank assets. It accounted for 73 percent of "risk assets."[34] By this measure also, New York was evidently at the center of all things financial.

Other central banks also expanded after September 2008, though not to this enormous scale. Proportionally to its size, however, the Bank of England expanded even more than the Federal Reserve in late 2008, when it more than tripled its debt holdings.[35] There were other historic departures. Central-bank interest rates, again following a Japanese precedent, were reduced to the lowest levels in their history. Gold prices reached historic highs, peaking in August and September 2011 at over $1,900 per ounce, an increase of fifty-four times over the $35 level of 1934–71. Formally, gold no longer has the slightest monetary role. Nonetheless, the central banks that manage the world's money and credit continue to hold immense volumes of gold, and they seem to want to hold it physically in their own vaults.

The US bubble itself was a massive transfer of wealth, to the wealthiest part of American society. This social aspect of financial bubbles is also in need of detailed study. The disposition of the bubble after the fact also constituted an extraordinary financial coup, which was conducted by and for many of the same big institutional players that had created the bubble in the first place. The biggest banks have been the channel for extraordinary stimulus policies, sometimes described as a kind of financial Keynesianism. Meanwhile, more "peripheral" social sectors have experienced austerity policies that recall the era of the Great Depression. The context of all of this is a world in which, as of 2015, the richest 1 percent appear to own some 50 percent of the world's wealth.[36] As before, the issues at stake in "global financial governance" are enormous. The challenges to open, accountable functioning in this institutional field are great. The challenges to truly democratic functioning are even greater. Many of the institutional structures, practices, and ideologies at work are historically entrenched. History teaches us, however, that these arrangements have changed and will change, and in profound ways.

Finally, concerning the place of Japan, we conclude by noting the international reemergence of Japanese finance in the aftermath of the New York– and London-centered bubble. Japanese banks, after a long period of reducing their holdings of bad loans, were in 2011 back to a number-three position internationally (measured by credits outstanding), after the United States and the United Kingdom.[37] In 2013, according to a BIS report, Japanese banks became the world's biggest suppliers of cross-border bank credit. As the authors of the report noted, "this marks a return of Japanese banks to the position that they held in the international banking market in the second half of the 1980s." During the banking crisis of the 1990s, Japanese banks pulled back sharply from their overseas operations. Their share of the international lending market reached a low in 2007, when the New York–London bubble was at its peak. In the rebound since then, "Japanese banks funded their cross-border expansion mainly through financing raised in Japan. . . . Their cross-border claims increased to $4 trillion in the first quarter of 2013." In 2015, BIS data indicated that Japanese banks were back in "pole position in cross-border lending."[38]

Was this surge of international credit creation a side-effect of unsustainable Japanese government stimulus policies, again run through the banking sector? Certainly, the persistence and recovery of Tokyo's international financial position has been helped by extraordinary subsidies, provided directly by the Bank of Japan and indirectly by the rest of Japanese society. What this kind of financial leveraging may mean for Japan's own future is a subject of intense speculation. In any case, no matter how the problems of the present may appear in the historical retrospect of another century, there are important reasons to keep our eyes on these three central places in international finance.

Appendix

Reference Material

TABLE A.1. Bank of England reserves and Bank of Japan accounts, 1904–1916 (in thousands of British pounds; continuation of table 2.1 in chapter 2)

		A	B	C	D
			Bank of England gold reserve	Bank of Japan "A" account (red-inked under "other private deposits")	BoJ balances as a proportion of BoE gold reserve ($C/B \times 100$) (%)
Date (year in quarters)		Total BoE reserves			
1904	Sep. 1	34,872	26,409	2,785	11
	Dec. 1	30,533	23,530	1,724	7
1905	Mar. 1	37,074	29,852	1,405	5
	June 1	35,923	26,683	1,224	5
	Sep. 1	34,550	24,922	2,601	10
	Dec. 1	31,255	22,375	3,516	16
1906	Mar. 1	35,490	27,304	2,795	10
	June 1	31,740	22,164	4,085	18
	Sep. 1	36,860	27,442	2,696	10
	Dec. 1	31,504	22,839	2,981	13

(*Continued*)

TABLE A.1. (Continued)

Date (year in quarters)		A Total BoE reserves	B Bank of England gold reserve	C Bank of Japan "A" account (red-inked under "other private deposits")	D BoJ balances as a proportion of BoE gold reserve ($C/B \times 100$) (%)
1907	Mar. 1	34,289	25,808	1,203	5
	June 1	33,793	24,451	1,472	6
	Sep. 2	36,494	26,645	3,643	14
	Dec. 2	31,465	21,590	3,448	16
1908	Mar. 2	37,774	29,162	2,300	8
	June 1	36,716	27,401	2,047	7
	Sep. 1	36,646	27,097	1,816	7
	Dec. 1	32,923	24,007	1,580	7
1909	Mar. 1	36,216	27,232	1,593	6
	June 1	35,823	26,138	1,712	7
	Sep. 1	38,704	28,928	1,022	4
	Dec. 1	35,035	25,776	1,163	5
1910	Mar. 1	34,923	26,335	915	3
	June 1	39,312	30,517	705	2
	Sep. 1	38,293	29,316	1,193	4
	Dec. 1	34,374	25,439	781	3
1911	Mar. 1	37,063	29,081	772	3
	June 1	37,564	28,491	1,806	6
	Sep. 1	40,010	29,299	972	3
	Dec. 1	36,002	26,409	778	3
1912	Mar. 1	37,721	29,306	3,277	11
	June 1	38,231	29,145	444	2
	Sep. 2	40,755	30,976	617	2
	Dec. 2	35,536	26,365	456	2
1913	Mar. 1	36,197	27,589	582	2
	June 2	36,143	27,440	534	2
	Sep. 1	41,792	32,178	611	2
	Dec. 1	35,100	26,090	422	2
1914	Mar. 2	40,459	31,831	619	2
	June 2	34,421	25,284	458	2
	Sep. 1	43,335	27,118	973	4
	Dec. 1	71,734	54,926	458	1
1915	Mar. 1	59,395	44,609	527	1
	June 1	59,316	45,309	533	1
	Sep. 1	67,466	54,558	543	1
	Dec. 1	51,100	35,414	469	1
1916	Mar. 1	55,235	41,253	549	1
	May 2	56,116	41,210	474	1

Source: Bank of England Daily Accounts, C1/44 to C1/64, Bank of England Archives, London.

TABLE A.2. Bank of England borrowings from the Bank of Japan (full series) (red-inked at bottom of Daily Account pages)

Date (mm/dd/yy)	Amount (in thousands of British pounds)
December 1904–January 1905	
12/28/04 to 1/11/05	970
1/12/05	470
September 1905–April 1906	
9/20/05 to 10/4/05	1,000
10/5/05	1,600
10/6/05 to 10/9/05	3,850
10/10/05 to 10/11/05	4,450
10/12/05 to 10/19/05	5,550
10/20/05 to 10/25/05	3,300
10/26/05 to 11/2/05	3,100
11/3/05 to 11/11/05	2,900
11/12/05 to 11/13/05	2,800
11/14/05	1,600
11/15/05 to 11/16/05	4,000
11/17/05 to 11/29/05	3,900
11/30/05	2,250
12/1/05 to 12/12/05	1,750
12/13/05	1,550
12/14/05	4,000
12/15/05	8,400
12/16/05 to 12/18/05	8,850
12/19/05 to 12/20/05	8,800
12/21/05	8,600
12/22/05 to 12/27/05	8,800
12/28/05 to 12/29/05	10,100
12/30/05 to 12/31/05	6,600
1/1/1906 to 1/8/06	4,600
1/9/06	4,550
1/10/06	4,400
1/11/06	4,900
1/12/06	4,600
1/13/06 to 1/14/06	7,450
1/15/06	8,400
1/16/06 to 1/17/06	9,650

(Continued)

Date (mm/dd/yy)	Amount (in thousands of British pounds)
1/18/06 to 1/23/06	10,850
1/24/06 to 1/28/06	7,300
1/29/06 to 2/1/06	6,800
2/2/06	9,900
2/3/06 to 2/7/06	10,150
2/8/06 to 2/15/06	9,150
2/16/06 to 2/20/06	7,950
2/21/06 to 2/25/06	4,600
2/26/06 to 2/28/06	2,600
3/1/06 to 3/15/06	1,600
3/16/06 to 4/1/06	600
June 1906	
6/11/06 to 6/24/06	450
August 1906	
8/14/06	500
8/15/06 to 8/20/06	750
8/21/06	350
September 1906–February 1907	
9/11/06 to 9/12/06	750
9/13/06	2,000
9/14/06	3,100
9/15/06	3,475
9/16/06 to 9/25/06	3,400
9/26/06 to 10/14/06	2,900
10/15/06	3,850
10/16/06 to 10/17/06	4,450
10/18/06	4,800
10/19/06 to 10/25/06	5,550
10/26/06 to 11/1/06	4,550
11/2/06 to 11/7/06	4,150
11/8/06 to 11/11/06	3,950
11/12/06 to 11/15/06	3,450
11/16/06 to 11/17/06	2,500
11/18/06	2,100
11/19/06	1,600
11/20/06	1,100

Date (mm/dd/yy)	Amount (in thousands of British pounds)
11/21/06 to 11/24/06	900
11/25/06 to 12/16/06	2,200
12/17/06 to 12/23/06	1,850
12/24/06 to 1/3/07	1,650
1/4/07 to 1/15/07	600
1/16/07	950
1/17/07	2,950
1/18/07 to 1/22/07	5,150
1/23/07 to 1/30/07	4,275
1/31/07 to 2/11/07	3,425
2/12/07 to 2/13/07	3,075
2/14/07	1,400
2/15/07	950
2/16/07 to 2/17/07	350
October 1907	
10/15/07	700
10/16/07 to 10/20/07	2,200
10/21/07	1,600
10/22/07	850
October 1909–December 1909	
10/15/09 to 10/16/09	400
10/17/09 to 10/24/09	4,520
10/25/09	4,620
10/26/09 to 10/28/09	5,220
10/29/09 to 11/1/09	5,720
11/2/09 to 11/3/09	5,770
11/4/09 to 11/7/09	6,120
11/8/09 to 11/10/09	6,520
11/11/09	7,370
11/12/09 to 11/18/09	7,770
11/19/09 to 11/30/09	6,270
12/1/09 to 12/6/09	5,870
12/7/09 to 12/9/09	5,820
12/10/09 to 12/15/09	5,720
12/16/09 to 12/19/09	5,520
12/20/09	4,320

(Continued)

TABLE A.2 (Continued)

Date (mm/dd/yy)	Amount (in thousands of British pounds)
12/21/09	3,920
12/22/09	3,370
12/23/09 to 12/27/09	3,070
12/28/09	2,270
12/29/09 to 12/30/09	700
October 1910–December 1910	
10/19/10	200
10/20/10	450
10/21/10 to 10/24/10	1,170
10/25/10 to 10/27/10	2,170
10/28/10 to 10/30/10	4,170
10/31/10	4,620
11/1/10	3,620
11/2/10	5,470
11/3/10 to 11/6/10	6,120
11/7/10 to 11/10/10	6,370
11/11/10 to 11/21/10	5,370
11/22/10 to 11/23/10	5,620
11/24/10 to 11/28/10	4,620
11/29/10	4,570
11/30/10	3,620
12/1/10	2,900
12/2/10 to 12/4/10	2,500
12/5/10	2,200
12/6/10	1,900
12/7/10	1,600
12/8/10	1,350
12/9/10	1,000
12/10/10 to 12/29/10	850

Source: Bank of England Daily Accounts, C1/44 to C1/64, Bank of England Archives, London.

TABLE A.3. Gold inflows to Japan from Korea, 1911–1936, compared to Japan's overall balance of gold shipments (in millions of yen)

Year	From Korea (net imports)	Overall balance of Japan's gold imports (+) and exports (−)
1911	9.1	−6.7
1912	9.1	−1.0
1913	10.0	−9.3
1914	10.2	−7.4
1915	11.4	−2.8
1916	15.6	+94.4
1917	9.5	+247.2
1918	5.7	+6.2
1919	3.5	+327.7
1920	22.7	+415.5
1921	7.2	+138.1
1922	3.9	+5.5
1923	5.6	+5.8
1924	3.3	+3.4
1925	3.4	−18.6
1926	5.8	−26.2
1927	4.4	−31.7
1928	3.0	+3.4
1929	5.8	+6.2
1930	26.6	−272.9
1931	39.4	−371.4
1932	18.3	−94.4
1933	20.5	−0.5
1934	31.0	+31.0
1935	31.4	+31.5
1936	50.5	+50.5

Source: Nihon Ginkō Tōkeikyoku 1966, 298–299.
Note: Gold was shipped from Taiwan during the first several years after Japanese colonization, after which Japanese gold imports from Taiwan became negligible. Korean gold exports were also sizable during the years before colonization; statistics are given by Schiltz 2012a, 120.

NOTES

Citations of archival materials refer to file and box numbers.

1. The Beginnings of Central Bank Cooperation

Epigraph: Clapham 1944, 1:379.

Simon Bytheway presented an early version of this chapter at the Institute of Financial and Monetary Studies (IMES), Bank of Japan; many thanks to the participants, Masato Shizume, and staff.

1. R. S. Sayers filed an early report on this relationship (Sayers 1936, 40–43; Sayers 1976, 1:31n2, 40–41). The present view is based on a reexamination of the "Histories of the Bank: Prof. R. S. Sayers Research Papers by B/E Staff" (ADM33/10–11, Bank of England Archives, London), which were closed until thirty years after the publication of Sayers's *The Bank of England, 1891–1944*. On completion of Sayers's work, which was commissioned by the Bank of England, some two-thirds of the material gathered for him was deemed redundant and destroyed by the BoE. Archivists fortunately saved important parts of Professor Sayers's notes and other materials, which make up the file today. Sayers thus had full access to three times the material we have today, including day-to-day records, correspondence, and other sources. He was assisted by a team of researchers and archivists, and the Bank of England retained editorial control. In the case of the Bank of Japan, a large part of the historical archive was lost in the great Tokyo earthquake and fire of 1923.

2. Kajima 1976, 264; Matsukata 1899, 166–167. As specified in "Draft No. 2 on the Method and Process and Payment of the War Indemnity," a kuping tael represented 579.84 grains, or 37.5729 grams of silver (Matsukata 1899, 171).

3. Matsukata 1899, 168–171; Muroyama 2005, 259–269; also Bytheway 2001; Bytheway 2005; Schiltz 2012b. Matsukata served as Japan's minister of finance a total of five terms from 1881 to 1900 (Kokushi Daijiten 1979, 555; Ericson 2014 and Ericson forthcoming, for background).

4. Matsukata 1899, 168–171; Matsukata 1900, 214–234.

5. Meiji Zaiseishi Henshūkai 1905, 218–220.

6. Governor to Chancellor of the Exchequer, December 18, 1896, Secretary's Letter Book, G23/87, BoE, 167–169. This was a time when BoE contacts with the exchequer were highly personal, often handled by the BoE governor alone (Sayers 1976, 1:13–14).

7. Daily Accounts–Deputy Governor (Governor's Daily Books), Bank of England [hereafter BoE], C1/44: 66. For the Franco-Russian financial relationship see Kindleberger 1993, 221–223.

8. Kynaston 1995, 126.

9. Platt 1968, 281–283, 294–295; Overlach 1976, 253–254; Kann 1926, 79.

10. Dayer 1988, 36–39.

11. For Japan's central bank cooperation with Germany see Imada 1990, 156.

12. Addis, circa 1896, quoted in Dayer 1988, 39.

13. Esherick 1976.

14. Yokohama Specie Bank 1976, 175.

15. Itoh 1994, 235–237; Tamaki 2005, 128–130.

16. Metzler 2006, 11; Inoue Junnosuke Ronsō Iinkai 1935, 39.

17. Daily Accounts–Deputy Governor (Governor's Daily Books), BoE, C1/44: 66; Nihon Ginkō Chōsakyoku 1897, 1–18.

18. There is still conjecture about what the "A" and "B" accounts denote; they were not referred to in any other specific way. When combined (with other foreign holdings added) they represent the BoJ's foreign specie reserve (zaigai seika), the meaning of which is also still contested among scholars.

19. B. Strong to J. D. Case, March 10, 1921; YSB to FRBNY, March 11, 1921; and "Memorandum on Business Conditions for the Bank of Japan," March 6, 1922; all in Japanese Govt. 1919–50, c.261, Federal Reserve Bank of New York archives; further detail in chap. 7.

20. Nihon Ginkō Kin'yū Kenkyūsho (1993, 61–62, 64–74) describes the history of research concerning these overseas balances. Matsuoka (1936) provides a significant early statement.

21. Governor to Chancellor of the Exchequer, December 18, 1896, Secretary's Letter Book, G23/87, BoE, 167–169; Bytheway 2014, 70–71.

22. Imada 1990, 146–148; Kynaston 1995, 386–408, esp. 387–389.

23. Daily Accounts–Deputy Governor (Governor's Daily Books), BoE, C1/44: 66, C1/45: 66, C1/46: 68.

24. Daily Accounts–Deputy Governor (Governor's Daily Books), BoE, C1/44 to C1/46, and Nihon Ginkō Chōsakyoku 1897, 1–18.

25. Foxwell 1900, 232–245; Matsukata 1900, 217; Tamaki 2005, 129–130. As indicated in the 1900 report issued under Matsukata's name, the Japanese government methodically reserved gold and foreign currencies to supply the Yokohama Specie Bank with "all necessary financial facilities" for making international payments. At the same time, in order to maintain a sufficient gold reserve for the Bank of Japan's convertible notes, "the Bank was to take every pains [sic] to absorb gold" (Matsukata 1900, 251). For the "postwar management" policy see Nagaoka 1973, 111–158, and for a complete Japanese policy history of gold and foreign currency, Saitō 2015.

26. Matsukata 1899, 219–225. Exactly how and when the Chinese indemnity funds were employed is unclear. According to Matsukata's "post-bellum" financial report, the "disposal and disbursement" of indemnity funds went primarily for military expenditure and expansion, with significant funds also allocated to the Imperial Household, a Calamities Reserve, and an Education Fund. Pointedly, Matsukata also emphasized that the Indemnity Fund was used "for supplying a large gold reserve" in order to carry out "the coinage reform of 1897" (Japan's adoption of the gold standard) and "was not in the least part spent off" (Matsukata 1900, 220–221).

27. Wakatsuki (1950) 1983, 121–125.

28. Bytheway 2007, 41–53; Bytheway 2015. It is possible that gold bullion was exported to the Japanese government from the Royal Mints of Sydney and Melbourne between 1896 and 1902,

but records of such a transaction have yet to be found. Given that the Australian Royal Mints preferred to sell gold minted as sovereign coins, and that all significant recorded Japanese gold purchases between 1896 and 1902 were in the form of bullion, the possibility seems unlikely.

29. For financial aspects of the Anglo-Japanese alliance, Bytheway 2014; Hunter 2004. For Russo-Japanese War loans, Suzuki 1994, 69–74, 83–127; Bytheway 2005, 111–117; Bytheway 2014, 75–77, 96–104; Metzler 2006, 45–52, 68–80; Smethurst 2007, 130–133, 141–187; Takahashi 1976, 547–78.

30. Nihon Ginkō 1908, 198.

31. Sayers 1936, 124; Metzler 2013, 254n13. As Lindert (1969, 28) explained it, "Borrowers in the London capital markets were commonly required to keep a certain share of their [loan] proceeds on deposit in London. (For colonies of the lending country, an extra commitment was implied.)" These funds were kept with the banks that extended the loans.

32. Daily Accounts–Deputy Governor (Governor's Daily Books), BoE, C1/52 to C1/64.

33. Ibid.

34. Sayers 1936, 42, 51.

35. Schiltz 2006; Nihon Ginkō 1982, 119, 138–139 (detailed comparisons of regulations on pp. 173–182 and 186–207). For the wider history of institutional emulation and adaptation see Westney 1987.

36. Chernow 1990, 73–77.

37. Schiltz 2012a, chap. 1.

38. Bytheway 2005, 237; Metzler 2006, 30–35; Bryan 2010, 167–172; Schiltz 2012b. For the more general point see Bordo and Rockoff 1996; also Mitchener, Shizume, and Weidenmier 2010 and Bytheway 2014.

39. Ikeda 1949, 60; Asai 1985, 5–10; also Asai 1982, 54–55. Edwin Dun, "the father of the Hokkaido dairy industry," had served in the Hokkaido Development Commission (Kaitakushi) as an agricultural adviser from 1873 to its abolishment in 1882 and was involved in many publicly lauded enterprises, including the construction of Hokkaido's first horse racing track and the establishment of a beer brewery.

40. Asai 1985, 5–10; *Long-Term Economic Statistics of Japan,* vol. 7, for budget figures.

41. See Matsumura 2009.

42. For the loan negotiations and subsequent friendship between Takahashi Korekiyo and Jacob Schiff see Smethurst 2007, 141–187; Bytheway 2005, chap. 6; Metzler 2006, 45–50; Best 1972. Schiff's letters to Takahashi are held in the Takahashi Korekiyo monjo, Kenseishiryōshitsu, National Diet Library, Tokyo.

43. Iriye 1972.

44. Metzler 2006, 55–59. For the South Manchurian Railway see Matsusaka 2001.

45. Clapham 1944, 2:421.

46. Quoted in Sayers 1976, 1:29.

47. Hawtrey 1962b, 1–39; Sayers 1936, 19–48; Sayers 1957, 1–19; Sayers 1976, 1:37–43.

48. Clapham 1944, 2:378.

49. Sayers 1936, 47–53.

50. Sayers 1936, 19–48; Sayers 1976, 1:37–41. India's gold standard reserve was transferred to London in 1902; the British Treasury also intervened at this point to block the construction of a gold mint in Bombay (De Cecco 1974, 69–71).

51. De Cecco 1974, 71–74.

52. Sayers (1936, 42) noted reports in the *Economist* of October 7, 1905, October 20, 1906, and January 19 and February 2, 1907. Reports also appeared in the *Statist.*

53. "Histories of the Bank—Prof. R.S. Sayers," M124.21, BoE, ADM33/11, 23A: 1–2; "Research Papers by B/E Staff," 11–20, M124.21, BoE, ADM33/10, 16C: 1–2; ibid., 21–24; Bytheway 2014, 80–81.

54. Cairncross 1995, 59; Hawtrey 1962b, 115–118.

55. Takahashi 1954, 1:3–5; Fujino 1965, 62; Metzler 2006, 81–83; Clapham 1944, 2:390.

56. Hawtrey 1932, 115–118; Friedman and Schwartz 1963, 156; Sayers 1976, 1:44–45, 55.

57. Clapham 1944, 2:379, 389.

58. Metzler 2006, 69–71. Current research by Michael Schiltz and others on the role of the Yokohama Specie Bank may help clarify these relations.

59. Suzuki 1994, 10–12. Toshio Suzuki's modestly titled book is perhaps the best account available of the actual mechanics of foreign loan issuing in London.

60. Lindert 1969, table 2 (converting Lindert's totals from dollars back into pounds). Sterling holdings thus constituted 80 percent of Japan's total reported foreign exchange holdings in all foreign currencies in 1913. That latter total, reckoned in US dollars, came to $78.3 million for the Bank of Japan, $41.9 million for the government, and $115.7 million for the Yokohama Specie Bank. Russia was in 1913 the only country with larger foreign reserves than Japan; these were mainly French balances, held in Paris. For India's position, see Balachandran 1994, 1996, 2001, 2008, and the classic studies by De Cecco (1974) and Saul (1960).

61. See, among others, Flandreau 1997; Cottrell 1995; Mouré 1992; Eichengreen 1987, 1984; Clarke 1967; and the works cited in chapters 3 and 5.

2. World War and Globalization

Epigraph: Warburg 1914, 160, 163–164, emphasis added.

1. Influential statements include those by Jeffrey Williamson and coauthors (e.g., Williamson 1996) and Jeffry Frieden (2006). Frieden writes, in a major survey of the history of globalization: "It took only a few months for the entire edifice of globalization to collapse. World War One broke out in August 1914 and swept away the foundations of the preexisting global order. . . . For eighty years after 1914 global economic integration existed only in the imagination of theorists and historians" (2006, xvi). Boyce (2009) presents a view closer to the one we offer here.

2. Broz (1997) gives a detailed survey.

3. Myers 1931.

4. The standard biography of Strong is the 1958 study by Lester Chandler. Even at 495 pages, however, it is brief relative to the scope of the subject. Important studies have since been made of Strong's international policies, including the notable contribution of Priscilla Roberts (2000), who also provides a comprehensive index to the literature. Allan Meltzer's 2003 history of the early Federal Reserve also treats Strong extensively; see also Wueschner 1999.

5. Chandler 1958, 25–30.

6. The US Treasury first went to the aid of Wall Street on October 24, 1906, by depositing $25 million in New York banks; J. P. Morgan then stepped in to organize an equally large funding pool for the banks (Friedman and Schwartz 1963, 159–160; also Chernow 1990, 122–127; Greider 1987, 273–274).

7. Chernow 1993, 133–137; Chandler 1958, 31–41 (quotations from Strong to Hahn, December 26, 1913, and Strong to Warburg, November 17, 1916).

8. For Hoover and Strong see Wueschner 1999.

9. Toniolo 2005, 16–18; Borio and Toniolo 2006, 9, and 2008, 27. R. Roberts (2013) gives a full account of the 1914 financial crisis. The BoE, backed up by the Treasury, purchased a volume of bills that peaked at £133 million on September 4, 1914, at a time when the size of the entire London discount market was estimated to be £350 million (R. Roberts 2013, 157–158).

10. Flandreau 1997; Eichengreen 1992, 7–9, 30–31, 42–54; Mouré 1992, 260; Cassis 2011, 113–121; see also Mouré 2002, 145–179; Singleton 2011, 91–109; and for a counterview, Parent 2008.

11. Keynes 1914 offers an interesting early statement of the official view. Keynes also charged that the big joint-stock banks lacked "public spirit" by hoarding sovereigns and depleting the

BoE's reserves (R. Roberts 2013, 48–69, 230; also De Cecco 1974, chap. 7); we return to this question in chapter 7. On the British financial moratorium in August 1914 see Sayers 1976, 1:70–78.

12. "Sir John Clapham's Account of the Financial Crisis in August 1914," in Sayers 1976, appendixes, 31–45 (quotation, 45).

13. Hennessy 1992, 236.

14. Hankey (1860, 49–53) gives an early statement on this originally domestically oriented institution; also Francis 1888, 179–183.

15. Hennessy 1992, 236. The India Office (IO) long supported the Bank of England in this way. At its inception in 1859, the India Office's BoE non-interest earning account had an agreed minimum of £0.5m. In many years the IO lost £11 thousand to £16.5 thousand in foregone interest; it appealed "on bended knee" to the BoE to reduce the balance or provide some compensating returns, but without success. Moreover, in November 1913, the IO's BoE non-interest earning account had a revised minimum of £1m, to which was added a quarter of any amount up to £6m borrowed from London's financial market, and an additional fifth on amounts between £6m and 10m (Sunderland 2013, 190–206). As another instance, at the outbreak of the 1914 war the National Bank of Australasia "realized that it might have to borrow heavily in an emergency, and it opened a current deposit account with the Bank of England and deposited £100,000 in order to be on the bank's 'list of favoured customers'" (Blainey 1958, 273).

16. P. Roberts (1998, 619) concluded also that the war enabled the FRBNY "to strengthen its position vis-à-vis the rest of the [Federal Reserve] System through collaboration with the Morgan firm and cooperative relationships with the Bank of England and the Banque de France."

17. Dayer 1988, 81, 92.

18. Chandler 1958, 30–31, 94–97; T. Lamont 1933, 59–60; "Correspondence with Great Britain: Letters to/from Montagu Norman, Deputy Governor, Bank of England (1916–1920)," file 1116.1, Benjamin Strong papers, (hereafter Strong papers), held in the archives of the Federal Reserve Bank of New York.

19. Boyle 1967 for a biography.

20. Chandler 1958, particularly 260–261, and Norman's emotional final letter to Strong on September 6, 1928, shortly before Strong's death (472–473): "renew your life and spirit as none other can do so well as you. And remember—when the time comes—let me be near to hold your hand and to watch the coming as well as the going.—God bless you and my love now and ever."

21. "The select few in New York were privileged to know more about the Bank of England's intentions than any Englishman outside of the Treasury and the Bank itself" (Sayers 1976, 1:121).

22. Strong to Norman, January 19, 1917, file 1116.1, Strong papers; *Federal Reserve Bulletin* 3 (January 1, 1917): 5.

23. *Federal Reserve Bulletin* 3 (March 1, 1917): 175. Reciprocal accounts between the FRBNY and the Bank of France were opened only later (Norman to Strong, September 10, 1918, file 1116.1, Strong papers).

24. P. Roberts 1998, 605–607.

25. Shimazaki 1989, 119.

26. Schiltz 2012a, 90–117, 152; Metzler 2006, 52–54; *Nihon Ginkō hyakunenshi*, 2:462–465.

27. US Bureau of the Census 1960, 537.

28. Strong to Tokyo Ginko Club, May 24, 1920, file 1000.4 (1), Strong papers. This was part of an explanation Strong made to the Tokyo Bank Club during his 1920 trip, described in chapter 5.

29. Federal Reserve System 1943, 539; gold valued at $20.67 per fine ounce.

30. "Development of the Acceptance Business," *Federal Reserve Bulletin* 1 (May 1, 1915): 52–54; Chandler 1958, 60–63, 88–93. For the echoes of the July–August 1914 financial crisis in New York see R. Roberts 2013, 208–212.

31. On the element of Anglo–American rivalry see, e.g., Withers 1918, 98–109; also Burk 1992.

32. Memorandum, January 6, 1916, by Mr. Montagu Norman re Mr. Strong's letter of December 10, 1915, file 1116.1, Strong papers. Norman wrote: "The fact that the dividing line [between commercial bills and finance bills] had been defined by tradition rather than words has contributed, I should maintain, in no small degree to its success when considered over a number of years. Its elasticity and even uncertainty have allowed to a wonderful extent a constantly shifting basis for the approval of Bills (by the Bank of England) which has been modified from week to week, or month to month, to suit the particular needs or dangers of the moment. From which it may be argued that the shadow or fear of the 'big stick' is apt to be more effective than its definition in black and white."

33. Ferderer 2003, 667.

34. Ibid., 672, 692. According to Federal Reserve estimates, total acceptances outstanding in the London market in November 1918 were roughly $500 million, while those in New York now came to $365 million ("Bankers' Acceptances in London and New York," *Federal Reserve Bulletin* 5 (January 1, 1919): 21–22.

35. Federal Reserve Board, *Federal Reserve Bulletin* (1915–).

36. P. Roberts 1998.

37. P. Roberts 1998, 602–604. Significantly, Paul Warburg and Benjamin Strong neatly reversed positions after the war. Then, Warburg supported looser rules for acceptance credits, with the idea of simultaneously funding both European reconstruction and American exports. (In this, Warburg anticipated the logic of the Marshall Plan after the Second World War.) Strong after the war rejected looser financing and enforced monetary contraction and deflation (P. Roberts 1998, 617–618).

38. Chernow 1993; Reifer (2000) for more on Wall Street's early and influential backing of the war.

39. Mayer 1973; Cleveland and Huertas 1985, 77–84; see also Prasad 1999.

40. Cleveland and Huertas 1985, 34, 40–42, 55–57.

41. Asahi Shinbunsha 1925; Cleveland and Huertas 1985, 45.

42. Cleveland and Huertas 1985, 61, 68–70.

43. For the wider context, Rosenberg 1999, esp. 81–93; for Haiti, *Foreign Relations of the United States*, 1914, 362–382.

44. "Foreign Business of the National City Bank of New York," *Federal Reserve Bulletin* 4 (October 1, 1918): 942–947; Scheiber 1969, 487.

45. Cleveland and Huertas 1985, 81, 123, 150; Citigroup, "Citigroup's History" (2005), at www.citigroup.com/citigroup/corporate/history/citibank.htm; Bytheway 2014, chaps. 5–6.

46. Chernow 1990, 186–200. During the war, Morgan's London partner E.C. Grenfell stopped in daily at the British Treasury and then sent instructions by cable to Morgan & Company in New York (Burk 1979a, 352; Burk 1982, 90). Grenfell was also a member of the Bank of England's Court of Directors.

47. Metzler 2006, chap. 8; also Mitani 1975, 2009.

48. Paxson 1920, 74–75, emphasis added. For Britain's experience, Burk 1982.

49. Strong to Tokyo Ginko Club, May 24, 1920, file 1000.4 (1), Strong papers. Concerning "window guidance" and "daily fund guidance" by the Bank of Japan after the Second World War, see Patrick 1962, 141–157; also Metzler 2013, 191–192. For Japan's wartime state-bank complex, Metzler 2013, chap. 8.

50. Sayers 1976, 1:120; Burk 1979b, 415.

51. Strong to Tokyo Ginko Club, May 24, 1920, file 1000.4 [1], Strong papers.

52. Chandler (1958, 124–132) introduces this credit-control episode, about which many more questions could be asked. The detailed histories given by Friedman and Schwartz (1963, 217–222) and Allan Meltzer (2003, 84–90) both discuss the wartime period without discussing this

extraordinary episode. Friedman and Schwartz did say they were puzzled at the anomalous behavior of wartime monetary aggregates.

53. Strong to Tokyo Ginko Club, May 24, 1920, file 1000.4 (1), Strong papers.

3. Japan Emerges as an International Creditor, 1915–1918

Epigraph: Strong to Tokyo Ginko Club, May 24, 1920, file 1000.4 (1), Strong papers.

Simon Bytheway presented an earlier version of this chapter at the Asian Studies Conference Japan, Sophia University; many thanks to the participants, discussants, and organizers.

1. For two major studies of US–British financial and political relations during this transition see Hogan 1977 and Watt 1984; also Orde 1996. For the larger question, see Arrighi 2010 and Kindleberger 1996.

2. See Katō and Yamaguchi 1988, 58–144, esp. 136, 146–207, 326–351, and 354–397.

3. Inoue, June 19, 1918, in *Inoue Junnosuke ronsō* 2:155–156; Metzler 2006, 109. Inoue's statement can be compared to McKay's (2014) review of current characteristics of international financial centers. Examples of current discussion on that question are Patterson 1916 and Wyse 1918.

4. Okazaki and Sawada 2007; Shizume 2012, 215–217.

5. Schiltz 2012a, chaps. 1 and 2; also Horesh 2012 and Horesh 2014, chap. 6.

6. Inoue 1928, 436–442.

7. Warner 1991, 81.

8. Forrest, 2008.

9. Warner 1991, 82–83.

10. *Federal Reserve Bulletin* 5 (August 1, 1919): 731; Federal Reserve System 1943, 539; Metzler 2006, 104–105.

11. Itō 1989, 12–59; Nihon Ginkō 1983, 357–363. It was also in 1916 that Mitsui Bank established its first overseas branch, in Shanghai, simultaneously posting representatives to New York and London (Ogura 2002, 16).

12. Nihon Ginkō 1983, 367–368; Itō 1979, 62; table 3.1.

13. P. Roberts 1998, 607–617.

14. Ōkurashō 1940, 618; *Federal Reserve Bulletin* 5 (August 1, 1919): 734.

15. Ōkurashō 1940, 616–621, 634–635. These numbers as reported in 1940 by the Japanese Ministry of Finance were considerably less than the numbers reported at the time. Up to April 1918, as the BoJ reported to the FRBNY, Japan had lent ¥748 million to Great Britain, ¥254 million to Russia, and ¥156 million to France. For the role of the Deposit Bureau see Ferber 2002.

16. Ōkurashō 1940, 621–625, 635–638.

17. Berton 2012, 30, 66–69, 85–86; N. Kawamura 2000, 118.

18. Ōkurashō 1940, 625–634, 638.

19. Berton 2012, 69; Inoue 1928, 436–437; Warner 1991, 84–86.

20. N. Kawamura 2000, 118.

21. Dayer 1988, 95–98, 100. Montagu Norman, writing to Benjamin Strong in February 1921, discussed the question of title to and sale of Russian gold in London (Confidential addendum in Norman to Strong, February 17, 1921, file 1116.2 (2), Strong papers). In later letters to Strong, Norman made repeated oblique references to the question of Russian gold, which seems to have been laundered in the London market as "South African gold." Strong's letter to Norman of April 5, 1921, refers to the possibility of handling "the socalled South African gold" in New York.

22. Borton 1955, 285, 287; LaFeber 1997, 119; Nish 2002, 22–23; Dunscomb 2011.

23. Morley 1954, 23–27.

24. Brooks 2000, 25–28, and on the larger context, Dickinson 1999, 158–168, and Smethurst 2007, chap. 11.

25. Lascelles to Kimberley, July 10, 1895, F.O. 181/729 (2), British National Archives, emphasis added.

26. Horesh 2014, 186–196.

27. Kajima 1968, 368–378; Nish 1972, 152–157; Dickinson 1999, 201.

28. Borton 1955, 283–285.

29. N. Kawamura 2000, 70. For Nishihara himself see Duus 1995, 347–350, and Schiltz 2012a, 135–137. Schiltz (2012a, chap. 3) discusses the larger subject of the Nishihara loans.

30. Shōda 1972, 146–181; Suzuki 1972, 277–350.

31. Borton 1955, 284, 296; Schiltz 2012a, 121–154; Yanaga 1966, 362–364.

32. Overlach 1976, 193–195, emphasis added; Shinobu 1974, 281–282; LaFeber 1997, 112–116.

33. Shinobu 1974, 290.

34. Itō 1979, 62–64; Nihon Ginkō 1983, 367–368; Noji and Omori 1986, 70–71; Sarasas 1940, 262–33l; Suzuki 1972, 141–165.

35. Suzuki 1972, 141–165.

36. Itō 1979, 64–67; Shōda 1972, 178–180.

37. Metzler 2006, 106–109, and sources cited there.

38. Noji and Omori 1986, 71–73; Suzuki 1972, 197–274.

39. Matsusaka 2001, 208.

40. Suzuki 1972, 197–274; N. Kawamura 2000, 73–74; Matsusaka 2001, 208–226; Schiltz 2012a, 121–154.

41. Shōda 1972, 8.

42. Matsusaka 2001, 211.

43. Gull 1943, 211–234; Schiltz 2012a, 121–154.

44. At the Tariff Conference of Peking, from October 1925 to July 1926, Japan vigorously attempted to recover its outstanding unsecured loans. The meeting collapsed before the issue was resolved (Nish 2002, 54–55).

45. According to one surmise, the Anfu regime used the bulk of Japanese funds to suppress revolutionary movements in southern China (Shinobu 1974, 291).

46. The Bank of Japan's research bureau conducted extensive research on Japan's outstanding loans to China, mostly in Japanese but in special cases in English, evidently to support diplomatic efforts to recover the loans. See Bank of Japan 1930.

47. Yanaga 1966, 362–364.

48. Ōkurashō 1940, 616–638; Noji and Omori 1986, 71–73; Shōda 1972, 178–180; Shinobu 1974, 289–291; Suzuki 1972, 197–274.

49. Inoue, June 19, 1918, in *Inoue Junnosuke ronsō* 2:193–195.

4. Postwar Alignment

Epigraph: Inoue Junnosuke, manuscript of July 1930, in *Inoue Junnosuke ronsō*, 4:265.

1. Headrick 1991.

2. Ahamed 2009 provides a group biography.

3. Iriye 2002, 18–31; Woolf quoted on p. 18, emphasis added.

4. Adapted from Cooper 2006, 2, and Cooper 2008, 78–80.

5. Cooper 2006; Cooper 2008; see also Goodhart 1995, 205–215.

6. See Knafo 2013, 173–174, and Bagchi 2007, 4–8.

7. Clarke 1967. For a counterargument see Simmons (1996, 407–443), who builds upon Nurkse 1944, particularly pp. 66–88. The "BIS view" is developed by Toniolo 2005.

8. Constituent Charter of the Bank for International Settlements (January 20, 1930), at http://www.bis.org/about/charter-en.pdf; McGarrah 1931.

9. Abstracted from Toniolo 2005, 1–4.

10. See also Boyce 1997, 142–143.

11. Metzler, *Lever of Empire*, treats Inoue extensively. Accounts in Japanese begin with his official biography (*Inoue Junnosuke den*, Tokyo, 1935), which excerpts many primary materials. For Inoue's activity in the Institute of Pacific Relations see Akami 2001.

12. "Eikoku ni okeru ginkō gyōmu" and "Rondon shijō no tegata nakakaigyō" (1900–1902), reprinted in *Inoue Junnosuke ronsō*, 4:48–102.

13. "Notes on Japan," July 1920, file 1000.4, Strong papers.

14. *Inoue Junnosuke den*, 131–144; *Nihon Ginkō hyakunenshi*, 2:487–503, 519–530; Odate 1922, 37–41, 71–75.

15. Odate 1922, 63–64. The scholarly debate over these questions is discussed in Nihon Ginkō Kin'yū Kenkyūjo 1993, 96–98, and *Nihon Ginkō hyakunenshi*, 2:491–503.

16. *Inoue Junnosuke ronsō*, 1:328; *Inoue Junnosuke den*, 145.

17. For the boycott of banknotes, Horesh 2012 and Horesh 2014, 190–196.

18. *Federal Reserve Bulletin*, July 1, 1919: 611, 615–617.

19. For the idea of "gold restoration depressions," Metzler 2006, esp. chap. 8; for an authoritative survey of the failure of the restored gold standard of the 1920s see Eichengreen 1992, and for a setting of this movement in world context, Tooze 2014, chap. 19.

20. Keynes (1925) 1931.

21. According to BoJ director Fukai Eigo (Fukai 1941, 152–154).

22. Bank of Japan data, given in Nihon Ginkō Tōkeikyoku 1966, 298–299. Gold inflows to Japan for 1919–21 were ¥885 million, while gold outflows were ¥4 million.

23. Hawtrey 1922a, 237. Hawtrey expressed a parallel fear of large gold flows to India (Balachandran 1996, 95).

24. Federal Reserve System 1943, 539. In 1921, the United States actually imported $2 million in gold from Japan (net). Bank of Japan numbers recorded only ¥100,000 in whole-world gold exports for 1921, against an inflow of ¥138.2 million (=US$69 million).

25. In the Bank of England's encyclopedic four-volume in-house history, Japan is only briefly mentioned under the rubric of "Central Banking and Central Banks Cooperation." The same work exhaustively discusses foreign gold production, shipments, and holdings, providing detailed intelligence on the gold positions of Madeira, Malta, and the Malay States, for example (*The Bank of England, 1914–1921*, M 7/156, Bank of England Archives, London).

26. Wholesale prices: Bank of Japan index, Statist index, and US Bureau of Labor Statistics, in E. B. Schumpeter 1940, table 4 (book pocket).

27. Howson 1974, 97–98.

28. Eichengreen 1992, 109–112.

29. Strong to Case, May 29, 1920, file 1000.4 (1), Strong papers.

30. In itself, the co-movement of discount rates was not new, but rather was typical of the final decades of the classical gold standard. As noted by Bloomfield (1959, 35), "in larger movements at least, the discount rates of virtually all the [central] banks tended to rise and fall together."

31. Strong to Norman, October 20, 1919; Norman to Strong, October 21, 1919; Norman to Strong, November 6, 1919; Strong to Norman, November 6, 1919, file 1116.1, Strong papers. Enigmatically, Norman told Strong that the reduction of the BoE's Banking Reserve to near £20 million "has been the *ostensible* reason for the [November 6] rise in the Bank Rate" (Norman to Strong, November 6, 1919, emphasis added).

32. *Nihon Ginkō hyakunenshi*, Shiryō-hen: 374; Sayers 1976, appendixes, 347; Federal Reserve System 1943, 439–440. The FRBNY began to raise rates on November 3, 1919 (Meltzer 2003, 27). Beginning November 26, the FRBNY increased its rate on acceptances, which Strong had kept below even the rate on US Treasury certificates. It then increased rates on Treasury certificates beginning December 30 (Meltzer 2003, 102–103).

33. On BoE–FRBNY coordination see Sayers 1976, 1:120–126.

34. Bank of England, "Memorandum as to Money Rates, 10 February 1920," in Sayers 1976, Appendixes, 65–68.

35. Metzler 2006, 131–132, 159–173.

36. On this point see esp. Kirshner 2007.

37. For the gendered aspect of this moral economy of deflation, Metzler 2004.

38. Federal Reserve Board 1943, 330; Ferderer 2003, 670–672, 686.

39. Spalding 1922, chap. 11.

40. For the case of Siam, Bytheway 2003, 249–252.

41. *Economist*, January 17, 1920, p. 119; *Economist*, January 24, 1920, p. 163.

42. Friedman and Schwartz 1963, 237; Greider 1987, 289–293; Meltzer 2003, 120.

5. Wall Street Discovers Japan, Spring 1920

Epigraph: Strong to Pierre Jay, July 19, 1920, file 1000.4 (1), Strong papers. Mark Metzler presented an earlier version of material in this and the following chapter at the Bank of Japan Institute for Monetary and Economic Studies (IMES); many thanks to the participants and especially to Masato Shizume.

1. Smethurst 2007, chaps. 8–9; Metzler 2006, 46–49, 149; Pak 2013, 162–165.

2. The China consortium part of the story has been dealt with in the greatest detail in English. The standard history is Field 1931; also W. I. Cohen 1978, 1982, and Takeshi Matsuda's excellent unpublished 1979 PhD dissertation, which makes extensive use of US, Japanese, and British sources.

3. Metzler 2006.

4. A one-hundred-page account of the trip was given by Henry W. Taft (1932).

5. Taft 1932, 11, 13.

6. The history of Shibusawa's business diplomacy is given by Kimura Masato (1991), who has written extensively on the subject. John Sagers is now writing a new study of Shibusawa; see also Sagers 2014.

7. Schiltz 2012a, chap. 2; Metzler 2006, 52–55.

8. In order, these company presidents were Baron Kondo Renpei, Baron Ōkura Kihachirō, Fujiyama Raita, N. Kajiwara, S. Asano, M. Kushida, K. Inoue, and K. Yukawa (Taft 1932). Concerning the political organization of Japanese business and its relationship to the state, see the excellent account given by William Miles Fletcher (1989).

9. Vanderlip's books included *The American "Commercial Invasion" of Europe* (1902), *What Happened to Europe?* (1919), *What Next in Europe?* (1922), and *Tomorrow's Money: A Financial Program for America* (1934). These were all translated promptly into Japanese as *Beikoku shōgyō no Yoroppa shinryaku* (1902), *Ōshū no keizaikai wa dō natta ka?* (1920), *Ōshū no shōrai* (1922), and *Amerika kin'yū seido kaikakuron* (1935).

10. Taft's account was written mainly during the summer of 1931 and published in April 1932; it concluded with an apologetic account of the recent Japanese assaults in Manchuria and Shanghai. To that extent at least, Taft too had been converted into a "friend of Japan."

11. Strong to Jay, May 11, 1920; Strong to Jay, July 19, 1920; Strong to Case, May 29, 1920; all in file 1000.4 (1), Strong papers.

12. *Nihon Ginkō hyakunenshi*, 2:462–465; Strong to Pierre Jay, May 11, 1920, file 1000.4 (1), Strong papers.

13. *Nihon Ginkō hyakunenshi*, 2:466; B. Strong to J. D. Case, March 10, 1921; YSB to FRBNY, March 11, 1921; "Memorandum on Business Conditions for the Bank of Japan," March 6, 1922; all in Japanese Govt. 1919–1950, c.261, FRBNY archives.

14. *Nihon Ginkō hyakunenshi*, 2:465–468, which has further details concerning BoJ deposits at the FRBNY.

15. Strong to Fukai, October 31, 1921, file 1330.1 [2], Strong papers. For "The Family" see Bacevich 1982; also Schuker 1976, 284n. Much information on the larger state-capital nexus is collected in Reifer 2000.

16. Strong to Jay, July 19, 1920, and Strong to Jay, July 21, 1920, file 1000.4 (1), Strong papers.

17. Strong to Jay, May 11, 1920, and Strong to Case, May 29, 1920, file 1000.4 (1), Strong papers.

18. Strong to Jay, May 11, 1920, file 1000.4 (1), Strong papers.

19. Strong to Jay, August 4, 1920, file 1000.4 (1), Strong papers. On Matsukata see Ericson 2014 and Ericson, forthcoming.

20. Strong to Tokyo Ginko Club, May 24, 1920, file 1000.4 (1), Strong papers.

21. "Copy of Notes in Handwriting of Benjamin Strong made in Japan in the Spring of 1920" [hereafter, "Notes on Japan"], file 1000.4 (1), Strong papers; T. Lamont 1921, 172.

22. Strong to Jay, July 21, 1920, file 1000.4 (1), Strong papers.

23. Strong, "Notes on Japan," July 1920, file 1000.4, Strong papers.

24. On the "Eastern establishment," the work of Priscilla Roberts (e.g., 1997, 1998) is highly significant. The British financial and governing elite is analyzed by Cain and Hopkins 2001 and by Cassis 1994; Antony Hopkins's forthcoming study of American empire treats this question of emulation in multiple dimensions. Strong's own tight web of connections is explained by Chandler 1958; also T. Lamont 1933. The history of Japan's governing and owning elites has had little systematic study in English, and one must put together the story from the incidental information in biographical and other studies.

25. Dayer 1976. Hata (1988, 283) called the Washington system "a daring offensive to roll back Japan's position in Asia and to restore their prewar position."

26. "Notes on Japan," July 1920, file 1000.4, Strong papers.

27. The issue of immigration was later intensified by the gratuitously insulting anti-Japanese legislation passed by the U.S. Congress in 1924; see Stalker 2006; also Azuma 2005, esp. 61–85. Lamont also deplored the anti-Japanese movement on the US West Coast.

28. "Notes on Japan," July 1920, file 1000.4, Strong papers.

29. Strong to Case, May 29, 1920, file 1000.4 (1), Strong papers. For Fukai, see also Smethurst 1997.

30. Strong to Jay, July 19, 1920, file 1000.4 (1), Strong papers.

31. Strong to Jay, August 4, 1920, file 1000.4 (1), Strong papers.

32. "Confidential Memorandum in Regard to Japanese Foreign Balances Sent to the Federal Reserve Bank of New York by Governor Strong under Date of August 4, 1920," file C261, August 1917–1920, "Japan–Bank of Japan: Policies and Procedures," Strong papers.

6. Putting the Program into Action, 1920–1928

Epigraph: Strong to Fukai, January 21, 1921, file 1330.1 (2), Strong papers.

1. *Federal Reserve Bulletin* 7 (February 1921): 209.

2. Takahashi and Morigaki (1968) 1993, 65; and for an English-language account, Metzler 2006, 129–137.

3. Luthringer 1934, 127–169. Although the sources of the crisis were surely better located in New York than in Manila, Strong's friend Leonard Wood, who was appointed governor general of the Philippines in 1921, characteristically described the bubble and bust as a matter of Filipino malfeasance and unreadiness for self-government.

4. "1920–21 World Trip–Part 3," file 1000.4 (3), Strong papers; Sugihara 1996; Korthals Altes 1991, 73–74. Balances at the Javasche Bank increased from 19 million florins in 1915 to 123 million in 1919 (*Federal Reserve Bulletin* 5 [January 1, 1919]: 643, 647).

5. File 1000.4 (4), Strong papers; King 1988, 21.

6. Balachandran 1993; Gadgil 1971, 254; Pillai 1923–1924, 248–249; Kaul 1924–1925.

7. Metzler, "The Correlation of Crises, 1918–1920," forthcoming.

8. Sauerbeck-Statist index, given in E. Schumpeter et al. 1940, table 4 (book pocket); Jastram 1977, 117; Tooze 2014, 359–360; Garside 1990.

9. "Foreign Countries: Trip around the World (April 1920–January 1921)," file 1000.4 (5), Strong papers, emphasis added.

10. Ibid.

11. Quoting point 16 in the Resolutions of the Commission on Currency and Exchange, Brussels Conference, October 1920 (in Sayers 1976, Appendixes, 69–73).

12. Cottrell 1997, 33–34.

13. "Central Banking," February 16, 1921, in Norman to Strong, February 17, 1921, file 1116.2 (2), Strong papers; Norman's "manifesto" is also printed in Sayers 1976, Appendixes, 74–75; see also Toniolo 2005, 19, and for more on Norman's ideas of central banking, Clay 1957, 282–299. (Point 10 in the draft sent to Strong is missing in the version given by Sayers.) Many of Norman's formulations concerning central banking originated in a "seminar by correspondence" that Norman conducted with Henry Strakosch, also in early 1921: see Cottrell 1997, esp. 31–35. On the question of the London office of the Imperial Bank of India see Bagchi 1997, 556–563, 582, 595. In the end, Bagchi explained, "the [IBI's] London office was not allowed to infringe upon the Bank of England's exclusive privilege of handling the sterling loans of the Government of India nor would it be permitted freely to deal in the bills of exchange between India and Britain" (595).

14. Strong to Norman, March 21, 1921; Norman to Strong, April 2, 1921; both in file 1116.2 (2), Strong papers.

15. Quoted and paraphrased from Montagu Norman, "Resolutions Proposed for Adoption by the Central and Reserve Banks Represented at Meetings to Be Held at the Bank of England" (1921), in Sayers 1976, appendixes, 75.

16. Diary entry of October 19, 1926, in Moreau 1991, 126. See also Ghosh 2007, 39–41.

17. Sayers 1976, appendixes, 343. These were profits after taxes and before payment of dividends (which were also extremely large). See also Sayers 1976, 1:18–19.

18. Balachandran 1994; Balachandran 1996, 6; see also Knafo 2013.

19. Cottrell 1997, 30–34.

20. Norman to Strong, March 14, 1921, file 1116.2 (2), Strong papers. The South African Reserve Bank's first governor was W.H. Clegg, who had been the Bank of England's chief accountant.

21. Norman to Strong, March 14, 1921, file 1116.2 (2), Strong papers.

22. Reserve Bank of Australia, www.rba.gov.au; also Blainey 1958, 315–316.

23. For Europe, two standard histories are Clarke 1967 and Meyer 1970. Among more recent accounts, Péteri 2002 is especially revealing.

24. Drake 1989; essays by Paul Drake and Barry Eichengreen, in Drake 1994; Rosenberg 1999; Schuker 2003.

25. Strong to Inoue, November 17, 1921, file 1330.1 (1), Strong papers.

26. Dayer 1988, 110–111, 124, 172–176. Tomotaka Kawamura (2015) explores the British "Eastern" exchange banks in their wider regional and global contexts. King's multivolume history provides a mass of detail on the history of the Hongkong and Shanghai Bank.

27. Strong to Inoue, November 17, 1921, file 1330.1 (1), Strong papers.

28. Dayer 1976; see also O'Brien 2004b. For the end of the Anglo-Japanese alliance and the Washington system see, among others, Dickinson 2004, Nish 1972, and Iriye 1965.

29. Strong to Inoue, November 17, 1921, file 1330.1 (1), Strong papers.

30. Fukai 1941, 162–173.

31. B. Strong to J. D. Case, March 10, 1921; YSB to FRBNY, March 11, 1921; "Memorandum on Business Conditions for the Bank of Japan," March 6, 1922; all in "Japanese Govt. 1919–1950," c.261, FRBNY archives; *Nihon Ginkō hyakunenshi*, 2:467.

32. Norman to Strong, April 2, 1921, file 1116.2 [2], Strong papers.

33. Strong to Inoue, August 29, 1921, file 1330.1 (1), Strong papers. See also Meltzer 2003, 114–116.

34. Strong to Inoue, December 19, 1922, file 1330.1 (1), Strong papers.

35. Sayers 1976, 1:111, also quoted in Toniolo 2005, 18.

36. K. Miller 2001.

37. James 1996, 18; for Japan's de facto gold exchange standard, Metzler 2006, 35–44.

38. The Genoa resolutions were written mainly by R. G. Hawtrey of the British Treasury (see Hawtrey 1922b; Mouré 2002, 53–54; Clarke 1973) and are reported also in *Federal Reserve Bulletin* 8 (June 1922): 678. Although the Genoa Conference has been considered a political failure, the Genoa financial resolutions present the clearest political statement of the new central-bank program as it was actually realized; see also Metzler 2006, 163–165.

39. *Nihon Ginkō hyakunenshi*, 3:342–343; Fukai 1941, 186–189. The version of Norman's principles transmitted to the BoJ, and received positively by Inoue, was filed under the heading "Chūō ginkō kaigi" and is summarized in *Nihon Ginkō hyakunenshi*, 3:343.

40. Strong to Fukai, January 14, 1922, and Fukai to Strong, June 23, 1925, both in file 1330.1 (2), Strong papers; Fukai 1941, 187–188. On the 1922 preparations for a return to the gold standard, Metzler 2006, 138–145.

41. Eichengreen 1992, 187–192.

42. Keynes (1925) 1931.

43. Quoted in Costigliola 1977, 925–926. Norman's response to Churchill's concern: "In connection with a gold 1925, the merchant, manufacturer, worker, etc., should be considered (but not consulted any more than about the design of battleships)" (in Boyce 1997).

44. Dalgaard 1981; Ally 1994.

45. Fukai to Strong, June 23, 1925, file 1330.1 (2), Strong papers.

46. For Katō's British-aligned policy, Duus 1968. For Japan's "shadow gold standard" in the 1920s, see chapter 8, this volume, and Metzler 2006, 250–251.

47. Warner 1991, 94–96.

48. Nihon Ginkō Tōkeikyoku 1966, 169.

49. Dayer 1988, 67.

50. Bytheway 2014, chap. 6; Warner 1991, 94–96. As we have seen, the Bank of Japan had before the war cooperated with the Bank of England by depositing special security funds. Japanese borrowers followed similar practices in relations with other British and French banks with whom they did business (Kobayashi 1922, 186).

51. Metzler 2006, 148.

52. Bytheway 2014, 106–111, 117–122; Itō 1989, 149–150.

53. Strong to Fukai, March 11, 1924, file 1330.1 (2), Strong papers, emphasis added; Metzler 2006, 165.

54. See also Keynes 1923, 167.

55. Garrett 1995, 615–618. Even seventy years after the fact, Garrett's revelations are remarkable. Norman avowed in public that his actions were "always of course subject to the supreme authority of the government" (Norman, 1926, cited in Collins 1993, 154).

56. Keynes 1928, 327–328. For related considerations, see Bryan 2015.

57. Klein 1997, 78–84.

58. Garrett 1995, 615.

59. Garrett 1995, 615, 618, 622.

60. Inoue, "Sengo ni okeru sekai no kin'yū," July 27, 1917, in *Inoue Junnosuke ronsō*, 2:101.

61. Bytheway 2014, 109–110. For this momentous history, see James 1985, 1986; McNeil 1986; Schuker 1988.

62. Federal Reserve System 1943, 538.

63. Strong to Fukai, January 12, 1925, file 1330.1 (2), Strong papers.

64. Kindleberger 1986, 54–61.

65. Strong to Inoue, November 1, 1923, materials held at the Bank of Japan.

66. Tsushima 1963, 202–205, 213; *Inoue Junnosuke den*, 265; Inoue to Strong, January 31, 1924, file 1330.1 (2), Strong papers. In a note to Strong on March 19, 1924, Inoue mentioned the comprehensive personal views Strong expressed in a letter of February 20 in regard to the loan business. (This letter, referred to also in *Inoue Junnosuke den*, 282, may not be extant.) Strong's letter to Inoue of November 1, 1923 (Materials held at the Bank of Japan) also discussed the loan.

67. Bytheway 2014, 110–111.

68. Inoue (July 1930) and Inoue (1926) in *Inoue Junnosuke ronsō*, 4:266–268, 239–240. For Strong's trip, "Secret Trip to London & Paris, April–May 1924," file 1000.5, Strong papers.

69. Metzler 2006, 175–183.

70. Inoue to Strong, January 25, 1924; Strong to Inoue, May 10, 1927, file 1330.1 (1), Strong papers, emphasis added. For bank consolidation after 1927, Okazaki and Sawada 2007.

71. Moggridge 1972.

72. Vasudevan 2008.

73. *Nihon Ginkō hyakunenshi*, 3:345–346.

74. Lamont to Stimson, June 25, 1929, quoted in Costigliola 1972, 614.

75. Fukai to Strong, June 23, 1925, file 1330.1 (2), Strong papers.

76. *Nihon Ginkō hyakunenshi*, 3:346–348; Clarke 1967 for the return to the gold standard in Belgium, Poland, and Romania; for Romania see also Cottrell 2003 and Racianu 2011.

77. Mouré 1992, 267–269.

78. *Nihon Ginkō hyakunenshi*, 3:346–348.

79. Ahamed 2009, 294–298; Boyce 2009, 209–212.

80. Strong to Inoue, August 8, 1927, file 1330.1 (1), Strong papers.

81. For example, Kindleberger 1986, 53.

82. Strong to Inoue, August 8, 1927, file 1330.1 (1), Strong papers, emphasis added.

83. Beckhart, Smith, and Brown 1932, 67–69; Strong to Jay, August 4, 1927, quoted in Boyce 2009, 212 (evidently referring to n25 (p. 497), not n24 as given in the text).

84. Garrett (1995, 615n16) suggests that it was Norman who was manipulating other central bankers at their meeting of 1927. In the spring of 1928, Strong may have avoided Norman during his annual trip to Europe—the last of his life—because of these concerns (Boyce 1997, 158).

85. Chandler 1958, 438 et seq.; Clarke 1967, 123–125; Kindleberger 1986, 50–53; Eichengreen 1992, 212–215.

86. For which see Murphy 1997, chap. 8.

87. Kindleberger 1986, 294; Eichengreen 1992, 204–221; also Friedman and Schwartz 1963, 412–414, 692–693. This view goes back at least to Irving Fisher (quoted by Friedman and Schwartz).

88. Metzler 2002.

89. Strong to Inoue, August 10, 1928, C261 (Japan–Bank of Japan, Policy and Procedures, 1928–1932), Strong papers.

7. Making a Market

Epigraph: Schumpeter 1939, 2:675–676.

An earlier version of this chapter was presented by Simon Bytheway at the Fifty-Sixth Market History Conference, Osaka University; many thanks to the participants, discussants, and organizers.

1. See also Patterson 1916, 270–272.

2. We use "Rothschilds" here as shorthand to refer to the merchant bank N. M. Rothschild & Sons of London, as do internal documents of N. M. Rothschild & Sons, Bank of England, and other archives. In different contexts, Rothschilds might loosely refer to the network of Rothschild cousins working together in finance throughout Europe.

3. Financial anthropologist Rachel Harvey (2013) presents a study of this highly ritualized market during the postwar period.

4. Estimates in Federal Reserve Board 1943, 542–543.

5. English purchasing power of gold index, from Jastram 1977, 34–37.

6. For an inspired introduction to monetary history see Galbraith 1975; also Knafo 2013, 81–101.

7. Twelve was the magic number, with a dozen pence to a shilling, 240 pence to a pound, and gold purity measured on a scale from 1 to 24 (two dozen) carat. Despite fierce competition from ten, twelve still is a very useful number.

8. Kindleberger 1993, 23–24, 61.

9. Memoranda on the Gold Market for the Years 1919–1935, Rothschild Archive Library (hereafter RAL), XI/35/64: 1. See also Ugolini 2013, 64–67.

10. Williams 1968, 266–297, esp., 286, emphasis added.

11. Memoranda on the Gold Market for the Years 1919–1935, RAL, XI/35/64: 2–3.

12. See Sayers 1936, esp. chap. 4, "Direct Operations on the Gold Market."

13. Brown 1929, 75–82; see also Bertola 2001.

14. Judging from the BoE's in-house history, Japan's gold operations after the First World War appear to have been a glaring omission in the BoE's focus or intelligence (*The Bank of England, 1914–1921*, M 7/156, Bank of England Archives, London).

15. Memoranda on the Gold Market for the Years 1919–1935, RAL, XI/35/64: 3; for official "disenchantment" with the banks see R. Roberts 2013, 48–69, 230.

16. South African criticisms were forceful. For example, Samuel Evans, writing in the final weeks of the war: "It would be difficult to conceive a more unbusinesslike and extravagant arrangement than the one which has hitherto prevailed as regards the disposal of S[outh] A[frican] gold" ("Disposal of SA Gold Bullion [by Samuel Evans]," October 5, 1918, 1–7, RAL).

17. Blagg 2012, 73–76; Green 2010, 30.

18. Ally 2001, 79–95; Ally 1994; Grewe 2013, 119–129.

19. Memoranda on the Gold Market for the Years 1919–1935, RAL, XI/35/64: 3. Significantly, upon legislating the Gold and Silver (Export Control) Act of 1920, the Bank of England appointed Rothschilds to oversee the distribution of export licenses. See Blagg 2012, 77–78.

20. Memoranda on the Gold Market for the Years 1919–1935, RAL, XI/35/64: 4.

21. Ibid.

22. See the London Bullion Market Association (LBMA) website for further information, http://www.goldfixing.com.

23. See Hobson 1954, 86–88.

24. Memoranda on the Gold Market for the Years 1919–1935, RAL, XI/35/64: 4–5. Bank of England commentary explains that "once or twice—but only once or twice it is asserted—the price has been altered by a penny or twopence to suit the convenience of other dealers in the market, where Messrs Rothschild have been absolutely convinced of there being justifiable reasons for such a change" ("London Market Price for 'Export' Gold," Private and Confidential, March 23, 1921, in Gold Bullion file, C43/135, vol. 1, Bank of England [hereafter BoE]).

25. Bank of England commentary explains that the cost of freight "of course, is practically invariable, and (b) [insurance] changes but little, remaining the same for months even years; but (c) [interest] varies according to the date of the next sailing and the speed of the vessel. (d) [the

charge in the US] is very small, is really slightly variable, but for this purpose is taken at 3d fixed" ("London Market Price for 'Export' Gold," Private and Confidential, March 23, 1921, in Gold Bullion file, C43/135, vol. 1, BoE.

26. Memoranda on the Gold Market for the Years 1919–1935, RAL, XI/35/64: 5; "London Market Price for 'Export' Gold," Private and Confidential, March 23, 1921, in Gold Bullion file, C43/135, vol. 1, BoE.

27. Memoranda on the Gold Market for the Years 1919–1935, RAL, XI/35/64: 5; Arnold 2016, 21; Green 1968, 104.

28. "London Market Price for 'Export' Gold," Private and Confidential, March 23, 1921, in Gold Bullion file, C43/135, vol. 1, BoE. When the British colonial government of India was keen to purchase large amounts of gold, there was "for a time" an arrangement under which it paid a premium to Rothschilds on condition that half of Rothschilds' gold supplies were provided for Indian purchase. "In this case the published price for the day represented the price at which the other half of the gold was offered. The price of the day in fact remained unaffected by the Indian Government's special contract and the premium they paid was calculated *on* that price of the day. This was of course an exceptional transaction."

29. For example, on September 12, 1919, £1 equaled $4.17. Thus, the sterling price of gold equaled the US statutory price of gold ($20.67183) divided by 4.17, to provide the first historical gold fix at £4.9572 (or 99 shillings [*s*] 1.75 pence [*d*]), per troy ounce fine (995). The price actually paid to the sellers of gold in London was therefore 99/1.75*d*, less expenses of 7.75*d* for freight, insurance, interest, packing in London, handling in New York, and commissions, to become 98/6 (4*l* 18*s* 6*d*), or £4.92—"the standard price."

30. For the potential benefits gleaned by the London gold market's founding brokers, particularly Mocatta & Goldsmid, see Arnold 2016.

31. Memoranda on the Gold Market for the Years 1919–1935, RAL, XI/35/64: 7–11; Federal Reserve System 1943, 539–540.

32. "Memoranda on the Realisation of Gold," July 24, 1919, Memoranda on the Realisation of Gold, 1919–1920, RAL, XI/111/154.

33. "Agreement," June 11, 1920, Memoranda on the Realisation of Gold, RAL, XI/111/262. See also files RAL, XI/111/152, RAL, XI/111/r153, and RAL, XI/111/262.

34. "Draft Memorandum on Gold Market," October 1937, Memoranda on the Gold Market for the Years 1919–1935, RAL, XI/35/64: 4, 7–11.

35. Carosso 1987, 453. After the Second World War, the boot was on the other foot. Edmund de Rothschild "was made to feel very much the poor relation" during his apprenticeship with Kuhn, Loeb & Company in New York (Ferguson 1999, 480).

36. Ernest "Windsor" Cassel was a well-known, international financier whose success extended deep into the social and political spheres of English life. He was a prominent society personality enjoying a close friendship with King Edward VII and the royal family, hence the "Windsor" appellation. He was also an influential adviser to the Treasury who actively worked with the Foreign Office to further British interests. See Thane 1986, 80–99.

37. "Memorandum, re: Kuhn, Loeb & Co.," January 1921, Kuhn, Loeb & Co. re: Joint Business Transactions, 1921–1930, RAL, XI/111/422.

38. "Memorandum, re: Kuhn, Loeb & Co.," January 1921, and "Kuhn, Loeb & Co. to Rothschilds," February 1, 1921, both in Kuhn, Loeb & Co. re: Joint Business Transactions, 1921–1930, RAL, XI/111/422.

39. "Rothschilds to Kuhn, Loeb & Co.," February 17, 1921, Kuhn, Loeb & Co. re: Joint Business Transactions, 1921–1930, RAL, XI/111/422.

40. "Kuhn, Loeb & Co. to Rothschilds," Confidential, March 3, 1921, Kuhn, Loeb & Co. re: Joint Business Transactions, 1921–1930, RAL, XI/111/422.

41. Kynaston 1999, 72.

42. Ferguson 1999, 455–456, 462.

43. Norman to Strong, April 2, 1921; also Strong to Norman, April 18, 1921, file 1116.2 [2], Strong papers.

44. Blagg 2009, 48–53.

45. Gold Standard Act of 1925; "The Packing of Bar Gold for Export," Memorandum, November 28, 1928, Gold Bullion file, C43/136, vol. 2, BoE.

46. Matsuoka 1936; Metzler 2006, 35–44.

47. For example see "Memoranda on the proposed est. of refinery in SA," 1919, RAL, XI/111/152. There was a history of tension here. In 1919, Rothschilds had opposed the construction of a separate South African mint, stating that they were not interested in "helping the South Africans to cut their own throats" and "could on no account join in establishing or running a refinery at that distance from London" ("Refinery in SA— proposed est.," June 23, 1919, 2).

48. Kynaston 1999, 88.

49. Memoranda on the Gold Market for the Years 1919–1935, RAL, XI/35/64: 5–6; Ally 1994 for the larger story. Refinery operations were, in effect, licensed by the Bank of England, in that refusal by the Bank of England to accept the bullion of a mint as good for delivery would prevent it from being traded on the London gold market.

50. "Gov. SARB (W. H. Clegg) to BOE, Chief Cashier (C. P. Mahon)," February 22, 1926, SA Reserve Bank, C44/214, BoE. The South African Reserve Bank governor, Clegg, had himself formerly been the chief cashier of the Bank of England.

51. "Disposal of Gold in London Market," Memorandum, September 29, 1926, London Gold Market file, C52/15, BoE.

52. Memoranda on the Gold Market for the Years 1919–1935, RAL, XI/35/64: 7–11; Balachandran 2001, 199–229.

53. Einzig 1931, 61–66. See also Einzig 1929, 379–387, and 1930, 56–63.

54. Memorandum, April 28, 1927, Gold Bullion file, C43/135, vol. 1, BoE. In 1926, Rothschilds is said to have sold gold worth £35,000 weekly, with Johnson, Matthey & Co. selling the same. See "Disposal of Gold in London Market," Memorandum, November 29, 1926, London Gold Market file, C52/15, BoE.

55. Before the Russian Revolution, British capital was heavily invested in the Lena goldfields, which were the site of a 1912 strike and massacre. By 1928, however, German gold refineries were competing on almost equal footing with the London refineries, and in the 1930s, German refineries took over the business of treating unrefined Soviet gold. For more detail on London's gold trade with the Soviet Union see Blagg 2012, 102–109.

56. Memoranda on the Gold Market for the Years 1919–1935, RAL, XI/35/64: 7–11.

57. The notion of "unquestioned tradition" is taken from Kynaston 1999, 371.

58. See Green 2010.

8. The Rush for Gold

Epigraph: Hawtrey 1932, 233, emphasis added.

1. Rothermund 1996 offers a valuable global survey.

2. For war debts see Moulton and Pasvolsky 1932.

3. Fisher 1933, 345–346, emphasis in original.

4. Paul Warburg, "Annual Report to the International Acceptance Bank," in Warburg 1930, 823–826; also quoted in Beckhart, Smith, and Brown 1932, 124–125, emphasis added.

5. Kreps 1952, 22; Ferderer 2003, 669–673, 676–677, 679, 689.

6. Ferderer 2003, 666, 671.

7. Warburg, "Annual Report to the International Acceptance Bank," in Warburg 1930, 823–826.

8. Irving Fisher (1935, 7, 43) later also used the image of an "inverted pyramid."

9. Clapham 1944, 2:421; see also Sayers 1976, 1:8–9.

10. Clapham 1944, 2:418.

11. *Nihon Ginkō hyakunenshi*, 3:355–356.

12. Saint-Simon/Iggers 1972, 105–107.

13. Costigliola 1972, esp. 614–616; Toniolo 2005, esp. 44–48, 61–63; Simmons 1993.

14. Sayers 1976, 1:352–358.

15. *Nihon Ginkō hyakunenshi*, 3:351–359; Tsushima 1963, 2:326–327. The initial capital of the BIS was 500 million Swiss francs, divided into 200,000 shares. Of these shares, 112,000 were divided equally among the seven core members, and the remainder were privately held.

16. Bank for International Settlements, *First Annual Report, for the Business Year Ended March 31, 1931* (Basel, 1931).

17. Nihon Ginkō Tōkeikyoku 1966, 299; table A.1, this volume.

18. This discussion summarizes conclusions argued in Metzler 2006, chap. 9. Duus (1968) describes the liberal and conservative valences of these two parties, and Metzler (2015) analyzes the timing of these policy swings.

19. Juichi Tsushima, "(Draft) Return of Japan to the Gold Standard" (Tokyo: Japanese Government Press, 1930), Bank of England, OV 16/2: 19.

20. Garrett 1995, 617, 630–631.

21. Kindleberger 1986, 85, 89; Rothermund 1996, 82–86.

22. Nihon Ginkō Tōkeikyoku 1966, 301; Federal Reserve System 1943, 542.

23. Bytheway 2014, chaps. 5–7; Cleveland and Huertas 1985, 124–125, 150–151. In 2015, NCB's successor Citibank sold its Japanese operations to Sumitomo Mitsui Banking Corporation (SMBC).

24. Metzler 2006, 218–220; Fukai 1941, 244–245; *Nihon Ginkō hyakunenshi*, 3:423–424; Cleveland and Huertas 1985, 77–84, 123.

25. *Nihon Ginkō hyakunenshi*, Shiryōhen, 329.

26. Nihon Ginkō Tōkeikyoku 1966, 299. Federal Reserve Board records show the United States received net gold inflows from Japan of $157 million in 1930, $199 million in 1931, and $50 million in 1932 (Federal Reserve System 1943, 540).

27. Bryan (2010) compares Japanese and Argentinian experience with the gold standard around the turn of the twentieth century.

28. Federal Reserve Board 1943, 540. Heavy US gold shipments to France began in 1928 and continued as follows (net gold exports, in millions of dollars): 1928: $308 m.; 1929: $65 m.; 1930: $74 m.; 1931: $345 m.; 1932: $442m.; 1933: $216 m.

29. The literature on the 1997–98 financial crisis is too vast to begin to cite here, but Stiglitz 2003 offers an excellent starting point. For the mutually cooperative response of Asian central banks (with leadership from Tokyo) see Grimes 2009.

30. Kindleberger 1986, 146–153; Eichengreen 1992, 264–278; Federal Reserve System 1943, 646.

31. Boyce 2009, 318–323.

32. Sayers 1976, appendixes, 355; Kindleberger 1986, 154–158; Federal Reserve System 1943, 638.

33. Smethurst 2007 gives a full appreciation of Takahashi's policy.

34. Memoranda on the Gold Market for the Years 1919–1935, RAL, XI/35/64: 6.

35. Ibid., 7.

36. Clavin 1992, 285–286.

37. "Rothschilds' Commission on Sales of Gold," Memorandum, December 7, 1931, London Gold Market file, C52/15, BoE. The new arrangement was a standard 1/8 per mille (0.125%) commission on all gold Rothschilds sold for the Bank of England; a reduced 1/16 (0.0625%) commission

when the buyer was provided to Rothschilds by the Bank of England; and no commission whatsoever on gold sold by the Bank of England if purchased for Rothschilds' own account.

38. Commission earned by Rothschilds on these transactions equaled about £23,000, and about £11,000 of that had to be shared with its own agents in "two way" transactions for realization in New York or Paris ("Statement of gold transactions effected through N. M. Rothschild and Sons from 1st October 1932—30th November 1932," and "Statement of gold transactions effected through N. M. Rothschild and Sons from 1st December 1932—31st December 1932," London Gold Market file, C52/15, BoE).

39. Schumann 1938.

40. Balachandran 1996, 172–173, 180–183; Dayer 1988, 239–240.

41. Memoranda on the Gold Market for the Years 1919–1935, RAL, XI/35/64: 1–2, 7–11; Rothermund 1992, 47–57; *Federal Reserve Bulletin* 19 (December 1933): 756. British authorities had fixed the rupee's exchange rate at 1*s* 6*d*, or £0.075. For fuller context see Rothermund 1992 and Balachandran 1994 and 2001.

42. Gold Bullion file, Secret, C43/139, BoE.

43. *Federal Reserve Bulletin* 19 (December 1933): 755.

44. Meltzer 2003, 386n, citing Lionel Robbins, *The Great Depression* (1934), on BoE reserves.

45. Feis 1966, 113–131; Kindleberger 1986, 196–201.

46. P. Roberts 1998, 620; Friedman and Schwartz 1963, 445–446n.

47. Brown 1940, 2:1087–1091.

48. "1933 Gold," Memoranda on the Gold Market for the Years 1919–1935, RAL, XI/35/64: 6.

49. Kindleberger 1986, 222–224; Memoranda on the Gold Market for the Years 1919–1935, RAL, XI/35/64: 7–11.

50. Federal Reserve Board 1943, 541.

51. Mouré 2002, 221–231.

52. Kynaston 1999, 388; Memoranda on the Gold Market for the Years 1919–1935, RAL, XI/35/64: 11.

53. E. Miller 2007, 55–74; Federal Reserve Board 1943, 541.

54. The London gold market reopened on March 22, 1954, with N. M. Rothschild & Sons continuing to serve as its chair until 2004. As of April 1, 1968, the "fix" was no longer quoted in pound sterling, but in US dollars, with a second "gold afternoon fix" for traders in New York. Even so, the relevance of the London gold fix came increasingly into question, and subsequently the market was reformed into the London Bullion Market Association in 1987 (Bott 2013b; Harvey 2013).

55. Metzler, "The Correlation of Crises, 1918–1920," forthcoming.

56. Clapham 1944, 2:421.

57. Iida 1997, 129–130.

58. Dayer 1988, 240–241. Eichengreen (1992, 293–294) writes that the Bank of France held £62.5 million in sterling on September 19, 1931, and took a 35 percent loss on it (equivalent to a loss of US$106 million).

59. Murphy 1997, 165–194.

60. Suter 1989; Suter 1992, appendix.

61. See also Clavin 1992.

62. Meltzer 2003, 546n.

63. British officials were aware of this potential from at least as early as 1911, fearing that a Japan not in alliance with Britain would be "quite likely to seek such assistance elsewhere, in a quarter least convenient for ourselves" (quoted in Chapman 2004, 82).

64. For a fuller account of Japanese business cycles, Metzler 2006. A standard study in Japanese is Fujino 1965.

65. Takahashi 1954, 1:5.
66. Smethurst 2007; Metzler 2006, chap. 12; Sugihara 1989.
67. Bytheway 2013, 412.
68. Shimazaki 1989, 397–401, 428; Yamamoto 2011, 175–177; Metzler 2013, 144–145.
69. Akita and White 2010b; Sugihara (2010) emphasizes that autarky did not become pronounced in practice until 1939.

Conclusion

Epigraph: Fisher to Warburton, July 23, 1946, excerpted in Cargill 1992, 1274.
1. Lewis and Wigen (1997) address the question of metageographies, though in a different sense; see also Beaverstock, Smith, and Taylor 2000. How the "weightless," virtual world of finance connects to the construction of social and physical infrastructures is an open question.
2. See, among others, Hobsbawm 1989, 315.
3. Chapman 2004, 82.
4. As appears, for instance, in central banks' discussions surrounding the London Economic Conference of 1933 (Clavin 1992).
5. Eichengreen 1992, 188–191.
6. Pauly 1997; Clavin 2013.
7. For example, T. Lamont 1951.
8. Kemmerer's tabulation is given in Eichengreen 1992, 188–191. For Kemmerer's international monetary advising see, among others, Rosenberg 1999, Drake 1989, and essays in Drake 1994.
9. In this we agree with the thrust of Ahamed's 2009 narrative; see also Eichengreen and Temin 2000. Compare Hawtrey in 1932: "The calamities of the past three years have been caused not by mere absence of co-operation, but by a disastrously synchronized unwisdom" (1932, 248). What we emphasize here is that this disastrous synchronization dates from 1919, and that the disaster did not involve technical details of implementation so much as the nature of the vision itself.
10. Cassis 2010; Cassis and Bussière 2005; also Jaffe and Lautin 2014, 124–189. We must leave it to other scholars to integrate Paris into this account, as Cassis does, and to bring in other international financial centers as well. Shanghai especially should be brought into the story, in its connections to Tokyo, London, and New York; here, Niv Horesh's work provides a basic starting point. Spufford 2006 provides a deep historical account of European financial history.
11. Rozman 1974; McClain, Merriman, and Ugawa 1994.
12. On Tokyo-centrism as it developed in the early twentieth century see Young 2013, chap. 2.
13. Lindert 1969, table 2.
14. Cain and Hopkins 2001.
15. Sylla 2011, 174–176.
16. Wójcik 2011; A.G. Hopkins's forthcoming study of American empire will greatly extend this picture.
17. As Bertola (2001, 145) notes, "The dominant position that the US had attained in the world economy by 1944 and its dominant share of the western world's monetary reserves of gold enabled it to play the leading role in shaping the Bretton Woods Agreement in 1944," which "formalised US pre-eminence in the monetary system of the post-war capitalist world economy." The centralizing holding of gold in this system also conforms to Paul Warburg's 1914 vision: "Implicit in the structure of the system was a restricted monetary role for gold, and a fixed dollar price for the metal that, together with a fixed gold parity for currencies, also translated as a fixed dollar parity. Specifically, under the Bretton Woods Agreement control of gold was to be central to the planned, co-operative regulation of exchange through a network of central banks and the International Monetary Fund (IMF)."

18. Sassen 1991, 171–172, 327; see also Helleiner 1989; Sassen 2002b, 20; Smith and Timberlake 2002; Slater 2004; Sassen 2006. R. B. Cohen (1981, 308), drawing on data of the late 1970s, may be the earliest statement of the idea that "New York, Tokyo and London are predominant as world centers of corporations and finance." On the Tokyo–New York connection since the 1970s, Murphy (1997) is a good starting point. On the limitations of the yen's internationalization see Grimes 2003 and 2009.

19. US Treasury data, at ticdata.treasury.gov/Publish/mfh.txt, accessed January 12, 2016; "Foreign Portfolio Holdings of U.S. Securities as of June 30, 2014" (Department of the Treasury/Federal Reserve Bank of New York/Board of Governors of the Federal Reserve System, April 2015).

20. Cain and Hopkins (2001) is a foundational study; see also the numerous works of Ranald Michie.

21. The central banks' emergency, highly discretionary purchase of private debt claims is normalized in a 2011 IMF report as a new part of central banks' "standard policy toolkit" (Stone, Fujita, and Ishi 2011; Le Maux and Scialom 2010 for historical perspective; Helleiner 2014b for the larger policy prospect).

22. Metzler 2008; Metzler 2015 for a comparative chronology.

23. Garside 2012; Shiratsuka 2009; Arai and Hoshi 2006.

24. Shiratsuka 2009, 5, 25.

25. Takagi 2011, 83–84; McCauley 2011, 94–95; Hattori and Shin 2009.

26. Wójcik 2011.

27. Iwamoto 2006; Schaede 2008.

28. Stella 2009; Le Maux and Scialom 2010.

29. Stella 2009 gives a very clear summation; quotation from p. 4.

30. Stella 2009, 16–17.

31. Robin Harding, "NY Fed President Floats Change to Exit Strategy," *Financial Times*, May 20, 2014.

32. Goldberg, Kennedy, and Miu 2010, 6–9, 27–29; Stella 2009, 15, 24; Helleiner 2014b, 38–43.

33. Fowler 2014, 827.

34. Stella 2009, 27.

35. Shiratsuka 2009, 24.

36. *Credit Suisse Global Wealth Report*, cited in www.bbc.com/news/business-30875633 (January 19, 2015).

37. "Just How 'Mega' Are Megabanks?," *Nikkei Weekly*, June 18, 2012 (referring to BIS data, as of the end of 2011). For the larger question, see again Arrighi 2010.

38. Adrian van Rixtel and Jeff Slee, "The Return of Japanese Banks," in *BIS Quarterly Review*, September 2013, 15–17; "Japan's Banks Return to Pole Position for Cross-Border Lending," FT.com, July 28, 2015.

References

Archival Materials

Bank of England archives, London.
FRBNY archives: Federal Reserve Bank of New York archives, New York City. Much of the material relevant to this study can now be accessed at fraser.stlouisfed.org.
Thomas W. Lamont papers, Baker Library, Harvard Business School.
Materials held at the Bank of Japan: Bank of Japan archives (Nihon Ginkō Kin'yū Kenkyūjo), Tokyo.
N. M. Rothschilds and Sons archives, London.
Benjamin Strong papers, Federal Reserve Bank of New York.

Books and Articles

Liaquat AHAMED. 2009. *Lords of Finance: The Bankers Who Broke the World*. New York: Penguin.
Tomoko AKAMI. 2001. *Internationalizing the Pacific: The United States, Japan and the Institute of Pacific Relations in War and Peace, 1919–1945*. London: Routledge.

Shigeru Aкіта and Nicholas J. Wнıтε, eds. 2010a. *The International Order of Asia in the 1930s and 1950s*. Farnham, UK: Ashgate.

——. 2010b. "The International Order of Asia in the 1930s and 1950s: Contexts, Hypotheses and Scope." In Akita and White 2010a, 1–13.

Russell Aliy. 1991. "War and Gold—the Bank of England, the London Gold Market and South Africa's Gold, 1914–19." *Journal of Southern African Studies* 17 (June): 221–238.

——. 1994. *Gold and Empire: The Bank of England and South Africa's Gold Producers, 1886–1926*. Johannesburg: Witwatersrand University Press.

——. 2001. "Gold, the Pound Sterling and the Witwatersrand, 1886–1914." In McGuire, Bertola, and Reeves 2001, 97–122.

Yoichi Arai and Takeo Hoshi. 2006. "Monetary Policy in the Great Stagnation." In *Japan's Great Stagnation: Financial and Monetary Policy Lessons for Advanced Economies*, edited by Michael M. Hutchison and Frank Westermann, 157–181. Cambridge, MA: MIT Press.

Anthony John Arnold. 2016. "Business Returns from Gold Price Fixing and Bullion Trading on the Interwar London Market." *Business History* 58 (2): 238–308.

Giovanni Arrighi. 2010. *The Long Twentieth Century: Money, Power, and the Origins of Our Times*. Updated edition. London: Verso.

Asai Yoshio. 1982. "Jūzoku teikokushugi kara jiritsu teikokushugi e—gaishi dō'nyū o chūshin to shita Nihon no taigai keizai kankei, 1895–1931 nen." *Rekishigaku kenkyū*, no. 511 (December).

——. 1985. "Nisshin sensōgo no gaishi dō'nyū to Nihon Kōgyō Ginkō." *Shakai keizai shigaku* 50 (February).

Eiichiro Azuma. 2005. *Between Two Empires: Race, History, and Transnationalism in Japanese America*. New York: Oxford University Press.

Andrew J. Bacevich. 1982. "Family Matters: American Civilian and Military Elites in the Progressive Era." *Armed Forces and Society* 8:405–415.

Amiya Kumar Bagchi. 1997. *The Evolution of the State Bank of India*. Vol. 2, *The Era of the Presidency Banks, 1876–1920*. New Delhi: State Bank of India / Sage Publications.

——. 2007. "Global Financial Integration—I: The Overlooked Historical Context of the Current Period." In Bagchi and Dymski 2007, 3–20.

Amiya Kumar Bagchi and Gary A. Dymski, eds. 2007. *Capture and Exclude: Developing Economies and the Poor in Global Finance*. New Delhi: Tulika.

G. Balachandran. 1993. "Britain's Liquidity Crisis and India, 1919–1920." *Economic History Review* 46 (3): 575–591.

——. 1994. "Towards a 'Hindoo Marriage': Anglo-Indian Monetary Relations in Interwar India, 1917–35." *Modern Asian Studies* 28 (July): 615–647.

——. 1996. *John Bullion's Empire: Britain's Gold Problem and India between the Wars*. Richmond, Surrey: Curzon. [Reprint: Routledge, 2013].

——. 2001. "The Gold Exchange Standard and Empire: India, 1900–1940." In McGuire, Bertola, and Reeves 2001, 199–229.

——. 2008. "Power and Markets in Global Finance: The Gold Standard, 1890–1926." *Journal of Global History* 3 (November): 313–335.

Bank of Japan Research Bureau. 1930. *Japanese Loans to China*. Tokyo: Bank of Japan.

Jonathan V. BEAVERSTOCK, Richard G. SMITH, and Peter J. TAYLOR. 2000. "World-City Network: A New Metageography?" *Annals of the Association of American Geographers* 90 (March): 123–134.

Benjamin Haggot BECKHART, James G. SMITH, and William A. BROWN Jr. 1932. *The New York Money Market*. Vol. 4, *External and Internal Relations*. New York: Columbia University Press.

Patrick BERTOLA. 2001. "Cyclical Developments in Gold Mining at Kalgoorlie: 1893–1944." In McGuire, Bertola, and Reeves 2001, 123–152.

Peter BERTON. 2012. *Russo-Japanese Relations, 1905–1917: From Enemies to Allies*. London: Routledge.

Gary Dean BEST. 1972. "Financing a Foreign War: Jacob H. Schiff and Japan, 1904–05." *American Jewish Historical Quarterly* 61 (June): 313–324.

Michele BLAGG. 2009. "The Royal Mint Refinery, 1852–1968." *The Rothschild Archive: Review of the Year, April 2008–March 2009*, 48–53.

———. 2012. "The Royal Mint Refinery: The Business of Adapting to Change, 1919–1968." PhD diss., King's College, London.

Geoffrey BLAINEY. 1958. *Gold and Paper: A History of the National Bank of Australasia Limited*. Melbourne: Georgian House.

Arthur I. BLOOMFIELD. 1959. *Monetary Policy under the International Gold Standard, 1880–1914*. New York: Federal Reserve Bank of New York.

Michael D. BORDO and Hugh ROCKOFF. 1996. "The Gold Standard as a 'Good Housekeeping Seal of Approval.'" *Journal of Economic History* 56 (2): 389–428.

Claudio BORIO and Gianni TONIOLO. 2006. "One Hundred and Thirty Years of Central Bank Cooperation: A BIS Perspective." BIS Working Papers No. 197 (February).

———. 2008. "One Hundred and Thirty Years of Central Bank Cooperation: A BIS Perspective." In *Past and Future of Central Bank Cooperation*, edited by Claudio Borio, Gianni Toniolo, and Piet Clement. New York: Cambridge University Press, 16–75.

Hugh BORTON. 1955. *Japan's Modern Century*. New York: Ronald Press.

Sandra BOTT, ed. 2013a. *The Global Gold Market and the International Monetary System from the Late 19th Century to the Present: Actors, Networks, Power*. Houndmills, Basingstoke, UK: Palgrave Macmillan.

———. 2013b. "South African Gold at the Heart of the Competition between the Zurich and London Gold Markets at a Time of Global Regulation, 1945–68." In Bott 2013a, 109–138.

Robert BOYCE. 1997. "Britain's Changing Corporate Structure and the Crisis of Central Bank Control in the 1920s." In Cottrell, Teichova, and Yuzawa 1997, 142–163.

———. 2009. *The Great Interwar Crisis and the Collapse of Globalization*. Houndmills, Basingstoke, UK: Palgrave Macmillan.

Andrew BOYLE. 1967. *Montagu Norman: A Biography*. London: Cassell.

Barbara J. BROOKS. 2000. *Japan's Imperial Diplomacy: Consuls, Treaty Ports, and War in China, 1895–1938*. Honolulu: University of Hawai'i Press.

William Adams BROWN Jr. 1929. *England and the New Gold Standard, 1919–1926*. New Haven, CT: Yale University Press.

———. 1940. *The Gold Standard Reinterpreted, 1914–1934*. 2 vols. New York: National Bureau of Economic Research.

J. Lawrence BROZ. 1997. *The International Origins of the Federal Reserve System*. Ithaca, NY: Cornell University Press.

Steven BRYAN. 2010. *The Gold Standard at the Turn of the Twentieth Century: Rising Powers, Global Money, and the Age of Empire*. New York: Columbia University Press.

——. 2015. "Interwar Japan, Institutional Change, and the Choice of Austerity." *Asiatische Studien—Études Asiatiques* 69 (2): 451–476.

Kathleen BURK. 1979a. "The Diplomacy of Finance: British Financial Missions to the United States, 1914–1918." *Historical Journal* 22 (June): 351–372.

——. 1979b. "J. M. Keynes and the Exchange Rate Crisis of July 1917." *Economic History Review* 32 (August): 405–416.

——. 1982. "The Treasury: From Impotence to Power." In *War and the State: The Transformation of British Government, 1914–1919*, edited by Kathleen Burk, 84–107. London: George Allen & Unwin.

——. 1992. "The Lineaments of Foreign Policy: The United States and a 'New World Order,' 1919–39." *Journal of American Studies* 26 (December): 377–391.

Simon James BYTHEWAY. 2001. "Japan's Adoption of the Gold Standard: Financial and Monetary Reform in the Meiji Period." In McGuire, Bertola, and Reeves 2001, 79–95.

——. 2003. "International Monetary Reform and Siam, 1855–1939: A Brief History." In *Village Communities, States, and Traders: Essays in Honour of Chatthip Nartsupha*, edited by C. Baker and A. Nozaki, 241–258. Bangkok: Thai-Japanese Seminar and Sangsan.

——. 2004. "Japanese Capital Loans and 'Yen Diplomacy': 1915–1918." Paper presented at the Asian Studies Conference, Tokyo, June 19.

——. 2005. *Nihon keizai to gaikoku shihon, 1858–1939* [The Japanese economy and foreign capital, 1858–1939]. Tokyo: Tosui.

——. 2007. "Kin hon'isei jidai ni okeru Nichi-Gō kan no kin bōeki, 1897–1931 nen" [Australian gold exports to Japan during the era of the gold standard, 1897–1931]. *Nihon University Journal of Business* 76 (4): 41–53.

——. 2013. "Japan's Financial Diaspora: The Rise, Fall and Rise of a Global Banking Network, 1880–2012." In *Philosophy and Essence of History and Social Science: For Professor Chatthip Nartsupha at 72*, edited by P. Phongpaichit and C. Baker, 403–428. Bangkok: Sangsan.

——. 2014. *Investing Japan: Foreign Capital, Monetary Standards, and Economic Development, 1859–2011*. Cambridge, MA: Harvard University Asia Center.

——. 2015. "Between London, New York, and the Antipodean Deep Blue Sea: Japan, Australia, and the International Gold Trade, 1873–1940." In *In the Light of History: Essays in Honor of Yoshiteru Iwamoto, Eiichi Hizen, and Akira Nozaki*, edited by C. Nartsupha and C. Baker, 105–122. Bangkok: Sangsan.

P. J. CAIN and A. G. HOPKINS. 2001. *British Imperialism, 1688–2000*. 2nd ed. London: Longman.

A. CAIRNCROSS. 1995. "The Bank of England and the British Economy." In *The Bank of England: Money, Power and Influence, 1694–1994*, edited by R. Roberts and D. Kynaston, 56–82. Oxford: Clarendon.

Thomas F. Cargill. 1992. "Irving Fisher Comments on Benjamin Strong and the Federal Reserve in the 1930s." *Journal of Political Economy* 100 (Centennial Issue, December 1992): 1273–1277.

Vincent P. Carosso. 1987. *The Morgans: Private International Bankers, 1854–1913*. Cambridge, MA: Harvard University Press.

Youssef Cassis. 1994. *City Bankers, 1890–1914*. Cambridge: Cambridge University Press.

———. 2010. *Capitals of Capital: The Rise and Fall of International Financial Centres, 1780–2009*. 2nd ed. Cambridge: Cambridge University Press.

———. 2011. *Crises and Opportunities: The Shaping of Modern Finance*. Oxford: Oxford University Press.

Youssef Cassis and Éric Bussière, eds. 2005. *London and Paris as International Financial Centres in the Twentieth Century*. Oxford: Oxford University Press.

Lester V. Chandler. 1958. *Benjamin Strong, Central Banker*. Washington, DC: Brookings Institution.

John Chapman. 2004. "The Secret Dimensions of the Anglo-Japanese Alliance, 1900–1905." In O'Brien 2004a, 82–98.

Ron Chernow. 1990. *The House of Morgan: An American Banking Dynasty and the Rise of Modern Finance*. New York: Simon & Schuster.

———. 1993. *The Warburgs: The Twentieth-Century Odyssey of a Remarkable Jewish Family*. New York: Random House.

John Clapham. 1944. *The Bank of England: A History*. Two volumes. Cambridge: Cambridge University Press.

Stephen V. O. Clarke. 1967. *Central Bank Cooperation, 1924–31*. New York: Federal Reserve Bank of New York.

———. 1973. *The Reconstruction of the International Monetary System: The Attempts of 1922 and 1933*. Princeton, NJ: Princeton Studies in International Finance No. 33, Department of Economics, Princeton University.

Patricia Clavin. 1992. "'The Fetishes of So-Called International Bankers': Central Bank Co-operation for the World Economic Conference, 1932–3." *Contemporary European History* 1 (November): 281–311.

———. 2013. *Securing the World Economy: The Reinvention of the League of Nations, 1920–1946*. Oxford: Oxford University Press.

Henry Clay. 1957. *Lord Norman*. London: Macmillan.

Harold van B. Cleveland and Thomas F. Huertas. 1985. *Citibank, 1812–1970*. Cambridge, MA: Harvard University Press.

R. B. Cohen. 1981. "The New International Division of Labor, Multinational Corporations and Urban Hierarchy." In *Urbanization and Urban Planning in Capitalist Society*, edited by Michael Dear and Allen J. Scott, 287–315. London: Methuen.

Warren I. Cohen. 1978. *The Chinese Connection: Roger S. Greene, Thomas W. Lamont, George E. Sokolsky, and American–East Asian Relations*. New York: Columbia University Press.

———. 1982. "America's New Order for East Asia: The Four Power Financial Consortium and China, 1919–1946." In *Essays in the History of China and Chinese-American*

Relations, Asian Studies Center, East Asia Series, Occasional Paper No. 7. East Lansing: Michigan State University.

Michael Collins, ed. 1993. *Central Banking in History.* Aldershot, UK: Edward Elgar.

Richard N. Cooper. 2006. "Almost a Century of Central Bank Cooperation." BIS Working Papers No. 198 (February).

——. 2008. "Almost a Century of Central Bank Cooperation." In Borio, Toniolo, and Clement 2008, 79–112.

Frank Costigliola. 1972. "The Other Side of Isolation: The Establishment of the First World Bank, 1929–1930." *Journal of American History* 59.

——. 1977. "Anglo-American Financial Rivalry in the 1920s." *Journal of Economic History* 37 (December): 911–934.

P. L. Cottrell. 1995. "The Bank of England in Its International Setting, 1918–1972." In *The Bank of England: Money, Power and Influence, 1694–1994,* edited by R. Roberts and D. Kynaston, 83–139. Oxford: Clarendon.

——. 1997. "Norman, Strakosch and the Development of Central Banking: From Conception to Practice, 1919–1924." In *Rebuilding the Financial System in Central and Eastern Europe, 1918–1994,* edited by Philip L. Cottrell, 29–73. Aldershot, UK: Scholar Press.

——. 2003. "Central Bank Co-operation and Romanian Stabilisation, 1926–1929." In *Business and Politics in Europe, 1900–1970,* edited by Terry Gourvish, 106–143. Cambridge: Cambridge University Press.

P. L. Cottrell, Alice Teichova, and Takeshi Yuzawa, eds. 1997. *Finance in the Age of the Corporate Economy: The Third Anglo-Japanese Business History Conference.* Aldershot, UK: Ashcroft.

Bruce R. Dalgaard. 1981. *South Africa's Impact on Britain's Return to Gold, 1925.* New York: Arno Press.

Roberta Allbert Dayer. 1976. "The British War Debts to the United States and the Anglo-Japanese Alliance, 1920–1923." *Pacific Historical Review* 45 (November): 569–595.

——. 1988. *Finance and Empire: Sir Charles Addis, 1861–1945.* New York: Palgrave Macmillan.

Marcello de Cecco. 1974. *Money and Empire: The International Gold Standard, 1890–1914.* Oxford: Basil Blackwell.

Frederick R. Dickinson. 1999. *War and National Reinvention: Japan in the Great War, 1914–1919.* Cambridge, MA: Harvard University Press.

——. 2004. "Japan Debates the Anglo-Japanese Alliance: The Second Revision of 1911." In O'Brien 2004a, 99–121.

Paul W. Drake. 1989. *The Money Doctor in the Andes: The Kemmerer Missions, 1923–1933.* Durham, NC: Duke University Press.

——, ed. 1994. *Money Doctors, Foreign Debts, and Economic Reforms in Latin America from the 1890s to the Present.* Wilmington, DE: Scholarly Resources.

Paul E. Dunscomb. 2011. *Japan's Siberian Intervention, 1918–1922: "A Great Disobedience Against the People."* New York: Lexington Books.

Peter Duus. 1968. *Party Rivalry and Political Change in Taishō Japan.* Harvard East Asian Series 35. Cambridge, MA: Harvard University Press.

———. 1995. *The Abacus and the Sword: The Japanese Penetration of Korea, 1895–1910*. Berkeley: University of California Press.

Barry EICHENGREEN. 1984. "Central Bank Cooperation under the Interwar Gold Standard." *Explorations in Economic History* 21:64–87.

———. 1987. "Conducting the International Orchestra: Bank of England Leadership under the Classical Gold Standard, 1919–1939." *Journal of International Money and Finance* 6:5–29.

———. 1992. *Golden Fetters: The Gold Standard and the Great Depression, 1919–1939*. New York: Oxford University Press.

Barry EICHENGREEN and Marc FLANDREAU, eds. 1997. *The Gold Standard in Theory and Practice*. 2nd ed. London: Routledge.

Barry EICHENGREEN and Peter TEMIN. 2000. "The Gold Standard and the Great Depression." *Contemporary European History* 9 (July): 183–207.

Paul EINZIG. 1929. "Gold Points and Central Banks." *Economic Journal* 39 (September): 379–387.

———. 1930. "Some New Features of Gold Movements." *Economic Journal* 40 (March): 56–63.

———. 1931. "Recent Changes in the London Gold Market." *Economic Journal* 41 (March): 61–66.

Steven J. ERICSON. 2014. "The 'Matsukata Deflation' Reconsidered: Financial Stabilization and Japanese Exports in a Global Depression, 1881–85." *Journal of Japanese Studies* 40 (Winter): 1–28.

———. Forthcoming. "'The Dictates of Practical Expediency': Influences on the Matsukata Financial Reform." To appear in *Monumenta Nipponica*.

Joseph ESHERICK. 1976. *Reform and Revolution in China: The 1911 Revolution in Hunan and Hubei*. Berkeley: University of California Press.

FEDERAL RESERVE SYSTEM. 1943. *Banking and Monetary Statistics, 1914–1941*. Washington, DC: Federal Reserve System.

Herbert FEIS. 1966. *1933: Characters in Crisis*. Boston: Little, Brown.

Katalin FERBER. 2002. "'Run the State Like a Business': The Origin of the Deposit Fund in Meiji Japan." *Japanese Studies* 22 (2): 131–151.

J. Peter FERDERER. 2003. "Institutional Innovation and the Creation of Liquid Financial Markets: The Case of Bankers' Acceptances, 1914–1934." *Journal of Economic History* 63 (September): 666–694.

Niall FERGUSON. 1999. *The House of Rothschild: The World's Banker, 1849–1999*. Vol. 2. New York: Viking Penguin.

Frederick Vanderbilt FIELD. 1931. *American Participation in the China Consortiums*. Chicago: Institute of Pacific Relations.

Irving FISHER. 1933. "The Debt-Deflation Theory of Depressions." *Econometrica* 1 (4): 337–357.

———. 1935. *100% Money*. New York: Adelphi.

Marc FLANDREAU. 1997. "Central Bank Cooperation in Historical Perspective: A Sceptical View." *Economic History Review* 50:735–763.

William Miles FLETCHER. 1989. *The Japanese Business Community and National Trade Policy, 1920–1942*. Chapel Hill: University of North Carolina Press.

Timothy FORREST. 2008. "Kith but Not Kin: The Highland Scots, Imperial Resettlement, and the Negotiating of Identity on the Frontiers of the British Empire in the Interwar Years." PhD diss., University of Texas at Austin.

Stephen A. FOWLER. 2014. "The Monetary Fifth Column: The Eurodollar Threat to Financial Stability and Economic Sovereignty." *Vanderbilt Journal of Transnational Law* 47:825–860.

E. FOXWELL. 1900. "Report on the Adoption of the Gold Standard in Japan, by Count Matsukata Masayoshi, H.I.J.M.'s Minister of Finance." *Economic Journal* 10 (June): 232–245.

Joseph Hume FRANCIS. 1888. *History of the Bank of England*. Chicago: Euclid Publishing Co.

Jeffry A. FRIEDEN. 2006. *Global Capitalism: Its Rise and Fall in the Twentieth Century*. New York: W. W. Norton.

Milton FRIEDMAN and Anna Jacobson SCHWARTZ. 1963. *A Monetary History of the United States, 1867–1960*. Princeton, NJ: Princeton University Press.

FUJINO Shōzaburō. 1965. *Nihon no keiki junkan—junkanteki hatten katei no rironteki, tōkeiteki, rekishiteki bunseki* [Business cycles in Japan—theoretical, statistical, and historical analysis of the cyclical development process]. Tokyo: Keisō Shobō.

FUKAI Eigo. 1941. *Kaiko 70 nen* [Reminiscences of seventy years]. Tokyo: Iwanami Shoten.

D. R. GADGIL. 1971. *The Industrial Evolution of India in Recent Times, 1860–1939*. 5th ed. Bombay: Oxford University Press.

J. K. GALBRAITH. 1975. *Money: Whence It Came, Where It Went*. London: André Deutsch.

John R. GARRETT. 1995. "Monetary Policy and Expectations: Market-Control Techniques and the Bank of England, 1925–1931." *Journal of Economic History* 55 (September): 612–636.

W. R. GARSIDE. 1990. *British Unemployment, 1919–1939: A Study in Public Policy*. Cambridge: Cambridge University Press.

———. 2012. *Japan's Great Stagnation: Forging Ahead, Falling Behind*. Aldershot, UK: Edward Elgar.

Jayati GHOSH. 2007. "Central Bank 'Autonomy' in the Age of Finance: The Implications for Developing Countries." In Bagchi and Dymski 2007, 39–51.

Linda S. GOLDBERG, Craig KENNEDY, and Jason MIU. 2010. "Central Bank Dollar Swap Lines and Overseas Dollar Funding Costs." *Federal Reserve Bank of New York Staff Reports*, no. 429 (February).

E. A. GOLDENWEISER. 1929. "The Gold Reserve Standard." *Journal of the American Statistical Association* 24, Supplement (March): 195–200.

Charles A. E. GOODHART. 1995. *The Central Bank and the Financial System*. London: Macmillan.

Timothy GREEN. 1968. *The World of Gold*. London: Michael Joseph.

———. 2010. *History of the London Good Delivery List, 1750–2010*. London: LMBA.

William GREIDER. 1987. *Secrets of the Temple: How the Federal Reserve Runs the Country*. New York: Simon & Schuster.

Bernd-Stefan GREWE. 2013. "The London Gold Market, 1900–1931." In *The Foundations of Worldwide Economic Integration: Power, Institutions and Global Markets,*

1850–1930, edited by Christof Dejung and Niels P. Petersson, 112–132. New York: Cambridge University Press).

William W. Grimes. 2003. "Internationalization of the Yen and the New Politics of Monetary Insulation." In Kirshner 2003, 172–194.

———. 2009. *Currency and Contest in East Asia: The Great Power Politics of Financial Regionalism*. Ithaca, NY: Cornell University Press.

E. M. Gull. 1943. *British Economic Interests in the Far East*. New York: International Secretariat, Institute of Pacific Relations.

Thomson Hankey. 1860. *Banking: Its Utility and Economy*. London: private circulation.

Rachel Harvey. 2013. "Market Status / Status Markets: The London Gold Fixing in the Bretton Woods Era." In Bott 2013a, 181–198.

Ikuhiko Hata. 1988. "Continental Expansion, 1905–1941." Translated by Alvin D. Coox. In *Cambridge History of Japan*, vol. 6, edited by Peter Duus, 271–314. Cambridge: Cambridge University Press.

Masazumi Hattori and Hyun Song Shin. 2009. "Yen Carry Trade and the Subprime Crisis." *IMF Staff Papers* 56 (2): 384–409.

R. G. Hawtrey. 1922a. "The Federal Reserve System of the United States." *Journal of the Royal Statistical Society* 85 (March): 224–269.

———. 1922b. "The Genoa Conventions on Currency." *Economic Journal* 32 (September): 290–304.

———. 1932. *The Art of Central Banking*. London: Longmans, Green.

———. 1962a. *The Art of Central Banking*. 2nd ed. London: Frank Cass. [See Hawtrey 1932.]

———. 1962b. *A Century of Bank Rate*. 2nd ed. London: Frank Cass.

Daniel R. Headrick. 1991. *The Invisible Weapon: Telecommunications and International Politics, 1851–1945*. New York: Oxford University Press.

Eric Helleiner. 1989. "Money and Influence: Japanese Power in the International Monetary and Financial System." *Millennium—Journal of International Studies* 18:343–358.

———. 2014a. *Forgotten Foundations of Bretton Woods: International Development and the Making of the Postwar Order*. Ithaca, NY: Cornell University Press.

———. 2014b. *The Status Quo Crisis: Global Financial Governance after the 2008 Financial Meltdown*. Oxford: Oxford University Press.

Elizabeth Hennessy. 1992. *A Domestic History of the Bank of England, 1930–1960*. Cambridge: Cambridge University Press.

Eric Hobsbawm. 1989. *The Age of Empire, 1875–1914*. New York: Vintage.

O. R. Hobson. 1954. *How the City Works*. London: News Chronicle.

Michael J. Hogan. 1977. *Informal Entente: The Private Structure of Cooperation in Anglo-American Economic Diplomacy, 1918–1928*. Columbia: University of Missouri Press.

Niv Horesh. 2012. "Between Copper, Silver and Gold: Japanese Banks of Issue in Taiwan, Northeast China and Korea, 1879–1937." *China Report* 48 (4): 375–392.

———. 2014. *Chinese Money in Global Context: Historic Junctures between 600 BCE and 2012*. Stanford, CA: Stanford University Press.

Susan Howson. 1974. "The Origins of Dear Money, 1919–20." *Economic History Review*, 2nd series, vol. 27.

David Hume. 1970. *Writings on Economics*. Edited by Eugene Rotwein. Madison: University of Wisconsin Press.

Janet Hunter. 2004. "Bankers, Investors and Risk: British Capital and Japan during the Years of the Anglo-Japanese Alliance." In O'Brien 2004a, 176–198.

Takeshi Iida. 1997. "The Role of the Central Bank in Industrial Finance: A Comparative Study of the United Kingdom and Japan." In Cottrell, Teichova, and Yuzawa 1997, 129–141.

Ikeda Shigeaki. 1949. *Zaikai kaiko* [Reminiscences of the business world]. Tokyo: Sekai no Nihon Sha.

Imada Toshiyuki. 1990. "Senzenki ni okeru Nippon Ginkō to Ō-Bei chūō ginkō no kokusai kyōchō ni tsuite" [Concerning international cooperation between the Bank of Japan and European and American central banks in the prewar period]. *Kin'yū Kenkyū* 9 (July): 141–175.

Inoue [Inouye] Junnosuke. 1928. "The Financial Crisis in Japan." In *Problems of the Pacific, 1929*, edited by J. B. Condliffe, 436–442. Chicago: University of Chicago Press.

———. 1935. *Inoue Junnosuke ronsō* [Collected works of Inoue Junnosuke]. 4 vols. Edited by Inoue Junnosuke Ronsō Hensankai. Tokyo: Inoue Junnosuke Ronsō Hensankai.

Inoue Junnosuke Ronsō Iinkai. 1935. *Inoue Junnosuke den* [Biography of Inoue Junnosuke]. Tokyo: Inoue Junnosuke Ronsō Iinkai.

Akira Iriye. 1965. *After Imperialism: The Search for a New Order in the Far East, 1921–1931*. Cambridge, MA: Harvard University Press.

———. 1972. *Pacific Estrangement: Japanese and American Expansion, 1897–1911*. Cambridge, MA: Harvard University Press.

———. 2002. *Global Community: The Role of International Organizations in the Making of the Contemporary World*. Berkeley: University of California Press.

Itō Masanao. 1979. "Taigai kin'yū no kōzō—1920 nendai no gaikoku kawase, bōeki kin'yū ni kansuru yobiteki kentō." In *Ryōtaisenkan no Nihon shihonshugi*, edited by Andō Yoshio, 51–85. Tokyo: Tōkyō Daigaku Shuppankai.

———. 1989. *Nihon no taigai kin'yū to kin'yū seisaku: 1914–1936* [Japan's financial policy and foreign finances, 1914–1936]. Nagoya: Nagoya University Press.

K. Itoh. 1994. "The Yokohama Specie Bank in London." In *Britain and Japan: Biographical Portraits*, vol. 5, edited by H. Cortazzi, 233–254. London: Japan Society.

Yoshiyuki Iwamoto. 2006. *Japan on the Upswing: Why the Bubble Burst and Japan's Economic Renewal*. New York: Algora.

Steven H. Jaffe and Jessica Lautin. 2014. *Capital of Capital: Money, Banking and Power in New York City, 1784–2012*. New York: Museum of the City of New York.

Harold James. 1985. *The Reichsbank and Public Finance in Germany, 1924–1933: A Study of the Politics of Economics during the Great Depression*. Frankfurt am Main: Fritz Knapp Verlag.

———. 1986. *The German Slump, Politics and Economics, 1924–1936*. Oxford: Clarendon.

———. 1996. *International Monetary Cooperation since Bretton Woods*. New York: Oxford University Press.

Roy W. Jastram. 1977. *The Golden Constant: The English and American Experience, 1560–1976*. New York: Wiley & Sons.

Morinosuke KAJIMA. 1968. *The Emergence of Japan as a World Power, 1895–1925.* Tokyo: Charles E. Tuttle.

———. 1976. *The Diplomacy of Japan, 1894–1922.* Vol. 1. Tokyo: Kajima.

E. KANN. 1926. *The Currencies of China.* Shanghai: Kelly and Walsh.

KATŌ Toshihiko and YAMAGUCHI Kazuo, eds. 1988. *Ryōtaisen-kan no Yokohama Shōkin Ginkō* [The Yokohama Specie Bank in the period between the wars]. Tokyo: Nihon Keizaishi Kenkyūsho.

B. N. KAUL. 1924–25. "Some Indices of Prices of Securities and Their Relation to Money Market." *Indian Journal of Economics,* v. 5, 255–284.

Noriko KAWAMURA. 2000. *Turbulence in the Pacific: Japan-U.S. Relations during World War I.* Westport, CT: Praeger.

Tomotaka KAWAMURA. 2015. "British Exchange Banks in the International Trade of Asia from 1850 to 1890." In *Commodities, Ports and Asian Maritime Trade Since 1750,* edited by Ulbe Bosma and Anthony Webster, 179–197. Palgrave Macmillan.

J. M. KEYNES. 1914. "The City of London and the Bank of England, August, 1914." *Quarterly Journal of Economics* 29 (November): 48–71.

———. (1923) 1924. *A Tract on Monetary Reform.* London: Macmillan.

———. (1925) 1931. "The Consequences of Mr. Churchill." Reprinted in his *Essays in Persuasion.* London: Macmillan.

———. 1928. "The Amalgamation of the British Note Issues." *Economic Journal* 38 (June): 321–332.

———. (1930) 1997. "The Significance of the Gold Points." Reprinted in *The Gold Standard in Theory and History,* 2nd ed., edited by B. Eichengreen and M. Flandreau, 131–139. London: Routledge.

KIMURA Masato. 1991. *Shibusawa Eiichi, minkan keizai gaikō no sōshisha* [Shibusawa Eiichi, the originator of nongovernmental economic diplomacy]. Tokyo: Chūō Kōronsha.

Charles P. KINDLEBERGER. 1986. *The World in Depression, 1929–1939.* Berkeley: University of California Press.

———. 1993. *A Financial History of Western Europe.* 2nd ed. New York: Oxford University Press.

———. 1996. *World Economic Primacy: 1500 to 1990.* New York: Oxford University Press.

Frank H. H. KING. 1987. *The Hongkong Bank in Late Imperial China, 1864–1902.* Cambridge: Cambridge University Press.

———. 1988. *The Hongkong Bank between the Wars and the Bank Interned, 1919–1945.* Cambridge: Cambridge University Press.

Jonathan KIRSHNER. 2007. *Appeasing Bankers: Financial Caution on the Road to War.* Princeton, NJ: Princeton University Press.

Judy L. KLEIN. 1997. *Statistical Visions in Time: A History of Time Series Analysis, 1662–1938.* Cambridge: Cambridge University Press.

Samuel KNAFO. 2013. *The Making of Modern Finance: Liberal Governance and the Gold Standard.* London: Routledge.

Ushisaburo KOBAYASHI. 1922. *War and Armament Loans of Japan.* Carnegie Endowment for International Peace, Japan Monographs. New York: Oxford University Press.

Kokushi Daijiten Henshū Iinkai. 1979. *Kokushi daijiten*. Tokyo: Yoshikawa Hirobumi Kan.

W. L. Korthals Altes. 1991. *Changing Economy of Indonesia*. Vol. 12A, *General Trade Statistics 1822–1940*. Amsterdam: Royal Tropical Institute.

Clifton H. Kreps. 1952. "Bankers' Acceptances." In *Money Market Essays* (Federal Reserve Bank of New York), 22–26.

David Kynaston. 1995. *The City of London*. Vol. 2, *Golden Years, 1890–1914*. London: Chatto & Windus.

——. 1999. *The City of London*. Vol. 3, *Illusions of Gold, 1914–45*. London: Chatto & Windus.

Walter LaFeber. 1997. *The Clash: A History of U.S.–Japan Relations*. New York: W. W. Norton.

Thomas W. Lamont. 1921. "The Two Japans." *Nation*, February 2, 172–173.

——. 1933. *Henry P. Davison: The Record of a Useful Life*. New York: Harper & Bros.

——. 1951. *Across World Frontiers*. New York: Harcourt, Brace.

Laurent Le Maux and Laurence Scialom. 2010. "Central Banks and Financial Stability: Back to the Past or Jump to the Future?" www.economix.fr/pdf/seminaires/crise/Le-Maux-Scialom-2010lastversion-1.pdf.

Martin W. Lewis and Kären E. Wigen. 1997. *The Myth of Continents: A Critique of Metageography*. Berkeley: University of California Press.

Peter H. Lindert. 1969. *Key Currencies and Gold, 1900–1913*. Princeton, NJ: International Finance Section, Princeton University.

George F. Luthringer. 1934. *The Gold-Exchange Standard in the Philippines*. Princeton, NJ: Princeton University Press.

Charles S. Maier. 1988. *Recasting Bourgeois Europe: Stabilization in France, Germany, and Italy in the Decade after World War I*. Princeton, NJ: Princeton University Press.

Takeshi Matsuda. 1979. "Woodrow Wilson's Dollar Diplomacy in the Far East: The New Chinese Consortium, 1917–1921." PhD diss., University of Wisconsin–Madison.

Masayoshi Matsukata. 1899. *Report on the Adoption of the Gold Standard in Japan*. Tokyo: Government Press.

——. 1900. *Report on the Post-Bellum Financial Administration in Japan, 1896–1900*. Tokyo: Government Press.

Masayoshi Matsumura. 2009. *Baron Kaneko and the Russo-Japanese War (1904–05): A Study in the Public Diplomacy of Japan*. Translated by Ian Ruxton. Morrisville, NC: Lulu Press.

Matsuoka Koji. 1936. *Kin kawase hon'isei no kenkyū* [Research on the gold-exchange standard]. Tokyo: Nihon Hyōronsha.

Y. T. Matsusaka. 2001. *The Making of Japanese Manchuria, 1904–1932*. Cambridge, MA: Harvard University Press.

Robert Mayer. 1973. "The Origins of the American Banking Empire in Latin America: Frank A. Vanderlip and the National City Bank." *Journal of Interamerican Studies and World Affairs* 15 (February): 60–76.

Robert N. McCauley. 2011. "The Euro and the Yen as Anchor Currencies: Before and during the Financial Crisis." *Currency Internationalisation: Lessons from the Global*

Financial Crisis and Prospects for the Future in Asia and the Pacific, BIS Papers No. 61, 93–104.

James L. McClain, John M. Merriman, and Ugawa Kaoru, eds. 1994. *Edo and Paris: Urban Life and the State in the Early Modern Era*. Ithaca, NY: Cornell University Press.

Gates W. McGarrah. 1931. "The First Six Months of the Bank for International Settlements." *Proceedings of the Academy of Political Science* 14 (January): 25–36.

John McGuire, Patrick Bertola, and Peter Reeves, eds. 2001. *Evolution of the World Economy, Precious Metals and India*. New Delhi: Oxford University Press.

Huw McKay. 2014. "Tokyo's Ultimately Failed Bid for First-Tier International Financial Center Status: Why Did It Fall Short?" *Asian Economic Papers* 13 (3): 1–25.

William C. McNeil. 1986. *American Money and the Weimar Republic: Economics and Politics on the Eve of the Great Depression*. New York: Columbia University Press.

Meiji Zaiseishi Henshūkai. 1905. *Meiji zaiseishi* [Meiji financial history]. 2 vols. Tokyo: Maruzen.

Allan H. Meltzer. 2003. *A History of the Federal Reserve*. Vol. 1, *1913–1951*. Chicago: University of Chicago Press.

Mark Metzler. 2002. "American Pressure for Financial Internationalization in Japan on the Eve of the Great Depression." *Journal of Japanese Studies* 28 (Summer): 277–300.

——. 2004. "Woman's Place in Japan's Great Depression: Reflections on the Moral Economy of Deflation." *Journal of Japanese Studies* 30 (Summer): 315–352.

——. 2006. *Lever of Empire: The International Gold Standard and the Crisis of Liberalism in Prewar Japan*. Berkeley: University of California Press.

——. 2013. *Capital as Will and Imagination: Schumpeter's Guide to the Postwar Japanese Miracle*. Ithaca, NY: Cornell University Press.

——. 2015. "Partisan Policy Swings in Japan, 1913–1932." *Asiatische Studien—Études Asiatiques* 69 (2): 477–510.

——. Forthcoming. "The Correlation of Crises, 1918–1920." In *Asia after Versailles*, edited by Urs Matthias Zachmann. Edinburgh: Edinburgh University Press.

Richard Hemmig Meyer. 1970. *Bankers' Diplomacy: Monetary Stabilization in the Twenties*. New York: Columbia University Press, 1970.

Ranald Michie. 2012. "The City of London as a Centre for International Banking: The Asian Dimension in the Nineteenth and Twentieth Centuries." In Nishimura, Suzuki, and Michie 2012, 13–54.

Edward S. Miller. 2007. *Bankrupting the Enemy: The U.S. Financial Siege of Japan before Pearl Harbor*. Annapolis, MD: Naval Institute Press.

Karen A. J. Miller. 2001. "Dawes Plan and Republican Politics." Working paper, Oakland University.

Mitani Taichirō. 1975. "Wōru Sutoriito to kyokutō: Washinton taisei ni okeru kokusai kin'yū shihon no yakuwari" [Wall Street and the Far East: The role of international finance capital in the Washington system]. *Chūō kōron* 90 (September): 157–181.

——. 2009. *Wōru Sutoriito to kyokutō: seiji ni okeru kokusai kin'yū shihon* [Wall Street and the Far East: International finance capital in politics]. Tokyo: Tōkyō Daigaku Shuppankai.

Kris James MITCHENER, Masato SHIZUME, and Marc D. WEIDENMIER. 2010. "Why Did Countries Adopt the Gold Standard? Lessons from Japan." *Journal of Economic History* 70 (March): 27–56.

Feliks MLYNARSKI. 1929. *Gold and Central Banks*. New York: Macmillan.

D. E. MOGGRIDGE. 1972. *British Monetary Policy, 1924–1931: The Norman Conquest of $4.86*. Cambridge: Cambridge University Press.

J. W. MORLEY. 1954. *The Japanese Thrust into Siberia, 1918*. New York: Columbia University Press.

Harold G. MOULTON and Leo PASVOLSKY. 1932. *War Debts and World Prosperity*. New York: Century.

Kenneth MOURÉ. 1992. "The Limits to Central Bank Co-operation, 1916–36." *Contemporary European History* 1 (November): 259–279.

———. 2002. *The Gold Standard Illusion: France, the Bank of France, and the International Gold Standard, 1914–1939*. Oxford: Oxford University Press.

Émile MOUREAU. 1991. *The Golden Franc: Memoirs of a Governor of the Bank of France—the Stabilization of the Franc (1926–1928)*. Translated by Stephen D. Stoller and Trevor C. Roberts. Boulder, CO: Westview.

MUROYAMA Yoshimasa. 2005. *Matsukata Masayoshi*. Tokyo: Minerva.

R. Taggart MURPHY. 1997. *The Weight of the Yen*. New York: W. W. Norton.

Margaret G. MYERS. 1931. *The New York Money Market*. Vol. 1, *Origins and Development*. New York: Columbia University Press.

NAGAOKA Shinkichi. 1973. "Nisshin sengo no zaisei seisaku to baishōkin: 'sengo keiei' no seisaku kettei o megutte" [Indemnity and financial policy after the Sino-Japanese War]. In *Nihon keizai seisaku shi ron*, vol. 1, edited by Andō Yoshio, 111–158. Tōkyō Daigaku Shuppankai, 1973.

NIHON GINKŌ CHŌSAKOKUSAIKYOKU. 1908. *Rondon dairiten tokuyaku ōfuku shoruitei* [File of documents concerning the in-and-outgoing supervision of the London Agency]. Tokyo: Nihon Ginkō.

NIHON GINKŌ CHŌSAKYOKU. 1897. *(Kaigaichi) Dakan ginken hakkō junbikin* [(Overseas) Reserve for the issue of convertible silver banknotes], no. A-546. Tokyo: Nihon Ginkō.

NIHON GINKŌ HYAKUNENSHI HENSAN IINKAI. 1982–86. *Nihon Ginkō hyakunenshi* [One-hundred-year history of the Bank of Japan]. 6 vols. Tokyo: Nihon Ginkō.

NIHON GINKŌ KIN'YŪ KENKYŪJO (Bank of Japan, Institute of Monetary and Economic Research). 1993. *Nihon Ginkō seido, seisaku ron shi* [History of studies of the Bank of Japan system and policy]. Itaku kenkyū hokoku, 5. Tokyo: Nihon Ginkō.

NIHON GINKŌ TŌKEIKYOKU (Bank of Japan, Statistics Office). 1966. *Meiji ikō hompō shuyō keizai tōkei. Hundred-Year Statistics of the Japanese Economy*. [Tokyo:] Nihon Ginkō.

Ian NISH. 1972. *Alliance in Decline: A Study of Anglo-Japanese Relations, 1908–23*. London: University of London, Athlone Press.

———. 2002. *Japanese Foreign Policy in the Interwar Period*. Westport, CT: Praeger.

Shizuya NISHIMURA, Toshio SUZUKI, and Ranald MICHIE, eds. 2012. *The Origins of International Banking in Asia: The Nineteenth and Twentieth Centuries*. Oxford: Oxford University Press.

Noji Kiyoshi and Omori Tokuko. 1986. "Daiichiji taisenki no Nihon no tai Chūgoku shakan" [Japanese loans to China at the time of the First World War]. In *Nihon no shihon yūshutsu: tai Chūgoku shakan no kenkyū* [Japanese capital exports: Research into loans to China], edited by Kokka Shihon Yushutsu Kenkyūkai, 51–87. Tokyo: Taga Shuppan, 1986.

Ragnar Nurkse [League of Nations Economic, Financial and Transit Department]. 1944. *International Currency Experience: Lessons of the Inter-War Period.* [Geneva:] League of Nations.

Phillips Payson O'Brien, ed. 2004a. *The Anglo-Japanese Alliance, 1902–1922.* London: Routledge.

———. 2004b. "Britain and the End of the Anglo-Japanese Alliance." In O'Brien 2004a, 267–284.

Gyoju Odate. 1922. *Japan's Financial Relations with the United States.* New York: Studies in History, Economics, and Public Law, no. 224 (vol. 48, no. 2), Columbia University.

Tetsuji Okazaki and Michiru Sawada. 2007. "Effects of a Bank Consolidation Promotion Policy: Evaluating the 1927 Bank Law in Japan." *Financial History Review* 14 (1): 29–61.

Ōkurashō [Ministry of Finance], ed. 1940. *Meiji Taishō zaiseishi* [Meiji-Taisho financial history]. Vol. 17. Tokyo: Zaisei Keizai Gakkai.

[Ōkurashō] Rinji Chōsakyoku Kin'yūbu [Ministry of Finance, Temporary Survey Bureau, Finance Division]. 1917. *Sekai kin'yū chūshin shijō no idō ni kansuru shosetsu yoryō* [Summary of various opinions concerning the shift of the world's central financial market]. [Tokyo: Ōkurashō], August 1917. Held at Zaimushō Bunko.

Anne Orde. 1996. *The Eclipse of Great Britain: The United States and British Imperial Decline, 1895–1956.* Houndmills, Basingstoke, UK: Macmillan.

Kevin H. O'Rourke and Jeffrey G. Williamson. 1999. *Globalization and History: The Evolution of a Nineteenth-Century Atlantic Economy.* Cambridge, MA: MIT Press.

T. W. Overlach. 1976. *Foreign Financial Control in China.* New York: Arno Press, reprint.

Susie J. Pak. 2013. *Gentlemen Bankers: The World of J. P. Morgan.* Cambridge, MA: Harvard University Press.

Antoine Parent. 2008. "When Economists 'Tell Histories': The Truncated Story of Central Banks' Cooperation over the Bimetallic Period." *Historical Social Research* 33 (4): 264–273.

Hugh T. Patrick. 1962. *Monetary Policy and Central Banking in Contemporary Japan.* University of Bombay, Series in Monetary and International Economics, No. 5, Bombay: Bombay University Press.

E. L. Stewart Patterson. 1916. "London and New York as Financial Centers." *Annals of the American Academy of Political and Social Science* 68 (November): 264–277.

Louis W. Pauly. 1997. *Who Elected the Bankers? Surveillance and Control in the World Economy.* Ithaca, NY: Cornell University Press.

Frederic L. Paxson. 1920. "The American War Government, 1917–1918." *American Historical Review* 26 (October): 54–76.

György Péteri. 2002. *Global Monetary Regime and National Central Banking: The Case of Hungary, 1921–1929.* Wayne, NJ: Center for Hungarian Studies and Publications.

P. P. Pillai. 1923–24. "The Financing of Indian Industry." *Indian Journal of Economics* 4:225–267.

D. C. M. Platt. 1968. *Finance, Trade, and Politics in British Foreign Policy, 1815–1914.* Oxford: Clarendon.

Srinivas B. Prasad. 1999. "The Metamorphosis of City and Chase as Multinational Banks." *Business and Economic History* 28 (Winter): 201–211.

Laure Quennouëlle-Corre and Youssef Cassis, eds. 2011. *Financial Centres and International Capital Flows in the Nineteenth and Twentieth Centuries.* Oxford: Oxford University Press.

Ileana Racianu. 2011. "The Banque de France, the Bank of England, and the Stabilization of the Romanian Currency in the Late 1920s." In Quennouëlle-Corre and Cassis 2011, 198–208.

Thomas Ehrlich Reifer. 2000. "Violence, Profits and Power: Globalization, the Welfare-Warfare State and the Rise and Demise of the New Deal World Order." PhD Diss., Binghamton University, State University of New York.

Priscilla Roberts. 1997. "The Anglo-American Theme: American Visions of an Atlantic Alliance, 1914–1933." *Diplomatic History* 21 (Summer): 333–364.

——. 1998. "'Quis Custodiet Ipsos Custodes?' The Federal Reserve System's Founding Fathers and Allied Finances in the First World War." *Business History Review* 72 (Winter): 585–620.

——. 2000. "Benjamin Strong, the Federal Reserve, and the Limits to Interwar American Nationalism" (parts 1 and 2). *Federal Reserve Bank of Richmond Economic Quarterly* 86:61–98.

Richard Roberts. 2013. *Saving the City: The Great Financial Crisis of 1914.* Oxford: Oxford University Press.

Richard Roberts and David Kynaston, eds. 1995. *The Bank of England: Money, Power and Influence, 1694–1994.* Oxford: Clarendon.

Emily Rosenberg. 1999. *Financial Missionaries to the World: The Politics and Culture of Dollar Diplomacy, 1900–1930.* Cambridge, MA: Harvard University Press.

Dietmar Rothermund. 1992. *India in the Great Depression, 1929–1939.* New Delhi: Manohar.

——. 1996. *The Global Impact of the Great Depression, 1929–1939.* London: Routledge.

Gilbert Rozman. 1974. "Edo's Importance in the Changing Tokugawa Society." *Journal of Japanese Studies* 1 (Winter): 91–112.

John Sagers. 2014. "Shibusawa Eiichi, Dai Ichi Bank, and the Spirit of Japanese Capitalism, 1860–1930." *Shashi: The Journal of Japanese Business and Company History* 3 (November 26): n.p.; online.

C. H. de Saint-Simon. 1972. *The Doctrine of Saint-Simon: An Exposition, First Year, 1828–1829.* Edited and translated by Georg Iggers. New York: Schocken Books.

Saitō Hisahiko. 2015. *Kindai Nihon no kin/gaika seisaku* [The gold and foreign currency policies of modern Japan]. Tokyo: Keio University Press.

P. Sarasas. 1940. *Money and Banking in Japan.* London: Heath Crawton.

Saskia Sassen. 1991. *The Global City: New York, London, Tokyo.* Princeton, NJ: Princeton University Press.

——, ed. 2002a. *Global Networks, Linked Cities.* London: Routledge.

——. 2002b. "Introduction: Locating Cities on Global Circuits." In Sassen 2002a, 1–36.

——. 2006. "Locating Cities in Global Networks: Tokyo and Regional Structures of Interdependence." *Japan Focus* [*Asia Pacific Review*], posted August 14.

S. B. SAUL. 1960. *Studies in British Overseas Trade, 1870–1914*. Liverpool: Liverpool University Press.

R. S. SAYERS. 1936. *The Bank of England Operations, 1890–1914*. London: P. S. King and Son.

——. 1957. *Central Banking after Bagehot*. Oxford: Clarendon.

——. 1976. *The Bank of England, 1891–1944*. 3 vols. Cambridge: Cambridge University Press.

Ulrike SCHAEDE. 2008. *Choose and Focus: Japanese Business Strategies for the 21st Century*. Ithaca, NY: Cornell University Press.

Harry N. SCHEIBER. 1969. "World War I as Entrepreneurial Opportunity: Willard Straight and the American International Corporation." *Political Science Quarterly* 84 (September): 486–511.

Catherine R. SCHENK. 2013a. "The Global Gold Market and the International Monetary System." In Bott 2013a, 17–38.

——. 2013b. "The Hong Kong Gold Market during the 1960s: Local and Global Effects." In Bott 2013a, 139–158.

Michael SCHILTZ. 2006. "An 'Ideal Bank of Issue': The Banque Nationale de Belgique as a Model for the Bank of Japan." *Financial History Review* 13 (2): 179–196.

——. 2012a. *The Money Doctors from Japan*. Cambridge, MA: Harvard University Asia Center.

——. 2012b. "Money on the Road to Empire: Japan's Adoption of Gold Monometallism, 1873–97." *Economic History Review* 65 (August): 1147–1168.

Stephen A. SCHUKER. 1976. *The End of French Predominance in Europe: The Financial Crisis of 1924 and the Adoption of the Dawes Plan*. Chapel Hill: University of North Carolina Press.

——. 1988. *American "Reparations" to Germany, 1919–1933: Implications for the Third-World Debt Crisis*. Princeton Studies in International Finance, no. 61.

——. 2003. "Money Doctors between the Wars: The Competition between Central Banks, Private Financial Advisers, and Multilateral Agencies, 1919–39." In *Money Doctors: The Experience of International Financial Advising, 1850–2000*, edited by Marc Flandreau, 49–77. London: Routledge.

C. G. W. SCHUMANN. 1938. *Structural Changes and Business Cycles in South Africa, 1806–1936*. London: P. S. King and Son.

E. B. SCHUMPETER, ed. 1940. *The Industrialization of Japan and Manchukuo, 1930–1940: Population, Raw Materials and Industry*. New York: Macmillan.

Joseph A. SCHUMPETER. 1939. *Business Cycles: A Theoretical, Historical, and Statistical Analysis of the Capitalist Process*. 2 vols. New York: McGraw-Hill.

SHIMAZAKI Kyūya. 1989. *En no shinryakushi: en kawase hon'i seido no keisei katei* [The yen's invasion history: The process of formation of the yen exchange standard system]. Tokyo: Nihon Keizai Hyōronsha.

SHINOBU Seisaburō, ed. 1974. *Nihon gaikō shi* [History of Japanese diplomacy]. Vol. 1. Tokyo: Mainichi Shinbun.

Shigenori Shiratsuka. 2009. "Size and Composition of the Central Bank Balance Sheet: Revisiting Japan's Experience of the Quantitative Easing Policy." Discussion Paper No. 2009-E-25, Institute for Monetary and Economic Studies (IMES), Bank of Japan.

Masato Shizume. 2012. "The Japanese Economy during the Interwar Period: Instability in the Financial System and the Impact of the World Depression." In *The Gold Standard Peripheries: Monetary Policy, Adjustment, and Flexibility in a Global Setting*, edited by Anders Ögren and Lars Fredrik Øksendal, 211–228. London: Palgrave Macmillan.

Shōda Tatsuo. 1972. *Chūgoku shakan to Shōda Kazue* [Shōda Kazue and Chinese loans]. Tokyo: Daimondo.

Beth A. Simmons. 1993. "Why Innovate? Founding the Bank for International Settlements." *World Politics* 45:361–405.

——. 1996. "Rulers of the Game: Central Bank Independence during the Interwar Years." *International Organization* 50:407–443.

——. 2006. "The Future of Central Bank Cooperation." BIS Working Papers No. 200 (February), Monetary and Economic Department, Bank for International Settlements.

John Singleton. 2011. *Central Banking in the Twentieth Century*. Cambridge: Cambridge University Press.

Eric Slater. 2004. "The Flickering Global City." *Journal of World Systems Research* 10 (Fall): 591–608.

Richard J. Smethurst. 1997. "Fukai Eigo and the Development of Japanese Monetary Policy." In *New Directions in the Study of Meiji Japan*, edited by Helen Hardacre and Adam L. Kern, 125–135. Leiden: Brill Academic.

——. 2007. *From Foot Soldier to Finance Minister: Takahashi Korekiyo, Japan's Keynes*. Cambridge, MA: Harvard University Press.

David Smith and Michael Timberlake. 2002. "Hierarchies of Dominance among World Cities: A Network Approach." In Sassen 2002a, 117–141.

William F. Spalding. 1922. *The London Money Market: A Practical Guide to What It Is, Where It Is, and the Operations Conducted in It*. London: Pitman and Sons.

Peter Spufford. 2006. "From Antwerp and Amsterdam to London: The Decline of Financial Centers in Europe." *De Economist* 154 (2): 143–175.

Nancy Stalker. 2006. "Suicide, Boycotts, and Embracing Tagore: The Japanese Popular Response to the 1924 US Immigration Exclusion Law." *Japanese Studies* 26 (September), 153–170.

Peter Stella. 2009. "The Federal Reserve System Balance Sheet: What Happened and Why It Matters." IMF Working Paper WP/09/120 (May), International Monetary Fund.

Joseph Stiglitz. 2003. *Globalization and Its Discontents*. New York: W. W. Norton.

Mark Stone, Kenji Fujita, and Kotaro Ishi. 2011. "Should Unconventional Balance Sheet Policies Be Added to the Central Bank Toolkit? A Review of the Experience So Far." IMF Working Paper WP/11/145 (June), International Monetary Fund.

Kaoru Sugihara. 1989. "Japan's Industrial Recovery, 1931–6." In *The Economies of Africa and Asia in the Inter-war Depression*, edited by Ian Brown, 152–169. London: Routledge.

——. 1996. *Ajia-kan bōeki no keisei to kōzō* [Formation and structure of intra-Asian trade]. Tokyo: Mineruva Shobō.

——. 2010. "The Formation of an Industrialization-Oriented Monetary Order in East Asia." In Akita and White 2010b, 61–102.

David SUNDERLAND. 2013. *Financing the Raj: The City of London and Colonial India, 1858–1940*. Woodbridge: Boydell Press.

Christian SUTER. 1989. "Long Waves in the International Financial System: Debt-Default Cycles of Sovereign Borrowers." *Review (Fernand Braudel Center)* 12 (1): 1–49.

——. 1992. *Debt Cycles in the World Economy: Foreign Loans, Financial Crises, and Debt Settlements, 1820–1990*. Boulder, CO: Westview.

SUZUKI Takeo, ed. 1972. *Nishihara shakan shiryō kenkyū* [Research into historical sources on the Nishihara loans], 277–350. Tokyo: Tokyo University Press.

Toshio SUZUKI. 1994. *Japanese Government Loan Issues on the London Capital Market, 1870–1913*. London: Athlone.

Richard SYLLA. 2011. "Wall Street Transitions, 1880–1920: From National to World Financial Centre." In Quennouëlle-Corre and Cassis 2011, 161–178.

Henry W. TAFT. 1932. *Japan and America: A Journey and a Political Survey*. New York: Macmillan.

Shinji TAKAGI. 2011. "Internationalising the Yen, 1984–2003: Unfinished Agenda or Mission Impossible?" *Currency Internationalisation: Lessons from the Global Financial Crisis and Prospects for the Future in Asia and the Pacific*, BIS Papers No. 61, 75–92.

TAKAHASHI Kamekichi. 1954–55. *Taishō Shōwa zaikai hendō shi* [Fluctuations of the business world in the Taishō and Shōwa eras]. 3 vols. Tokyo: Tōyō Keizai Shinpo.

TAKAHASHI Kamekichi and MORIGAKI Sunao. (1968) 1993. *Shōwa kin'yū kyōkō shi* [History of the Shōwa financial panic]. Tokyo: Kōdansha.

TAKAHASHI Korekiyo. (1936) 1976. *Takahashi Korekiyo jiden* [Autobiography of Takahashi Korekiyo]. 2 vols. Edited by Uetsuka Tsukasa. Tokyo: Chūkō Bunko.

Norio TAMAKI. 2005. "Japan's Adoption of the Gold Standard and the London Money Market, 1881–1903: Matsukata, Nakai and Takahashi." In *Britain and Japan: Biographical Portraits*, vol. 1, edited by Ian Nish, 121–132. London: Global Oriental.

Pat THANE. 1986. "Financiers and the British State: The Case of Sir Ernest Cassel." *Business History* 28 (1): 80–99.

Gianni TONIOLO, with Piet CLEMENT. 2005. *Central Bank Cooperation at the Bank for International Settlements, 1930–1973*. Cambridge: Cambridge University Press.

Adam TOOZE. 2014. *The Deluge: The Great War, America, and the Remaking of the Global Order, 1916–1931*. New York: Viking.

TSUSHIMA Juichi. 1963. *Mori Kengo-san no koto*. Vol. 2. Tokyo: Hōtō Kankōkai.

Stefano UGOLINI. 2013. "The Bank of England as the World Gold Market Maker during the Classical Gold Standard Era, 1889–1910." In Bott 2013a, 64–87.

U.S. DEPARTMENT OF COMMERCE, BUREAU OF THE CENSUS. 1960. *Historical Statistics of the United States, Colonial Times to 1957*. Washington, DC: Government Printing Office.

Ramaa VASUDEVAN. 2008. "The Borrower of Last Resort: International Adjustment and Liquidity in a Historical Perspective." *Journal of Economic Issues* 42 (December): 1055–1081.

WAKATSUKI Reijirō. (1950) 1983. *Kofūan kaikoroku, Wakatsuki Reijirō jiden, Meiji, Taishō, Shōwa sekai hisshi* [Autobiography of Wakatsuki Reijirō: The secret history of the Meiji, Taishō, and Shōwa eras]. Tokyo: Yomiuri Shinbunsha.

Paul WARBURG. 1914. "Circulating Credits and Bank Acceptances." Essays on Banking Reform in the United States. In *Proceedings of the Academy of Political Science in the City of New York* 4 (July): 159–172.

——. 1930. *The Federal Reserve System, Its Origins and Growth.* 2 vols. New York: Macmillan.

F. WARNER. 1991. *Anglo-Japanese Financial Relations: A Golden Tide.* Oxford: Basil Blackwell.

D. Cameron WATT. 1984. *Succeeding John Bull: America in Britain's Place, 1900–1975.* Cambridge: Cambridge University Press.

D. Eleanor WESTNEY. 1987. *Imitation and Innovation: The Transfer of Western Organizational Patterns in Meiji Japan.* Cambridge, MA: Harvard University Press.

D. WILLIAMS. 1968. "The Evolution of the Sterling System." In *Essays in Money and Banking in Honour of R. S. Sayers*, edited by C. R. Whittlesey and J.S.G. Wilson, 266–297. Oxford: Clarendon.

Jeffrey G. WILLIAMSON. 1996. "Globalization, Convergence, and History." *Journal of Economic History* 56 (June): 1–30.

H. WITHERS. 1918. *War and Lombard Street.* London: John Murray.

Dariusz WÓJCIK. 2011. "The Dark Side of NY-LON: Financial Centres and the Global Financial Crisis." Oxford University, Working Papers in Employment, Work and Finance, No. 11–12.

Silvano A. WUESCHNER. 1999. *Charting Twentieth-Century Monetary Policy: Herbert Hoover and Benjamin Strong.* Westport, CT: Greenwood.

Robert Callander WYSE. 1918. "The Future of London as the World's Money Market." *Economic Journal* 28 (December): 386–397.

YAMAMOTO Yūzō. 2011. *"Dai-TōA Kyōeiken" keizaishi kenkyū* [Research on the economic history of the "Greater East Asian Co-prosperity Sphere"]. Nagoya: Nagoya Daigaku Shuppankai.

C. YANAGA. 1966. *Japan since Perry.* Hamden, CT: Archon, reprint.

YOKOHAMA SHŌKIN GINKŌ [Yokohama Specie Bank]. 1976. Yokohama Shōkin Ginkō shi [History of the Yokohama Specie Bank]. Yokohama Shōkin Ginkō.

Louise YOUNG. 2013. *Beyond the Metropolis: Second Cities and Modern Life in Interwar Japan.* Berkeley: University of California Press.

Index

Note: Page numbers in *italics* indicate figures; those with a *t* indicate tables.

CPSIA information can be obtained
at www.ICGtesting.com
Printed in the USA
BVOW08*1331021216
469610BV00002B/6/P